What Jews Say About God

FROM BIBLICAL
TO MODERN TIMES

What Jews Say
ABOUT
GOD

FROM BIBLICAL
TO MODERN TIMES

Selected and annotated by
Alfred J. Kolatch

JONATHAN DAVID PUBLISHERS, INC.
Middle Village, New York 11379

WHAT JEWS SAY ABOUT GOD

Jonathan David Publishers, Inc.
68-22 Eliot Avenue
Middle Village, NY 11379
www.JonathanDavidOnline.com

2 4 6 8 10 9 7 5 3 1

Library of Congress Cataloging-in-Publication Data
What Jews say about God : from biblical to modern times / selected and Annotated
by Alfred J. Kolatch
    p. cm.
  Includes bibliographical reference and index
  ISBN 0-8246-0415-6
  1. God (Judaism)—Quotations, maxims, etc. 2. Judaism—Quotations,
maxims, etc. I. Kolatch, Alfred J., 1916–
BM610.W53   1999
296.3'11—dc21
                                               99-24290
                                                    CIP

Book design and composition by John Reinhardt Book Design

Printed in the United States of America

To my Grandpa Moses
And the other Wise Men of Israel
Who, like Rabbi Chanina, believed that
"the seal of God is Truth."

Contents

Introduction

THE OTHER DAY I was walking past a schoolyard next to the Reform Temple of Forest Hills, where thirty or forty screaming skullcap-clad Orthodox children were kicking small soccer balls around during a recess period from their classes in the Dov Revel Yeshiva. After I stood and watched for a while through the wire fence, two of the children approached me, and one of them asked, "Are you Jewish?"

"Yes," I said, and then countered, "are you Jewish?"

The boys looked at each other and laughed.

Then I said, "Are you in third grade?"

"No," they said, "we're in second grade."

"Are you studying Chumash [the Torah] yet?" I asked.

"Yes," they replied.

"And what *sidra* [weekly portion] are you studying now?"

"*Va-yeira*," they answered.

"Do you know the first words of the *sidra*?" I asked.

"*Va-yeira eilav Ha-Shem*," they answered in unison.

"And what do the words mean?" I asked.

"'Ha-Shem [God] appeared to him,'" they responded.

"And from where did He appear?" I asked. "Where is God?"

They both looked at each other, and as if the answer were choreographed, simultaneously pointed heavenward and said: "Ha-Shem [God] is up there. Ha-Shem knows everything. Ha-Shem is the ruler of the world!"

And with that they ran off to continue with their game of soccer.

.•.

It seems so easy for most youngsters to know where God is and to be certain of His great power. But for most older folks, the belief is not so certain and not so easy to come by. And this difficulty is not a new phenomenon. It is a dilemma that existed as far back as the days of Abraham and Moses, even as it did for the great Sages whose beliefs are known to us from the pages of the Talmud and Midrash.

In Exodus Rabba (5:9), for example, the Midrash quotes the verse from Exodus (20:15) that describes what happened immediately after the Ten Commandments were given to Moses on Mount Sinai: "Now all the people saw the *sounds* of thunder, the flashing fire, the sound of the *shofar* [ram's horn], and the mountain smoking. . . ." The question that puzzles the Rabbis was why the Torah speaks of the thunder in the plural. And Rabbi Yochanan offers this explanation: "The voice of God, as He spoke, split up into seven voices and the seven voices into seventy languages, so that all nations might hear it. When each nation heard the voice in their own language, their souls departed [they were filled with fear], except for Israel, who was not harmed."

Rabbi Tanchuma comments: "The Voice went forth and reached each Israelite in proportion to his capacity to receive it: the old according to their strength, the young according to their strength, to the children, and babes, and women according to their strength." And then he adds: "and even to Moses according to his capacity [to understand God's words]."

The disciples of Rabbi Ishmael arrive at the same conclusion as Rabbis Yochanan and Tanchuma. Based on the verse in the Book of Jeremiah, "And like a hammer that breaks the rock into pieces" (23:29), they conclude that "just as a hammer [when it strikes the anvil] emits many sparks, so did every single word that went forth from the Holy One, blessed be He, divide itself into many languages" (Shabbat 88b).

As one reads the Bible, one is struck before long by the many different names by which God is called. At the outset, in the Book of Genesis, He is first called Elohim; later he is called Jehovah (Yahweh), a name used as a substitute for Adonai (which was considered an ineffable name, too holy to be pronounced, except in prayer). He is also referred to in the Bible as El, Elo'ah, Shaddai, and Tzeva'ot. The use of such a variety of appellations is reflective of the fact that Jews have not always conceived of God in the same way.

The name by which God identified Himself to man is noted in the Book of Exodus (chapter 3), where God appears to Moses from the midst of the bush that burned but would not be consumed and instructs Moses to tell the Children of Israel that He will free them from the bondage of Egypt. Moses then asks, "When I come to the Israelites and say to them, 'The God of your fathers has sent me to you,' and they ask me, 'What is His name?' what shall I say to them?'" (Exodus 3:13).

God answers: "Eh-heh-yeh asher Eh-heh-yeh." Say to the Israelites, "Eh-heh-yeh [I will be who I shall be] sent me to you" (Exodus 3:14).

God identifies himself not as a Being of the moment but as a God of becoming; a God of the past, present and future. God is to be understood as our model of the past

This idea of an ever-evolving God is presented dramatically in Richard Buckmaster's book *No More Secondhand God* (1963). "God is a verb, not a noun," he writes. In *For Those Who Can't Believe* (1995), Rabbi Harold Schulweiss expresses the same thought: "We have been taught to think of God as a noun. . . . I propose a shift of focus from noun to verb, from subject to predicate, from God as person to godliness. . . ." Rabbi Ismar Schorsch also iterates this sentiment in the August 1996 issue of *Commentary* magazine: "God is a verb, not a noun, an ineffable presence that graces my life with a daily touch of eternity."

⋅◦⋅

Jews have many faces and God appears to them in many guises. From the ultra-Orthodox to the ultra-liberal to the secular, Jews experience God—indeed, conceive of God—in countless, oftentimes contradictory, ways. Nobel Prize-winning novelist Isaac Bashevis Singer (1904-1991) expresses this enigmatic complexity through a favorite yarn:

> I met a Jew who had grown up in a *yeshiva* and knew large sections of the Talmud by heart. I met a Jew who was an atheist. I met a Jew who owned a large clothing store with hundreds of employees, and I met a Jew who was an ardent communist. . . . It was all the same man.

Just as each human being is unique in his physical makeup, so is each individual in the way he or she experiences the entity called God. This distinctiveness is addressed by the Rabbis of the Midrash (Mechilta Ba-chodesh 4) when they comment on Exodus 19:19, which states that when the Israelites stood at the foot of Mount Sinai at the time the Torah was given to Moses, "the sound of the shofar grew louder and louder." The Rabbis observe: "Ordinarily the sound coming from a voice or instrument becomes weaker as it is prolonged. Here, the sound grew louder. Why was this? Why was it softer at first?" Their answer: "So the ear of the listener might become accustomed to the sound, each person in keeping with his hearing capacity."

Just as each individual senses the world in a highly individual way, so does each person sense the presence of God in an individual way. Each person must find God through his own inner voice and in his own time.

Action and Prayer

In Jewish thought the existence of God is axiomatic. Proof of God's existence, say traditionalists, is found in the very existence of the world, for only God could have the intelligence and power to put such a beautiful and complex universe into motion.

In the Bible and early Jewish writings, scant attention is paid to proving the existence of God or in articulating that conviction. Rather, the emphasis has been on demonstrating one's belief through action—namely, by carrying out the commandments (mitzvot) of the Torah. In the Jerusalem Talmud (Chagiga 1:7), the Rabbis quote God as saying, "It would have been far better had they [Israel] forsaken Me, but guarded [and lived by] the teachings of My Torah." Living up to the ideals of truth, justice, charity, kindness, and peace as detailed or implied in the teachings of the Torah is paramount. In the words of Isaac Bashevis Singer, "God is silent; God speaks in acts."

For Jews, fulfilling God's commandments, while essential, has never been sufficient to satisfy their spiritual need to reach God. In the talmudic tractate Taanit (2a), the Rabbis note that God must be reached not only through observance but also through prayer. Observance and prayer, the "service of the heart," are inextricably intertwined.

The formal liturgy as passed down through the generations is replete with expressions of adoration of God, as in *Adon Olam* ("Master of the Universe"), a hymn composed by the illustrious eleventh-century poet and philosopher Solomon ibn Gabirol; with supplications for forgiveness, as in the *Al Cheit* ("For the Sin") prayer, a confessional composed between the sixth and tenth centuries, recited on Yom Kippur; with proclamations of God's sovereignty, as in the *Aleinu* ("It Is Our Duty [to praise God]"), the formal conclusion of all prayer services; and with declarations of God's holiness, as in the Aramaic *Kaddish* (a form of the Hebrew word *kadosh*, meaning "holy") prayer, which is recited at several points during all prayer services.

Need for a Personal God

The formal synagogue service has provided a venue for people individually and for Jews as a group to make contact with God, although not all Jews attend religious services for the same purpose. Leib Goldhirsch (1860-1942), father of the brilliant humorist Harry Golden (1902-1981) was fond of relating a story about two Jews, recent immigrants to America, both of whom attended synagogue regularly. One was a devout; the other, an atheist.

When the atheist was asked why he, a nonbeliever, attended synagogue, he explained: "My beloved friend Dudya Silverberg goes to *shul* [synagogue] to talk to God, and I go to talk to Dudya."

Prayer in the Jewish tradition means more than simply asking God to fulfill one's own personal needs. "Whoever has it in his power to pray on behalf of his neighbor and fails to do so is called a sinner," says the Talmud (Berachot 12b). The needs of one's fellow man and the expectations of the community are paramount in Jewish prayer. According to the fourth-century Babylonian scholar Abaye, the correct way to pray is to include the whole congregation of Israel in one's prayers. One should say, "May it be Thy will, O Lord our God, to lead us forth in peace . . . " (Ibid. 29b-30a).

.•.

The ways in which Jews communicate with God outside of the formal synagogue setting are as diverse as they are individual. Throughout the centuries Jews have forged their own special relationships with God.

Chasidic rebbes have been known to talk directly to God and quite often to offer Him a tongue-lashing. One such anonymous rebbe, who surely believed in God's goodness and meant no disrespect, is reported to have addressed Him thusly:

> You [God] wish me to repent of my sins, but I have committed only minor ones. . . . But you, O Lord, have committed grievous ones: You have taken away babies from their mothers, and mothers from their babies. So let us make a truce. If You will forgive me, I will forgive You.

.•.

How a person sees God, where he sees God—indeed, whether he sees God at all—is reflected not only in the way he speaks to God but in the way he speaks about God.

David Lieber, past president of the University of Judaism in Los Angeles, conceives of God as "the Creative Power at work, bringing order out of chaos," but concedes, "Who or what God stands for— a process, a force—I do not know, nor does anyone else."

Novelist Norman Mailer contends: "I am a disbeliever in the omnipotence of God because of the Holocaust. . . ."

U. S. writer Anne Roiphe says, "I cannot accept God as the Good-Surgeon-in-the-Sky. Whatever tumors He may be removing, He also planted there."

The once-spurned Jewish philosopher Baruch Spinoza put it so well: "The mind's highest good is the knowledge of God, and the mind's highest virtue is to know God."

Professor Abraham J. Heschel wrote, "There are no proofs for the existence of God. There are only witnesses. You can think of Him by seeking to be present to Him."

Reform rabbi Joshua O. Haberman sees God as "the core source of all being. My God is personal, conscious, and self-revealing."

Reconstructionist rabbi Mordecai M. Kaplan said that "only by way of participation in human affairs and strivings are we to seek God."

Orthodox scholar Joseph B. Soloveitchik sees God "in every beam of light, in every bud and blossom, in the morning breeze, and the stillness of a starlit evening."

Professor Louis Finkelstein of the Jewish Theological Seminary once articulated his connection with God by saying, "When I pray, I talk to God; when I study, God talks to me."

. -•- .

What Jews Say About God brings together the most important statements made by Jews to God or about God from biblical times to the present. Culled from the writings and utterances of poets, philosophers, humorists, scientists, novelists, rabbis, politicians, and others, these expressions offer insight into the Jewish mind as it conceives of God and man's relationship to Him.

The quotations contained in this volume are divided into six chapters.

Chapter 1: The Essence and Nature of God deals with God as creator and ruler of the universe, His Oneness and uniqueness, His omniscience and omnipotence, and His many other attributes.

Chapter 2: Searching for and Experiencing God focuses on man's reach towards God through prayer, observance of the commandments, and leading a holy life.

Chapter 3: God, Jews, and the World-at-Large treats the ideas of convenance, chosen peoplehood, and partnership with God.

Chapter 4: Miracles, Messianism, and the World-to-Come deals with the Revelation, life after death, resurrection, and heaven and hell.

Chapter 5: A Personal God focuses on man's relationship with God on a one-to-one basis.

Chapter 6: Sin, Suffering, and Repentance explores the concepts of *teshuva*, freedom of will, accountability, and redemption.

For the most part, what Jews in this volume are saying about God is that God is within our grasp, yet beyond our grasp; that He is within our comprehension, yet beyond our understanding; that He is elusively immanent, yet transcendent. In a word: He is there for all who can feel His presence.

ALFRED J. KOLATCH
Forest Hills, New York
January 2, 1999

CHAPTER ONE

The Essence
and Nature of God

Introduction

F ROM ITS VERY INCEPTION Judaism has conceived of God as the sole
Creator of the universe, as the Power who sustains it and rules
over it in compassion and wisdom. As the gentle shepherd watches
over his tender flock, so does God provide loving care for His fragile
and vulnerable children. Unlike other belief systems, Judaism did
not concern itself with finding proof of God's existence and mas-
tery of the world; such belief was axiomatic. Unlike those who subscribe to polytheism, dualism, or trinitarianism, each day Jews affirm
the unity of God through the words of the Shema (Deuteronomy
6:4):

> Hear O Israel, the Lord is our God, the Lord is One.

Jews so passionately embraced the idea that one God, and He
alone, is Master of the universe that they tried to ensure that the
blight of idolatry not even remotely be associated with the father of
the Jewish people. For this reason, Abraham is portrayed in the
Midrash (Genesis Rabba 38:13) as an iconoclast who smashed the
idols of his father, Terah. This myth was created to help establish
Abraham as the innovator of the "One God" concept, as one who
adamantly rejected any contrary belief.

The Bible itself says nothing about Terah and his beliefs or mode
of worship, but the Midrash builds Abraham up as a monotheist
who is so staunch in his belief that he would even contend against

his father, portrayed as a manufacturer and worshiper of idols made of wood and stone, and destroy his gods. To prove that his father's idols are powerless, Abraham smashes most of them with a hatchet, which he then places in the hands of the largest idol.

When Terah sees what his son had done, he cries out, "What mischief have you done to my gods?"

"I have not done this," Abraham lies. "See, the hatchet is in the hands of your largest god! He did it. He did it because when I placed the savory meat before the idols, they all stretched out to take some first. The large idol was enraged because of their greed, and he smashed your idols." Abraham makes his point by showing how ridiculous is his father's belief in the power of the idols.

In a further attempt to establish the Jewish forbears as monotheists, the last book of the Bible, II Chronicles (4:18), depicts Moses as a leader who was pure and undefiled by the idolatry of the house of Pharaoh in which he grew up. To promote this idea, it proposes that Pharaoh's daughter, who found the infant Moses in the bulrushes along the shore of the Nile River was actually a Jewess. II Chronicles gives her name as Bitya, meaning "daughter of God." Under the scenario presented, Moses was brought up by a God-fearing Jewess, not by an Egyptian idolatress and her family.

In answer to the question of how it is possible to claim that Pharaoh's daughter was a Jewess, the Talmud offers the following explanation: "She went down to the river to cleanse herself of her father's idols" (Megilla 13a). To which Rabbi Yochanan adds: "Anyone who repudiates idolatry is a Jew."

·•·

What is the essence and nature of this One God who is the center of the Jewish belief system? Answering this question is difficult on many levels, particularly because of the limits of language in describing a nonphysical entity. Although God is anthropomorphized repeatedly in the Bible—He *expels* man from the Garden of Eden, *orders* Noah to build an ark, *smells* the pleasant odor of the offering brought by Noah, *confuses* the language of men when they decided to build the Tower of Babel, and so on—almost all Jewish philosophers and theologians are in agreement that God is not to be conceived of as having human form. This belief is based upon the biblical description of the Revelation on Mount Sinai: "You heard the sound of words, but you saw no form . . ." (Deuteronomy 4:12).

Moses Maimonides (1135–1204) was probably the first Jewish philosopher to state categorically that "whoever conceives of God as a corporeal being is an apostate" (Mishneh Torah, Hilchot Teshuva 3:7). One of his contemporaries, the French talmudist Abraham ben David of Posquières (1120–1190), also known by the acronym Ravad, argued that many good Jews believe that God has human form, and they are not to be considered heretics; they are simply in error for failing to understand that the anthropomorphic passages in Scripture and rabbinic literature were not meant to be taken literally.

David Ben-Gurion, in a conversation with confidant Moshe Pearlman that was recorded in Perlman's Ben-Gurion Looks Back (1965), revealed his feelings on anthropomorphizing God:

> I know what God is not. He is not a man. He has no ears, no eyes. . . . Nevertheless, I do believe that there must be a being, intangible, indefinable, even unimaginable, but something infinitely superior to all we know and are capable of conceiving.

Whether language can be used successfully to articulate the nature and essence of God has been the subject of endless discussion. Isaac Bashevis Singer expressed his feeling on the subject in his Coat of Many Colors: "Since He is a silent God, He talks in deeds, in events, and we have to learn this language."

This section contains a wide variety of quotations that relate to the essence and nature of God—His attributes and how He manifests Himself in the world.

Aaron ben Elijah

[c. 1300–1369]

KARAITE PHILOSOPHER AND EXEGETE

1. God created the physical world and was not Himself created.
2. God is formless and incorporeal, unique and unitary, comparable to nothing in existence.

Two of the Karaite ten principles of faith. From his Eitz Ha-chayim.

Abba ben Memel

THIRD-CENTURY PALESTINIAN SCHOLAR

God said: My name is according to My work: when I judge, it is *Elohim* [God]; when I war on the wicked, it is *Zebaot* [Hosts]; when I suspend judgment, it is *Shaddai* [Almighty], and when I show compassion, it is *Adonai* [Lord].

Quoted in Exodus Rabba (3:6).

Abba Saul

SECOND-CENTURY PALESTINIAN SCHOLAR

Just as He is gracious and compassionate, be thou gracious and compassionate.

Interpreting the verse "This is my God and I will honor Him; the God of my fathers, and I will exalt Him" (Exodus 15:2). Quoted in the talmudic tractate Shabbat (133b).

(Rabbi) Abbahu

Also known as Avahu

THIRD-CENTURY TALMUDIC SCHOLAR

God created other worlds and destroyed them before He created this one. He [God] said: "This one pleases me; the others did not."

A view based upon the statement in Genesis (1:31) "and God saw all that He had done and behold it was very good," implying that much activity preceded the creation of our world. Quoted in Genesis Rabba (3:7) and Midrash Yalkut Shimoni, Ecclesiastes 968.

.-•.

The first commandment ["I am the Lord thy God"] is to be compared to an earthly king who has a father or brother or son. But God said: "I am not like that [king] for I am first; I have no father . . . I have no brother . . . and I have no son.

Quoted in Exodus Rabba (29:4), an apparent refutation of the Christian concept of a trinity.

Abraham ben David

[1120–1198]

RABBI OF POSQUIÈRES, FRANCE

How can he [Maimonides] say such a thing? Many people wiser and better than he were led to believe the language of the Bible and the stories of the aggada which say that God has a body.

Criticizing Moses Maimonides for saying that anyone who believes that God is a corporeal being is a heretic.

Morris Adler

[1906–1996]

U.S. CONSERVATIVE RABBI, AUTHOR

Creation is not a completed event, permitting God to withdraw into a cosmic vastness outside of it. Creation is a dynamic, ongoing process.

From his May I Have a Word with You? (1967).

Jacob B. Agus

[1911–1986]

U.S. CONSERVATIVE RABBI, AUTHOR, SCHOLAR

The word of God in the heart of man is not an auditory hallucination, but a power, a deposit of energy, a momentary upsurge toward a higher level of being.

From an essay in Condition of Jewish Belief (1966), compiled by the editors of Commentary magazine.

Akiba ben Joseph
[c. 50–135]
LEADING TALMUDIC SCHOLAR, ACTIVIST

Beloved is man, for he was created in the image of God.
> Quoted in the Ethics of the Fathers (3:18).

·◆·

As a house implies a builder, a dress a weaver, a door a carpenter, so the world proclaims God its Creator.
> From the Midrash Temura (chapter 3). Quoted in Joseph L. Baron's A Treasury of Jewish Quotations (1956).

Joseph Albo
[c. 1380–c. 1435]
FIFTEENTH-CENTURY SPANISH RABBI, THEOLOGIAN

We cannot imagine that even God can make a part equal to the whole; or a diagonal of a square equal to one of its sides; or two contradictory propositions true at the same time.
> Addressing the philosophical question often asked: Can God make an object that is so heavy that He Himself cannot lift it? From his philosophical work Sefer Ha-Ikkarim (1428).

·◆·

A sage was asked if he knew the essence of God. He replied: "Had I known it, I should have been it."
> Ibid. Expressing the thought that only God can have knowledge of Himself. Man can know God only through His manifestation in the universe.

·◆·

The prophets had to speak in a language understood by the masses, . . . so they said that He is a jealous and avenging God.
> Ibid.

Woody Allen

[1935–]

U.S. ACTOR, WRITER, FILM DIRECTOR

If it turns out that there is a God, I don't think that He's evil. But the worst that you can say about him is that basically He's an underachiever.

From the 1975 film Love and Death.

Robert Alter

[1935–]

HEBREW SCHOLAR, LITERARY CRITIC

Language in the biblical stories is never conceived as a transparent envelope of the narrated events, or as an aesthetic embellishment of them, but as an integral and dynamic component—an insistent dimension—of what is being narrated. With language God creates the world; through language He reveals His design in history to men. There is a supreme confidence in an ultimate coherence of meaning through language which informs the biblical vision.

From an article in Commentary magazine, which he expanded upon in his Art of Biblical Narration (1981).

Amos

EIGHTH-CENTURY B.C.E. PROPHET OF ISRAEL

The lion has roared
who will not fear?
The Lord God has spoken
Who can but prophesy?

From the Book of Amos (3:8).

Anonymous

A man strikes many coins from the same mold, and each is a duplicate of the other. But although the King of Kings, the Holy One, blessed be He, fashioned every man from the mold of the first man [Adam] not a single person is exactly like his fellowman.

From the talmudic tractate Sanhedrin (37a).

.•.

If God does not approve, a fly won't make a move.

A Yiddish folk saying.

.•.

Man was created single for the sake of peace among men, so that no one might say to his fellow: "My father was greater than yours."

Emphasizing how important the establishment of peace is to God.

.•.

Adam was created [last of all beings] on the eve of the Sabbath, lest the Sadducees say: "God had a partner in man [when he created the world]."

Quoted in the talmudic tractate Sanhedrin (38a).

.•.

There are three partners in man: the Holy One, blessed be He, his father, and his mother. His father supplies the semen of the white substance out of which are formed the child's bones, sinews, nails, the brain in his head, and the white in his eye; his mother supplies the semen of the red substance out of which is formed his skin, flesh, hair, blood, and the black of his eye; and the Holy One, blessed be He, gives him the spirit and the breath, beauty of features, eyesight, the power of hearing and the ability to speak and to walk, understanding and discernment. When his time to depart from the world approaches, the Holy One, blessed be He, takes away his share and leaves the shares of his father and his mother with them.

Quoted in the talmudic tractate Nidda (31a).

.•.

Even those things which you may regard as completely superfluous to the creation of the world, such as fleas, gnats, and flies, even they too are included in the creation of the world, and the Holy One, blessed be He, carries out His purpose through everything, even through a snake, a scorpion, a gnat, or a frog.

Quoted in Midrash Genesis Rabba (10:7).

Israel Baal Shem Tov

[c. 1700–1760]

FOUNDER OF CHASIDISM

People should get to know what the unity of God really means. To attain a part of this indivisible unity is to attain the whole. The Torah and all its ordinances are from God. If I therefore fulfill but one commandment in and through the love of God, it is as though I have fulfilled them all.

Quoted in Solomon Schechter's Studies in Judaism (1896).

·◆·

Everything created by God contains a spark of holiness.

Quoted by Solomon Ansky in his play The Dybbuk (1918).

·◆·

Unless we believe that God renews the work of Creation every day, our prayers and our observance of the commandments become routine and jaded. As it is written in the Book of Psalms (71:9): "Cast me not off in the time of old age"—that is to say, do not let my world grow old.

Quoted in Nahum Glatzer's In Time and Eternity (1946).

·◆·

God never does the same thing twice. That which exists is unique, and it happens but once.

Explaining why he once stood at the threshold of a synagogue but refused to enter. Quoted in Martin Buber's Legends of the Baal Shem (1955).

·◆·

Man must think that all things in this world are permeated by the power of God; and all things accomplished through the thoughts of men, even the slightest of them, are done through His providence. It does not matter, therefore, whether the desire of a man is carried out or not, for God knows that it is better that it should not have been realized.

From his Testament of The Besht.

·◆·

The Shechina [God] permeates all four aspects [literally "worlds"] of nature: inanimate things, plants, living creatures, and man. Godliness is inbred in all creatures in the universe whether they be good or bad.

> *Quoted in the work* Toldot Yaakov Yosef, *by Jacob Joseph Palonnoge (died 1782), a disciple of the Besht.*

Leo Baeck
[1873–1956]
GERMAN REFORM RABBI, THEOLOGIAN

He is the One, and therefore man must decide for Him, in contrast to, and over and against all else, and must serve Him only . . . .

> *From his* Essence of Judaism (1936).

Bernard J. Bamberger
[1904–]
U.S. REFORM RABBI, BIBLE SCHOLAR

I hold to the faith—which does not seem to me unreasonable—that there is a cosmic root out of which man's values grow. I believe that man's strivings, above all his ethical strivings, are not irrelevant to the universe. I believe man has some kinship with ultimate reality. Or, in more traditional language—though no language is adequate—I believe in God as a living power.

> *From an essay in* Condition of Jewish Belief (1966), *compiled by the editors of* Commentary *magazine.*

·◆·

Spinoza was a pantheist—he identified God with the world. . . . To Spinoza the world *is* God. The mental and spiritual life of man is just as much a part of God as the rocks or the sea; but Spinoza's God has no conscious purpose, no relationship to humanity. He is not a loving Father; prayer cannot be addressed to Him.

> *From his* The Story of Judaism (1964).

Yosef Begun

RUSSIAN REFUSENIK

I can't say I am a strong Orthodox Jew now, but I continue to respect Jewish tradition and religion. It seems to me that a Jew cannot deny the existence of God. Maybe a Jew can be non-observant, but if a person decides that he wants to be a Jew, he cannot exist without the idea of God. . . . The Torah has seventy faces and every one of them is God.

> One of the most prominent refuseniks, from an interview with Walter Ruby. Begun was released from Christopol Prison in 1987. While there, he became a very observant Jew. From an article in The Jewish World, October 15–21, 1993.

Jack Bemporad

CONTEMPORARY U.S. REFORM RABBI

There is the problem of man's freedom in terms of his relation to God . . . The problem of freedom concerns itself with an attempt to reconcile God's omnipotence with human responsibility. To say that God is omnipotent—in the traditional sense—means that God has all possible power.
If God is all-powerful, then there can be no power other than God's.
If there is no power other than God's, then man can have no power.
If man has no power, then man can have no responsibility.

> From his essay "Toward a New Theology," in The American Judaism Reader (1967), edited by Paul Kresh.

David Ben-Gurion

[1886–1973]

FIRST ISRAELI PRIME MINISTER (1948–1953; 1955–1963)

I do believe in the existence of a spiritual, eternal, all-embracing superior being, but I cannot say that I share the belief of most of my orthodox friends. Is it not curious that even institutionalized religion nowhere describes God in any positive or recognizable way? . . .

Nevertheless, as I say, I do believe that there must be a being, intangible, indefinable, even unimaginable, but something infinitely superior to all we know and are capable of conceiving. Without such a being, there are certain phenomena which just cannot be explained.

Quoted in Ben-Gurion Looks Back: Talks with Moshe Pearlman (1965).

Eliezer Berkovits
[1908–1992]
U.S. ORTHODOX RABBI, SCHOLAR, AUTHOR

Man can only exist because God renounces the use of power on him. This . . . means that God cannot be present in history through manifest material power. Such presence would destroy history. History is the area of human responsibility and its product.

From his Faith After the Holocaust (1973).

· ◆ ·

God is mighty for He shackles His omnipotence and becomes *powerless* so that history may be possible.

Ibid.

· ◆ ·

The foundation of religion is not the affirmation that God *is*, but that God is concerned with man and the world; that, having created this world, He has not abandoned it, leaving it to its own devices; that He cares about His creation. It is of the essence of biblical religion that God is sufficiently concerned about man to address Himself to him; that God values man enough to render Himself approachable by him.

From his God, Man, and History (1959).

· ◆ ·

Judaism is essentially non-mystical because, according to it, God addresses Himself to man and He awaits man's response to the address. God speaks and man listens; God commands and man obeys. Man searches and God allows Himself to be found; man entreats and God answers. In the mystical union, however, there are no words and no law, no search and no recognition, because there is no separateness. Judaism does not admit the idea that man may rise "beyond Good and Evil," as it were, by drowning himself in the Godhead.

Ibid.

Daniel J. Boorstin
[1914–]
U.S. LIBRARIAN, HISTORIAN, AUTHOR

What preoccupies us, then, is not God as a fact of nature, but as a fabrication useful for a God-fearing society. God himself becomes not a power but an image.

From his Image (1961).

Eugene Borowitz
[1924–]
U.S. REFORM RABBI, THEOLOGIAN

Cohen's God, Baeck's mystery, Kaplan's peoplehood, Buber's Covenant and Heschel's Prophetic Sympathy, will not mesh together. The premises on which they are founded substantially contradict one another.

In his Choices in Modern Jewish Thought (1983), *arguing against the idea that a patchwork theology can be created by selecting the most appealing elements from prominent thinkers.*

Ruth Brin
CONTEMPORARY U.S. POET

When men were children, they thought of God as a father;
When men were slaves, they thought of God as a master;
When men were subjects, they thought of God as a king.
But I am a woman, not a slave, not a subject, not a child who longs for
    God as father or mother.
I might imagine God as a teacher or friend, but those images, like king,
    master, father or mother, are too small for me now.

From her A Woman's Meditation (1979).

···◆···

God is the force of motion and light in the universe.
God is the strength of life on our planet;
God is the power moving us to do good;
God is the source of love springing up in us.
God is far beyond what we can comprehend.

Ibid.

Martin Buber
[1878–1965]
GERMAN THEOLOGIAN, AUTHOR

Whether or not we know it, what we really mean when we say that a god is dead is that the images of God vanish and that therefore an image, which up to now was regarded and worshipped as God, can no longer be so regarded and so worshipped.

From his Israel and the World (1963).

···◆···

The Jewish teaching of the wholeness of life is the other side of the Jewish teaching of the unity of God.

Ibid.

···◆···

A man is a heathen to the extent to which he does not recognize God in His manifestations.

Ibid.

···◆···

If anyone tells you that he loves God and does not love his fellow man, you will know that he is lying.

From his Ten Rungs: Hasidic Sayings (1947).

Ephraim Z. Buchwald

CONTEMPORARY U.S. ORTHODOX RABBI, EDUCATOR

It's really a very meaningful religion irrespective of whether you believe in God or not. The mitzvahs make sense even if you could prove black and white there is not God. This is just a meaningful way of life.

Quoted in Tradition in a Rootless World (1991).

Sid Caesar

[1922–]

U.S. COMEDIAN

I believe in something. I don't know if there is a God. I believe there is an energy, a force. Everything is energy and nothing disappears. The conservation law is at work.

Quoted in Tim Boxer's Jewish Celebrity Hall of Fame (1987).

Rene-Samuel Cassin

[1887–1976]

FRENCH-BORN NOBEL PEACE PRIZE WINNER, AUTHOR

The monotheistic creed of the Jewish people, epitomized in the idea of one God, Father of all men, and strengthened by the bitter memories of slavery in Egypt, inspired in them rather early a vivid repugnance to serfdom. To them that institution is neither natural nor just.

From his essay "From the Ten Commandments to the Rights of Man," in Of Law and Man (1971), edited by Sholomo Shoham.

Marc Chagall

[1887–1985]

RUSSIAN-BORN ARTIST

When I am finishing a picture, I hold some God-made object up to it—a rock, a flower, the branch of a tree or my hand—as a kind of final test. If the painting stands up beside a thing man cannot make, the painting is authentic. If there's a clash between the two, it is bad art.

Quoted in the Saturday Evening Post, December 2, 1962.

Chama ben Chanina

THIRD-CENTURY PALESTINIAN TALMUDIC SCHOLAR

As He [God] clothes the naked, visits the sick, comforts mourners, and buries the dead, so you do likewise.

> Quoted in the talmudic tractate Sota (14a).

(Rabbi) Chanina

FIRST-CENTURY DEPUTY HIGH PRIEST, SCHOLAR

The seal of god is truth.

> Quoted in the talmudic tractates Shabbat (55a) and Yoma (69b).

.•.

One never injures a finger here on earth if it has not be so decreed from above.

> Commenting on a verse in the Book of Psalms (37:23). Quoted in the talmudic tractate Chulin (7b).

.•.

The seal of the Holy One, blessed be He, is emet, meaning "truth."

> Emet is spelled alef, mem, tav: the first middle and last letter of the alphabet. This led Samuel ben Nachmani to comment: "This describes the people who fulfill the Torah from alef to tav," from beginning to end. Quoted in the talmudic tractate Shabbat (55a).

Chanina ben Dosa

FIRST-CENTURY TALMUDIC SCHOLAR

He in whom his fellowman takes delight, God takes delight as well.

> From the talmudic tractate Ethics of the Fathers (3:10).

Chiya bar Abba

THIRD-CENTURY TALMUDIC SCHOLAR

God appeared to the people of Israel in keeping with the circumstance and need of each occasion. He appeared at the Red Sea as a mighty warrior, at Sinai as a teacher of children, in the prosperous times of Solomon as tall and sprightly as the cedars of Lebanon, and in Daniel's time as a Sage of the Torah.

From the Mechilta (II:231), edited by Lauterbach.

Hermann Cohen
[1842–1918]
GERMAN PHILOSOPHER, AUTHOR

We call God an idea, meaning the center of all ideas, the idea of truth.

Following in the footsteps of Kant. Quoted in Martin Buber's essay "The Love of God and the Idea of Deity," in his Israel and the World (1948).

⋅✦⋅

Worm that I am, consumed by passions, cast as bait for egoism, I must nevertheless love man. If I am able to do so, and so far as I am able to do so, I shall be able to love God.

Ibid.

⋅✦⋅

The love of men for God is the love of the moral idea. I can love only the ideal, and I can comprehend the ideal in no other way save by loving it.

Ibid.

⋅✦⋅

Even God's omnipotence is delimited by mathematical and logical reason.

Quoted in Reason and Hope: Selections from the Jewish Writings of Hermann Cohen (1971), translated by Eva Jospe.

Robert Cohen
WRITER, RADIO HOST

He healed people by telling them how precious they were and how unconditionally he and God loved them—a mode of outreach that evangelical Christians have found phenomenally successful over the years but that most Jewish professionals have strenuously avoided.

Describing the influence of Rabbi Shlomo Carlebach. In Moment magazine, August 1997.

17

David A. Cooper

CONTEMPORARY U.S. RABBI, AUTHOR, KABBALIST

What is God? In a way, there is no God. Our perception of God usually leads to a misunderstanding that seriously undermines our spiritual development. God is not what we think It is. God is not a thing, a being, a noun. It does not exist, as existence is defined, for It takes up no space and is not bound by time. Jewish mystics often refer to It as *Ein Sof*, which means "Endlessness."

From his God Is a Verb: Kabbalah and the Practice of Mystical Judaism (1997).

. ·•· .

The closest we can come to thinking about God is as a process rather than a being. We can think of it as "be-ing," as verb rather than noun. Perhaps we would understand this concept better if we renamed God. We might call It God-ing, a process, rather than God, which suggests a noun.

Ibid.

. ·•· .

This question [of how divine providence works] has plagued mystics and metaphysical thinkers for two thousand years. It is extremely difficult to address as long as we remain fixed on the old paradigm of God as a noun. However, once we move to the concept that God is a verb, and that the process of creation is relational, we gain new insight, for creation-ing cannot unfold without God-ing, and vice versa. It is like two gears turning against each other—if one gear is withdrawn, the other immediately stops.

Ibid.

Moses Cordovero

[1522–1570]

PALESTINIAN MYSTIC

Do not attribute duality to God. . . . Do not say, "This is a stone and not God." . . . Rather, all existence is God, and the stone is a thing pervaded by divinity.

From his Shi'ur Koma.

(King) David

SECOND KING OF ISRAEL, RULED C. 1000–C. 960 B.C.E.

The soul fills, carries, and survives the body, and the Holy One fills, carries, and outlives the universe. The soul is one, and the Holy One is one. The soul is pure, does not eat, sees and is unseen, and never sleeps, and the Holy One is pure, does not eat, sees and is unseen, and neither slumbers nor sleeps.

> Quoted in Leviticus Rabba (4:8), explaining why he praised God so often with his soul, as expressed in the Book of Psalms in Psalm 25:1 and scores of other verses.

Lucy S. Dawidowicz

[1915–   ]

HISTORIAN, TEACHER, AUTHOR

Judaism is a man's religion not only in substance and in practice but in its symbolic theology. God is male. Israel in relation to God is female: the bridegroom God and the Virgin Israel. The Shekhinah, the Divine Presence, represents the female potency within God. The Torah is female, the Sabbath is female. In relation to them, God is male. In the books of the prophets and, of course, in the Song of Songs, marriage and sexual relations symbolize the ties between God and Israel, Israel and the Sabbath, Israel and Torah.

> Quoted in The Jewish Presence: Essays on Identity and History (1977).

Alan M. Dershowitz

[1938–   ]

U.S. PROFESSOR, ATTORNEY, AUTHOR

Who would I like to meet if I could go back in time? I'd like to meet Job, and tell him he was right to complain about God. If the definition of chutzpah is a man who kills his parents and then demands mercy on the grounds that he is an orphan, the definition of an injustice is a God who authorizes the killing of innocent children, and then demands of their parents that they accept it as justice. I'd like to have patted Job on the back and said: "Even God was wrong in his final speech; you were right."

> From an interview with Eli Wohlgelernter in The Jerusalem Post, May 4, 1998.

Wayne Dosick

CONTEMPORARY U.S. CONSERVATIVE RABBI, AUTHOR

Ruach Elohim, the spirit, the breath of God "hovered over the waters" [Genesis]. And then God began to create. . . . The breath of God is the breath, the life force, of human beings. We exist, we live, we are because our breath is the breath of God.

From his Dancing With God (1997).

Albert Einstein

[1879–1955]
GERMAN-BORN U.S. SCIENTIST

Judaism is not a creed; the Jewish God is simply a negation of superstition, an imaginary result of its elimination.

From his World As I See It (1934).

·◆·

I believe in Spinoza's God who reveals Himself in the orderly harmony of what exists, but not in a God who concerns Himself with the fates and actions of human beings.

When asked if he believes in God.

·◆·

God is subtle, but He is not malicious.

A remark made in April 1921 during a visit to Princeton University.

·◆·

God is slick, but He ain't mean.

Restating in 1946 his earlier statement, "God is subtle, but he is not malicious."

(Rabbi) Eleazar

SECOND-CENTURY TALMUDIC SCHOLAR

Even at such times when God is filled with anger, He never fails to be compassionate.

Quoted in the talmudic tractate Pesachim (87b).

·•·

The manner of human beings is for the lofty to take notice of the lofty and not of the lowly. But the manner of God is not so: He is lofty and He takes notice of the lowly.

   Quoted in the talmudic tractate Sota (5a).

·•·

God grieves over every man who is haughty in spirit.

   Ibid.

Eleazar ben Simon
SECOND/THIRD-CENTURY PALESTINIAN SCHOLAR

God never found it necessary to converse with a woman, save one righteous one.

   Referring to Sarah, wife of Abraham. Quoted in Genesis Rabba (20:6).

Eleazar of Modin
FIRST/SECOND-CENTURY TALMUDIC SCHOLAR

If one wishes to adopt Judaism, in the name of God and for the sake of Heaven, welcome and befriend him, do not repel him.

   From the Midrash Mechilta to Exodus (18:6).

Emil L. Fackenheim
[1916–]
CONTEMPORARY U.S. REFORM RABBI, THEOLOGIAN, AUTHOR

The universe we find ourselves in is an infinitely more complex and more wonderful construction than a clock. Is it likely, as the atheists maintain, that, while the clock was made for a purpose and according to a craftsman's design, the universe is only an accidental collection of atoms? Only an insane person would say this about the clock. . . . Just as the clock is evidence for the clockmaker, the universe is evidence for a universemaker—for God.

   From his Paths to Jewish Belief (1968).

Edmond Fleg

[1874–1963]

FRENCH POET, PLAYWRIGHT

The Jew has suffered so much hurt, he has endured so many injustices, experienced so completely the misery of life, that pity for the poor and the humiliated has become second nature to him. And in his agonized wanderings, he has seen at close range so many men of all races, and of all countries, different everywhere and everywhere alike, that he has understood, he has felt in the flesh of his flesh, that Man is one as God is One. Thus was formed a people which may have the same vices and the same virtues as other peoples, but which is without doubt the most *human* of all peoples.

From his essay "Why I Am a Jew" (1929).

Evidence of God I have found in the existence of Israel.

Ibid.

Sigmund Freud

[1856–1939]

AUSTRIAN-BORN ORIGINATOR OF PSYCHOANALYSIS

The psychoanalysis of individual human beings, however, teaches us with quite special insistence that the god of each of them is formed in the likeness of his father, that his personal relation to God depends on his relation to his father in the flesh and oscillates and changes along with that relation, and that at bottom God is nothing other than an exalted father.

From his Totem and Taboo (1913).

Judaism had been a religion of the father; Christianity became a religion of the son. The old God the Father fell back behind Christ; Christ, the Son, took his place, just as every son had hoped to do in primeval times.

From his last book, Moses and Monotheism (1939).

Erich Fromm

[1900–1980]

U.S. PSYCHOLOGIST, AUTHOR

The logical consequence of Jewish monotheism is the absurdity of theology. If God has no name, there is nothing to talk about. However, any talk about God—hence all theology—implies using God's name in vain, in fact, it brings one close to idolatry.

From his You Shall Be As Gods (1967).

．．．

In the nineteenth century the problem was that God was dead; in the twentieth century the problem is that man is dead.

From his Sane Society (1955).

Aviv Geffen

CONTEMPORARY ISRAELI ROCK STAR

I value Judaism, but a Pink Floyd record turns me on more than the Western Wall. I believe we have created God. I am God. You are God. John Lennon is God. People make money out of God instead of honoring Him.

Israel's leading pop star speaking out, when asked about his feelings toward Judaism, in a September 1996 Rosh Hashana interview with Ma'ariv's youth magazine, after its readers voted him "Personality of the Year."

Neil Gillman

CONTEMPORARY U.S. CONSERVATIVE RABBI, THEOLOGIAN

If we cannot see God in any direct sensory way, then how do we become aware that God is present in history and in our lives? What we do see, in a direct sensory way, is nature and historical events. But everyone sees nature and history, and many people never make the leap from seeing all of this and acknowledging that God is present there. . . .

What then distinguishes believers from atheists? Only the interpretive structure, the metaphorical spectacles that we bring to our experience, our distinctive way of making sense of the world.

From his March 13, 1998 column in The Jewish Week.

.•.

We commit idolatry when we take our metaphors for God to be literally true. . . . But speak of God we must, so we resort to metaphors. These metaphors help us talk and think of God, they open the gates of prayer for us, but they remain metaphors, not photographs.

From a Torah lesson on Shabbat Nachamu/Va-etchanan in The Jewish Week, *August 7, 1998.*

Allen Ginsberg
[1926–1997]
U.S. POET, ACTIVIST

The Jews always complained, kvetching about false Gods, and erected the biggest false God, Jehovah, in the middle of western civilization.

From his poem "World Karma," which appeared in White Shroud (1986).

Samuel Goldwyn
[1882–1974]
U.S. FILM PRODUCER

God makes stars. I just produce them.

Quoted in London's Daily Express, *May 16, 1939.*

Abraham Golomb
[1888–1982]
YIDDISH WRITER

The first and most important principle of Jewish tradition is a negative one. "No graven images" keeps Jewishness from getting tied up with any fixed bodily idea. Everything in Judaism must remain fluid—streaming, changeable, on the running board of history; everything in Jewishness must be with and go with its people in exile; God Himself must.

From his essay "What Is Jewish Tradition?" Reprinted in Joseph Leftwich's anthology The Way We Think (1969).

Elliott Gould

[1938–]

U.S. STAGE AND SCREEN ACTOR

God, to me, is the mind all together all over. The universe is like a miraculous piece of music—every note, every molecule, every atom is part of a composition that wants to be played as well as it can be played. So, therefore, we must continue to practice. To live it. To live it with a conscience, a consciousness, an awareness of what we are in relation to that symphony.

Quoted in Larry King's Powerful Prayers (1998).

·•·

I pray [to God] in my own way every day for peace and harmony, for humanity, nature, and the environment. When I feel I'm being swept away by materialism, by pressures, and by stress, I will stop and pray just to get back in touch with my inner self. . . . Prayer helps to purify the soul, the heart, and the mind.

Ibid.

Arthur Green

CONTEMPORARY U.S. REFORM RABBI, AUTHOR

We seek a religious language that goes beyond the separation of "God", "world," and "self" that seems so ultimate in most of Western theology. The God of which we speak here is not the "wholly other," so widely familiar in our thought and yet so little tested by real understanding. We refer rather to a deity that embraces all of being, a single One that contains within it all the variety and richness of life, yet is also the Oneness that transcends and surpasses all.

From his Seek My Face, Speak My Name: A Contemporary Jewish Theology (1992).

·•·

Essentially I am a Jewish monist. I encounter life as a single reality. When seen from the viewpoint of unity, that whole of being is called Y-H-W-H (or that old pagan-rooted and misleading word "God," if you must). . . .

I do not know a Fellow or a Force "out there," beyond the world in some quasi-spatial sense, Who creates, reveals, redeems. But I do believe there is a deep consciousness that underlies existence, that each human mind is a part of the universal Mind, and that the Whole is sometimes accessible ("revealed") to its parts. The One of which I speak is transcendent, in that it is infinitely elusive and mysterious, while yet being deeply immanent, present throughout the world to those whose eyes are open.

From his essay in Commentary, August 1996.

·*·

I believe that the most essential message of Judaism is that each of us is created in the image of God. We exist for the purpose of teaching that message.

Ibid.

Heinrich Heine
[1797–1856]
GERMAN POET

The beginning and end of all things is God.

From an article in Die Romantische Schole, April 2, 1833.

Will Herberg
[1901–1977]
U.S. THEOLOGIAN, SOCIAL CRITIC

Morality ungrounded in God is indeed a house built upon sand, unable to stand up against the vagaries of impulse and the brutal pressures of power and self-interest.

From his Judaism and Modern Man (1951).

Joseph H. Hertz

[1872–1946]

CHIEF RABBI OF ENGLAND, SCHOLAR, AUTHOR

Trinitarianism has at times been indistinguishable from tritheism; i.e., the belief in three separate Gods. . . . Judaism recognizes no intermediary between God and man, and declares that prayer is to be directed to God alone, and to no other being in the heavens above or on earth beneath.

From his Pentateuch and Haftorahs (1961).

• • •

The Shema excludes pantheism, which considers the totality of things to be the Divine. The inevitable result of believing that all things are divine, and all equally divine, is that the distinction between right and wrong, between holy and unholy, loses its meaning. Pantheism, in addition, robs the Divine Being of conscious personality. In Judaism, on the contrary, though God pervades the universe He transcends it. . . . The Rabbis expressed the same thought when they said: "The Holy One, blessed be He, encompasses the universe, but the universe does not encompass Him."

Ibid.

Abraham Joshua Heschel

[1907–1972]

U.S. THEOLOGIAN, PROFESSOR, ACTIVIST

God is of no importance unless He is of supreme importance.

From his Man Is Not Alone (1951).

• • •

It is tragically true that we are often wrong about God, believing in that which is not God, in a counterfeit ideal, in a dream, in a cosmic force, in our own father, in our own selves. We must never cease to question our own faith and ask what God means to us.

Ibid.

• • •

It was not the aspiration of Israel to know the Absolute but to ascertain what He asks of man; to commune with His will rather than with His essence.

Ibid.

• •

There are no proofs for the existence of the God of Israel. There are only witnesses. You can only think of Him by seeking to be present to Him. You cannot define Him, you can only invoke Him. He is not a notion but a name.

Ibid.

• •

The ineffable Name; we have forgotten how to pronounce it. We have almost forgotten how to spell it. We may totally forget how to recognize it.

From his essay "Toward an Understanding of Halacha," included in
Seymour Siegel's Conservative Judaism and Jewish Law (1977).

• •

In exposing ourselves to God we discover the divine in ourselves and its correspondence to the divine beyond ourselves. That perception of correspondence, our discovering how acts of human goodness are allied with transcendent holiness, the sense of the sacred context of our candid compassion—is our most precious insight.

From his article in The Zionist Quarterly, Summer 1951.

• •

The pagan gods had animal passions, carnal desires . . . While the God of Israel has a passion for righteousness.

From his The Prophets (1962).

• •

We have no nouns by which to express His essence; we have only adverbs by which to indicate the ways in which He acts.

Quoted in Harold Schulweiss's For Those Who Can't Believe (1995).

Samson Raphael Hirsch
[1808–1888]
GERMAN ORTHODOX RABBI, SCHOLAR, AUTHOR

The foundation of Jewish life is not merely that there is only one God, but the conviction that this One, only, and true God is my God, my sole Ruler and Guide in all that I do.

From his comment on Exodus 20:2: "I am the Lord your God who brought you out of the land of Egypt."

Joseph ibn Caspi
[c. 1280–c. 1340]
PHILOSOPHER, GRAMMARIAN

How can I know God and that He is One, unless I know what knowing means and what constitutes unity? No one really knows the true meaning of loving God and fearing Him, unless he is acquainted with natural science and metaphysics, for we love not God as a man loves his wife and children, nor do we fear Him as we would a mighty man. I do not say that all men can reach this intellectual height, but I maintain that it is the degree of highest excellence, though those who stand below it may still be good. Strive, thou, my son, to attain this degree; yet be not hasty in commencing metaphysical studies, and constantly read moral books.

From his book Sefer Ha-musar. Quoted in Israel Abrahams's Jewish Life in the Middle Ages (1958).

Moses ibn Ezra
[c. 1055–1135]
SPANISH HEBREW POET

To remember the Sabbath is to remember that God created the world.

From his comment on the fourth commandment (Exodus 20:8).

Solomon ibn Gabirol

[*c.* 1021–*c.* 1056]

SPANISH POET, PHILOSOPHER

Thou art One, and Thou art exalted above abasement and falling—not like a man, who falls when he is alone.

From his Keter Malchut *("Kingly Crown").*

·•·

It is impossible to describe the divine Will. One may only approximate its definition by saying that it is a divine Power, creating matter and form and holding them together, and that it is diffused from the highest to the lowest. . . . It is this Power which moves and directs everything.

From his Fountain of Life.

·•·

Almighty God, on lofty throne
In wisdom Thou didst build the world,
Thy might the firmament unfurled
And Thou wast King ere kings were known.

Translated from the Hebrew by Israel Zangwill.

Bachya ibn Pakuda

[*c.* 1050–1120]

SPANISH PHILOSOPHER, AUTHOR

If a man were to produce a document with the kind of writing only possible when done with a pen and were to claim that the ink spilled over onto the paper so that the writing emerged of its own accord, . . . we would point out that the thing is impossible. Now if this is impossible even with regard to the forms of letters, how can we say of [the whole universe] that it came into being without a Maker's intention, the *wisdom* of a Mind, and the *power* of a Powerful Being?

From his Duties of the Heart, *translated by Edwin Collins (1905).*

·•·

Any representation of God forming itself in our minds applies to something other than God.

From his Chovot Ha-levavot.

Isaiah

EIGHTH-CENTURY B.C.E. PROPHET OF ISRAEL

Thus saith the Lord: The heaven is My throne, and the earth my foot-stool. Where is the house that you could build for me? And where is the place of My abode?

From the Book of Isaiah (66:1–2).

·•·

The Lord is a God of justice. Happy are all who trust in Him.

Ibid.

·•·

Holy, holy, holy
Is the God of Heaven's hosts,
Whose Presence fills all the earth!

Ibid.

(Rabbi) Ishmael's Disciples

POST-SECOND-CENTURY TALMUDIC SCHOLARS

Peace is a precious thing, for even God fudged on the truth for the sake of peace.

Quoted in the talmudic tractate Bava Metzia (87a) where they note that God did not report the part of Sarah's statement that referred to Abraham's old age (Genesis 18:13).

(Prophet) Jeremiah

SIXTH-CENTURY B.C.E. PROPHET OF ISRAEL

Thus said the Lord:
Let not the wise man glory in his wisdom;
Let not the strong man glory in his strength;
Let not the rich man glory in his riches.
But only in this should one glory:
In his earnest devotion to Me.
For I the Lord act with kindness, justice, and equity in the world;
For in these I delight.

From the Book of Jeremiah (9:22–23). It is on this note that Maimonides concludes his Guide of the Perplexed (III:54).

·◆·

I am the Eternal, the God of all flesh—is anything too difficult for me?
From the Book of Jeremiah (32:27).

Jeremiah ben Eleazar

THIRD-CENTURY PALESTINIAN SCHOLAR

God acted as best man for Adam.

Based on Genesis 2:22, which states that after creating Eve, God brought her to Adam. The lesson taught by this action is that "a man of eminence should associate himself with men of lesser stature in acting as best man, and the action should not be misconstrued." Quoted in the talmudic tractate Berachot (61a).

·◆·

When the Holy One, blessed be He, created Adam, He created him an hermaphrodite.

Commenting on the verse in Genesis 5:2. Quoted in Midrash Rabba on Genesis (8:1).

(Rabbi) Joseph

THIRD/FOURTH-CENTURY TALMUDIC SCHOLAR

Man should always learn from the example of his Creator. The Holy One, blessed be He, ignored all the mountains and high places and caused His divine presence (Shechina) to abide on Mount Sinai. And He ignored all the beautiful trees and caused His Shechina to abide in a bush.

Teaching man to associate with the humble. Quoted in the talmudic tractate Sota (5a).

Morris Joseph

[1848–1930]

BRITISH REFORM RABBI, THEOLOGIAN

Passover has a message for the conscience and the heart of all mankind. For what does it commemorate? It commemorates the deliverance of a people from degrading slavery, from most foul and cruel tyranny. And so, it is Israel's—nay, God's protest against unrighteousness, whether individual or national. Wrong, it declares, may triumph for a time, but even though it be perpetrated by the strong on the weak, it will meet with its inevitable retribution at last.

From his Judaism as Creed and Life (1903).

God has not made the world and left it to its fate. Exalted above the heavens, He yet takes a deep and loving interest in human joys and sorrows. It is impossible to think otherwise. The Supreme Being is bound by His own nature to care for His handiwork. An unsympathizing God is no God.

Ibid.

Joshua ben Karcha
SECOND-CENTURY TALMUDIC SCHOLAR

No place is devoid of God's presence, not even a thornbush.

Quoted in Midrash Exodus Rabba (2:5). In answer to the question: "Why did God choose a thornbush from which to speak to Moses?"

(Rabbi) Judah
SECOND-CENTURY TALMUDIC SCHOLAR

Of all [the creatures] that the Holy One, blessed be He, created in His world, He did not create a single thing without purpose. [Thus] He created the snail as a remedy for a scab; the fly as an antidote to the hornet['s sting]; the mosquito [crushed] for a serpent['s bite]; a serpent as a remedy for an eruption, and a [crushed] spider as a remedy for a scorpion['s bite].

Quoted in the talmudic tractate Shabbat (77b). The crushed insect was applied to the infected area as an antidote.

Judah ben Ezekiel

THIRD-CENTURY BABYLONIAN TALMUDIST

Of all the things God created in His world, not one did He create without a purpose.

> Quoting his teacher Rav in the talmudic tractate Shabbat (77b), where is detailed the purpose of the snail, the fly, etc.

Mordecai M. Kaplan

[1881–1983]

U.S. RABBI, RECONSTRUCTIONIST MOVEMENT FOUNDER

Modern scientific and philosophic thought regards all reality not as something static but as energy in action. When we say that God is Process, we select, out of the infinity of processes in the universe, that complex of forces and relationships which makes for the highest fulfillment of man as a human being, and identify it by the term God. In exactly the same way, we select, among all the forces and relationships that enter into the life of the individual, those which make for his highest fulfillment and identify them by the term person. God and person are thus correlative terms, the meaning of each being relative to and dependent on that of the other, like parent and child, teacher and pupil, citizen and state. God is the Process by which the Universe produces persons, and persons are the Processes by which God is manifest in the individual.

> From his Questions Jews Ask (1956).

．◆．

A magnetic needle, hung on a thread or placed on a pivot, assumes of its own accord a position in which one end of the needle points north and the other south. So long as it is free to move about, all attempts to deflect it will not get it to remain away from its normal direction. Likewise, man normally veers in the direction of that which makes for the fulfillment of his destiny as a human being. That fact indicates the functioning of a cosmic Power which influences his behavior. What magnetism is to the magnetic needle, Godhood or God is to man.

> Quoted in Contemporary Jewish Thought (1985), edited by Simon Noveck.

Menachem M. Kasher

[1895–1983]

POLISH-BORN ISRAELI AUTHOR, SCHOLAR

Ben Azzai laid down a fundamental teaching of Judaism. For in the verse quoted [Genesis 5:1], the scholar saw the basic declaration of human brotherhood. By tracing back the whole of the human race to one single ancestor, created by one God, the Bible taught that all men have *one* Creator—the heavenly Father—and *one* ancestor—the human father.

From his Encyclopedia of Biblical Interpretation (1953).

Walter Kaufmann

[1921–]

U.S. HUMANISTIC PHILOSOPHER

Faith in immortality, like belief in God, leaves unanswered the ancient question: Is God unable to prevent suffering, and thus not omnipotent? Or is He able and not willing it and thus not merciful? And is He just?

After turning to Lutheranism, he returned to Judaism, favoring a humanistic approach. From his Faith of a Heretic (1961).

Yehezkel Kaufmann

[1889–1963]

UKRAINIAN-BORN ISRAELI BIBLE SCHOLAR

The Bible itself attests indirectly to the fact that Israel's monotheism is postpatriarchal. Historical monotheism is associated always with certain phenomena which serve as its organic framework: apostolic prophecy, the battle with idolatry, and the name of YHWH. Patriarchal times know none of these. Genesis records divine manifestations and prophecies, but there is no trace of apostolic prophecy. No patriarch is charged with a prophetic mission; the first apostolic prophet is Moses.

From his Religion of Israel—Toldot Ha-emuna Ha-Yisraelit (1937).

Morality is an absolute value, for it is divine in essence. The God who demands righteousness, justice, kindness, and compassion is Himself just, kind and compassionate. Moral goodness makes man share, as it were, in the divine nature.

Ibid.

·•·

When was the battle against the pagan folk religion joined, out of which a monotheistic people emerged? The Torah literature testifies that this battle took place, not only before the time of the literary prophets, but even before the formation of the Torah literature itself. That no story of a battle with paganism is recorded before the age of Moses suggests a *terminus a quo*. Only with Moses does the contrast between the faith of YHVH and paganism appear. The struggle with paganism began with Moses.

Ibid.

Alfred Kazin
[1915–]
U.S. AUTHOR, BOOK REVIEWER, EDITOR

My overwhelming feeling about modern American Judaism is that it's not a question of belief but rather a question of belonging, of attachment. They are interested not in God but in Judaism, which I believe to be essentially ancestor worship.

From the prologue of his Mr. Sammler's Planet (1970).

Larry King
[1924–]
U.S. TALK-SHOW HOST, COLUMNIST

Do you really have a son?

When asked by Bryant Gumbel on the May 1, 1997, Larry King Show: "If you could ask God one question, what would it be?" King then added: "What if the answer is No?"

Jacob al-Kirkisani

TENTH-CENTURY IRAQI-BORN KARAITE SCHOLAR

Scripture as a whole is to be interpreted literally, except where literal interpretation may involve something objectionable or imply a contradiction. . . . Thus we are compelled to say that the verse, *And they saw the God of Israel* (Exodus 24:10), must not be understood literally and does not signify seeing with one's eye, since it is contrary to reason to assume that the Creator may be perceived with man's senses. Generally, however, the Karaites interpret the Bible literally.

Quoted in Leon Nemoy's Karaite Anthology (1952).

Kaufmann Kohler

[1843–1928]

BAVARIAN-BORN U.S. REFORM RABBI

The maintenance of the entire household of nature is one continuous act of God which can neither be interrupted nor limited in time. God in His infinite wisdom works forever through the same laws which were in force in the beginning and which shall continue through all the realms of time and space.

From his Jewish Theology (1918).

Irving Kristol

[1920–]

U.S. WRITER, EDITOR

If God is really dead, by what authority do we say that any particular practice is prohibited or permitted? Pure reason alone cannot tell us that incest is wrong. . . . Pure reason cannot tell us that bestiality is wrong; indeed, the only argument against bestiality these days is that, since we cannot know whether animals enjoy it or not, it is a violation of "animal rights."

Countering the Nietzschean "God is dead" philosophy. Quoted in David Dalin's American Jews and the Separationist Faith (1992).

William Kristol

CONTEMPORARY U.S. EDITOR, PUBLISHER

The future of American Jewry depends, first, on a rejection of the false idols of our times; second, on a willingness to "bend the knee and bow in worship" only to the Holy One, blessed be He; and, finally, on the ability to demonstrate and articulate reasonably the nobility and profundity of the religion into which we have had the good fortune to be born.

Quoted in Moment magazine, December 1997.

Norman Lamm

[1927–]

U.S. ORTHODOX RABBI, UNIVERSITY PRESIDENT

The God of the Bible is beyond, not within, nature: "In the beginning, God created heaven and earth."

From his Faith and Doubt: Studies in Traditional Jewish Thought (1986).

Fran Leibowitz

[1951–]

U.S. WRITER

All God's children are not beautiful. Most of God's children are, in fact, barely presentable.

From her Metropolitan Life (1978).

Michael Lerner

[1943–]

U.S. ENVIRONMENTAL EDUCATOR, AUTHOR, RABBI

Many Jews under 50 report they experience the Jewish world as conformist, materialistic, dominated by the wealthy and the fund-raisers, undemocratic, sexist, lacking in spirituality and defining everyone who criticizes Israeli policy as "self-hating." . . . Create an environment in which children growing up in the Jewish world see that the people who are respected, really have power and influence, are those with greatest sensitivity, caring for others (including non-Jews), spiritual vitality, Jewish learning, commitment to social change and alive to awe, wonder and radical amazement at God's presence in the world—and you'll guarantee the Jewish future.

From Hadassah Magazine, June-July 1993.

.•.

Conceptions of God in Judaism have changed and evolved along with our understanding of ourselves and our world. The God who takes a stroll in the Garden of Eden (Genesis 3:8) made little sense to the rabbis who constructed the Talmud, so they reinterpreted Bible stories in ways that made God into a spiritual entity without a body.

From his Jewish Renewal (1994).

.•.

I believe that God's energy permeates every ounce of Being and every moment of existence, that God is constantly sending us messages and constantly not only making possible our transcendence but demanding and begging us to join with Her/Him in this process.

Ibid.

Jon D. Levenson
HARVARD UNIVERSITY PROFESSOR, AUTHOR

Yes, I do believe in God, the God of Abraham, Isaac, and Jacob, Creator and Master of the world, Who has singled Israel out from all peoples and given them His Torah, and Who will redeem them and all the world in the messianic consummation.

From his essay in Commentary, August 1996.

(Rabbi) Levi
THIRD-CENTURY TALMUDIC SCHOLAR

Six organs serve a person; three are under his control and three are not under his control.

The eye, the ear, and the nose are not under a person's control: he sees what he doesn't want to see, hears what he doesn't want to hear, and smells what he doesn't want to smell.

The mouth, the hand, and the foot are under a person's control. If he wishes, he can use his mouth to study Torah; or if he wishes, he can use it to speak gossip and blasphemy. If he wishes, he can use his hand to distribute charity; or if he wishes, he can use it to steal and kill. If he chooses to, he can use his feet to walk to synagogues or houses of study; or, if he chooses to, he can walk to houses of bawdy entertainment or immorality.

Quoted in Midrash Genesis Rabba (67:3).

Levi ben Gershon [Gersonides]
[1288–1344]
FRENCH-BORN PHILOSOPHER, BIBLE SCHOLAR

God foreknows only the possibilities open to a man in his freedom, not the particular decisions he will make.

From his Sefer Milchamut Adonai ("Book of the Wars of the Lord"), a work severely criticized by traditionalists.

Levi Yitzchak of Berditchev
[1740–1809]
CHASIDIC RABBI

Whether a man really loves God can best be determined by the love he bears for his fellowman.

Quoted in Lothar Kahn's God: What People Have Said about Him (1980).

Emmanuel Levinas
[1905–]
FRENCH PHILOSOPHER, AUTHOR

My effort always consists in extricating from this theological language meanings addressing themselves to reason. . . . [This] consists, first of all, in a mistrust of everything in the texts studied that could pass for a piece of information about God's life, for a theosophy; it consists in being preoccupied, in the face of each of these apparent news items about the beyond, with what this information can mean in and for man's life.

> From his Four Talmudic Readings (1968). *Expressing his approach to rabbinic sources.*

Tehilla Lichtenstein

LEADER OF THE JEWISH SCIENCE MOVEMENT

One of the most important goals which you can set yourself to achieve is the realization of God's presence in your life. I deem it so important because if you can attain to this realization, you will be lifted above all the cares and anxieties of life, you will find that life no longer has the power to hurt you, you will find that life assumes wonderful meaning and joy, you will find yourself safe and secure even in the midst of the greatest vicissitudes and storms. . . .

> From her essay "God in the Silence," in Jewish Science Interpreter, vol. 21, no. 10 (1947).

David Lieber

[1925–]

U.S. CONSERVATIVE RABBI, SCHOLAR, EDUCATOR

God, the source of all existence, is unknown and forever unknowable. At the same time, He does seem to reveal himself in human experience in unexpected moments and in a variety of circumstances. In any case, He functions as the symbol of all human aspirations for self-transcendence, as the ideal limit of man's notion of supreme value. He is "the beyond" in our midst, and faith in Him is an awareness of the ideal possibilities of human life, and of man's ability to fashion his life in the light of them.

> From an essay in Condition of Jewish Belief (1966), *compiled by the editors of* Commentary *magazine.*

. .•. .

The issue is not whether I believe in God; I do. The question is what I mean by that. To me, "God" refers to the creative power at work bringing order out of chaos and maintaining the interrelatedness of all things. Who or what "God" stands for—a process, a being, a force—I do not know, nor does anyone else. What is clear is that "God" is a human construct which enables us to enter into a personal relationship with that power.

From his essay in Commentary, August 1996.

Joshua Loth Liebman
[1907–1948]
U.S. REFORM RABBI, AUTHOR

It is basic to Jewish tradition that God reveals himself anew in every generation, and some of the channels of this revelation in our day are in the healing principles and insights of psychology and psychiatry.

From his Psychiatry and Religion.

Max Lilienthal
[1815–1882]
GERMAN-BORN REFORM RABBI, EDUCATOR

Here are the three doctrines which shall be taught here as the essence of Judaism: First, there is a God, one, indivisible, eternal, spiritual, most holy and most perfect. Second, there is an immortal life and man is a son of eternity. Thirdly, love thy fellow men without distinction of creed or race as thyself.

From his Modern Judaism (1865).

Israel Salanter Lipkin
[1810–1883]
LITHUANIAN RABBI, MORALIST

In imitation of God, it is our duty not only to confer an act of kindness upon those who harm us, but to do it at the very moment we are wronged.

Quoted in Louis Ginzberg's Students, Scholars and Saints (1928).

Herbert M. Loewe

[1882–1940]

BRITISH SCHOLAR

What is false in science cannot be true in religion. Truth is one and indivisible. God is bound by His own laws.

From his Rabbinic Anthology (1938).

Moses Chaim Luzzatto

[1707–1746]

ITALIAN KABBALIST, HEBREW POET, AUTHOR

There is absolutely nothing that He [God] must necessarily do.

Quoted in his Derech Ha-Shem ("The Way of God") (1981).

Samuel David Luzzatto

[1800–1865]

ITALIAN SCHOLAR, PHILOSOPHER

Judaism looks upon all human beings as children of one Father; thinks of them all as created in the image of God, and insists that a man be judged not by his religion, but his action.

From his Yesodei Ha-Torah (1880).

Norman Mailer

[1932–]

U.S. NOVELIST, POLITICIAN

If God is all good, then he is not all powerful. If God is all powerful, then he is not all good. I am a disbeliever in the omnipotence of God because of the Holocaust. But for 35 years or so, I have been believing that He is doing the best He can.

Upon the publication of his The Gospel According to the Son.
Quoted in Time, May 5, 1997.

I've always been religious. I just have a God that's a little different from others. It's not because I'm special. It's just that it's the only thing that makes sense for me: the notion I have of an imperfect God doing the best that He or She can do. I've found it immensely useful as a religion, because self-pity used to be one of my vices.

> Commenting on the publication of his The Gospel According to the Son in The New York Times, April 24, 1997.

Moses Maimonides
[1135–1204]
SPANISH RABBI, PHYSICIAN, SCHOLAR, PHILOSOPHER, AUTHOR

God is one; He is not two, but one. The oneness of any of the single things existent in the Universe is unlike His Unity. He is not one as a species since this includes numerous individuals; nor one as a body since this is divisible into parts and sections, but a Unity which is unique in the world.

> From his Mishneh Torah, Yesodei Ha-Torah (1:7).

•—•

The basic principle of all basic principles and the foundation of all wisdom is to realize that there is a Prime Being who brought into being everything that exists and that all creatures in heaven and earth and between them only enjoy existence by virtue of His existence. If it could be imagined that He did not exist, then nothing else could have existed. But if it could be imagined that all beings were non-existent, He alone would still exist. For all beings need Him but He, blessed be He, needs not a single one of them.

> Ibid. (1:1).

•—•

I believe with complete faith in the existence of the Creator, blessed be He, who is perfect in all aspects of existence; that He is the cause of all things in existence, and nothing can exist without Him.

> Based upon his commentary to the Mishna Sanhedrin (10), in which he presents Thirteen Principles (Articles) of Faith in which every Jew must believe in order to be assured a place in the world-to-come. These principles were recast in poetic form by an unknown author; the composition is known as Ani Maamin ("I Believe"). Maimonides' Thirteen Principles is

also the basis of the Yigdal hymn, which was composed in the year 1300 by Daniel ben Judah and which is part of the daily morning (Shacharit) liturgy.

.•.

I believe with complete faith that the Creator, blessed be He, is One and totally unique, unlike any other species or entity. He alone is our God who was, is, and ever will be.

Ibid.

.•.

I believe with complete faith that the Creator, blessed be He, is not a physical being. Physical attributes such as movement and rest do not apply to Him.

Ibid.

.•.

I believe with complete faith that the Creator, blessed be He, is the absolute first, and everything else that exists is not first in relation to Him.

Ibid.

.•.

I believe with complete faith that the Creator, blessed be He—and may He be exalted—is the only One worthy of worship, and that his greatness should be made known to all.

Ibid.

.•.

Existence, life, power, wisdom and will, when applied to God, have not the same meaning as when applied to us. . . . It cannot be said that His [God's] existence is more stable, His life more permanent, His power greater, His wisdom more perfect, and His will more pervasive, and that the same definition applies to both of us. . . . There is no comparison between the essence of God and that of other beings.

From his Guide of the Perplexed (1190).

.•.

We can only obtain a knowledge of God through His works; His works give evidence of His existence.

Ibid.

The Ishmaelites [Mohammedans] are not considered pagans in any sense; no trace of paganism is left in their speech and in their hearts; they confess the Unity of God in its correct and unconditional meaning. People say that their houses of worship are pagan, that they contain pagan symbols which were revered by their ancestors. But this does not matter. Even if they still bow to them, their hearts are directed toward God. They may be deluded and in error in various matters, but concerning monotheism they are not at all mistaken.

From a responsum in Teshuboth ha-Rambam (1934), edited by A. Freimann.

Whoever conceives of God as a corporeal being is an apostate.

From his Mishneh Torah, Hilchot Teshuva (3:7).

It is manifest that God is identical with His attributes and His attributes with Him, so that it may be said that He is the knowledge, the Knower, and the Known, and that He is the Life, the Living, and the Source of His own life, the same being true of His other attributes. This conception is very hard to grasp. . . .

From his Eight Chapters (8), a preface to his comments on the Ethics of the Fathers.

(Prophet) Malachi
FIFTH-CENTURY B.C.E. PROPHET OF ISRAEL

Have we not all one Father?
Did not one God create us all?
Why then do we deal unkindly with one another?

From the Book of Malachi (2:10).

Daniel C. Matt

PROFESSOR OF MYSTICISM, RABBI, AUTHOR

This discovery demands that we continue to expand our understanding of God. That's the greatest challenge to spirituality, to avoid fixation on any one notion of God. This will be a healthy corrective . . . to see God as the energy which pervades all material existence.

Commenting on the August 1996 discovery of what may turn out to be primitive life on Mars.

Louis B. Mayer

[1885–1957]

U.S. MOTION PICTURE EXECUTIVE

If children get a love of God in their hearts they'll keep that love through their lives. Why is it that there are so few Catholic converts to Communism? It is because they learned the love of God when they were children. Why don't Jews and Protestants do the same thing?

From a speech at a Chamber of Commerce dinner in his honor in April 1954. Quoted in Neal Gabler's An Empire of Their Own *(1988).*

Marshall T. Meyer

[1930–1993]

U.S. CONSERVATIVE RABBI, EDUCATOR

What is so great about the fact that there is one God? Suppose there are 10 gods? Or 20 gods? Or none. . . . But if there is one creator God, there is a tremendous consequence. You and I are brothers and the Haitians are my brothers and sisters. Now that is a major difference that you don't get without the concept of God, and that is particularly Jewish.

Quoted in The Jewish Advocate, *January 1996.*

Michael A. Meyer

CONTEMPORARY U.S. WRITER

My belief in God approximates closely that of the German-Jewish Kantian thinker Hermann Cohen who understood God to be an Ideal to which human lives respond and to which the Jews have responded in unique fashion.

From his essay in Commentary, August 1996.

． ・•・

The God Who is our Ideal is clearly not a personal God except through the metaphors we necessarily employ in prayer. But such a god is incomparably relevant to our religious and moral lives. The Ideal is a source of imperatives for our conduct that are every bit as demanding as those issued by a personal God.

Ibid.

Arthur Miller

[1915–]

U.S. PLAYWRIGHT, NOVELIST

Whatever the inspiration from above, a poet or poets wrote Genesis, and some editor-rabbi made the decision to set it at the very opening of the holy books of the Jewish people. It had to be the first book because it tells why there has to be God, and thus makes the rest of the Bible necessary. Without the murder of Abel, the Bible is but one more clan history, a curio. It is this fratricide that anchors the Jewish religion in human life, just as the Crucifixion does in the Christian cosmos.

From his essay "The Story of Adam and Eve" in Genesis: As It Is Written (1996), edited by David Rosenberg.

Henry Miller

[1891–1980]

U.S. AUTHOR

Imagination is the voice of daring. If there is anything Godlike about God it is that He dared to imagine everything.

From his Sexus (1949).

Jacob Minkin

CONTEMPORARY U.S. CONSERVATIVE RABBI, AUTHOR

It came to him [the Baal Shem Tov] simply and naturally from his profound love and knowledge of nature that God did not create the world and then withdraw from it; creation is continuous, progressive, unending.

> Claiming that the Baal Shem Tov was a Spinozan pantheist without knowing it. From his Romance of Hassidism (1955).

Lily (Lilian) H. Montague

[1873–1963]

BRITISH SOCIAL WORKER, LIBERAL RELIGIOUS LEADER

I believe in God as the God of truth. . . . It matters infinitely what we think and believe, for thought and belief do affect conduct. We know that some of the best Jews the world has produced have been unlearned and that learning and the love of truth are not necessarily the same thing.

> From her Faith of a Jewish Woman (1958).

Claude G. Montefiore

[1858–1938]

BRITISH SCHOLAR, AUTHOR

Hard as it is for the world to explain with God, it is harder yet without Him.

> From his Liberal Judaism (1903).

Moses

BIBLE HERO, LEADER OF THE CHILDREN OF ISRAEL

Hear, O Israel! The Lord is our God, the Lord is one.

> Calling upon Israel to keep the commandments so as to be ensured that He will bring them good fortune and so that tenure in the Land will be long and fruitful. Quoted in the Book of Deuteronomy (6:4).

Joel Myers

EXECUTIVE VICE-PRESIDENT OF THE RABBINICAL ASSEMBLY

When all is said and done, there is much that matters deeply to us that is in God's hands alone, while at the same time, every day is filled with blessings large and small, for which we are grateful beyond words.

From a message in the Rabbinical Assembly Newsletter, September 1998.

Nachmanides (Moses ben Nachman)

[1194–1270]

SPANISH TALMUDIST, PHYSICIAN

You are not master of your words, nor have you power over your hand; everything is of the Lord, who forms your heart.

From a letter to his son, c. 1268.

Cynthia Ozick

[1928–]

U.S. AUTHOR, PLAYWRIGHT, ESSAYIST

The universal Creator is necessarily One, affirming the unity of humankind. . . . The universal Creator, as expressed in Judaism, is transcendent, incorporeal, un-imaged, never incarnate, never immanent, never enfleshed in any form imaginable by human conceptual powers. God's nature is hidden from us. . . .

All this is why I find the phrase "the love of God" intellectually perilous and spiritually demeaning. It leads inexorably to definition, which is to limit, to objectify-and to objectify in subjective terms. . . .

In Judaism the love of God is enacted through right conduct and the study of right conduct; the act of study, concerning itself with the modes of human civilization, is itself holy. The deep study of right conduct is equal to prayer and liturgy; it is the extension and augmentation of prayer.

From her essay "Love Is What We Do," in Portland: The University of Portland Magazine, winter 1977, in which she condemns the loose use of the term "love of God" as spiritually demeaning.

Arno Penzias

1978 NOBEL LAUREATE IN PHYSICS

By looking at the order of the world, we can infer purpose and from purpose we begin to get some knowledge of the Creator, the Planner of all this. I look at God through the works of God's hands and from those works imply intentions. From these intentions, I receive an impression of the Almighty.

Quoted in The God I Believe In (1994), by Joshua O. Haberman.

Isaac Leibush (I.L.) Peretz

[1852–1915]
POLISH–BORN YIDDISH NOVELIST, POET, CRITIC

Zeitlin once wrote: "Peretz has a heaven, but no God in heaven!" The first half of the phrase is a compliment, and I acknowledge it gratefully. And I confirm that the second half is true, too. I don't even know where to look for His dear Name! Before the world—He is its Creator? After the world—He slips out of it?

From his essay "Roads That Lead Away from Jewishness." Reprinted in Joseph Leftwich's The Way We Think (1969).

Philo

[c. 20 B.C.E.–40 C.E.]
ALEXANDRIAN PHILOSOPHER, BIBLE SCHOLAR, AUTHOR

The whole heaven and the whole world is an offering dedicated to God, and it is He who has created the offering; and all God-beloved souls, citizens of the world, consecrate themselves, allowing no mortal attraction to draw them in the opposite direction, and they never grow weary of devoting and sanctifying their own imperishable life.

From his essay "On the Eternity of the World."

Judith Plaskow

[1948–   ]

FEMINIST THEOLOGIAN, EDUCATOR

Because relationships among human beings are unique in containing the potential for the full mutuality and reciprocity that form the foundations of the moral life, it is important that we use anthropomorphic imagery [for God], and that we broaden it as far as possible. But our moral responsibility extends to the entire web of creation, all of which manifests and can symbolize divine presence and activity.

> From her essay "Spirituality and Politics: Lessons from B'not Esh," in Tikkun magazine, May–June 1995.

. .•. .

These images of God—lover, friend, companion, cocreator—are more appropriate metaphors for the God of the covenant than the traditional images of lord and king. Defining God's power not as domination but empowerment, they evoke a God who is with us instead of over us, a partner in dialogue who ever and again summons us to responsible action.

> From her Standing Again at Sinai: Judaism from a Feminist Perspective (1990).

. .•. .

When God is conceived of as a male, as a king ruling over the universe, male rule in society seems appropriate and right.

> Ibid.

Dennis Prager

CONTEMPORARY U.S. AUTHOR, EDITOR, RADIO TALK-SHOW HOST

First, and most important, this verse [in the Bible, Genesis 1:1] makes everything after it both logically tenable and morally necessary. Or, to put in the negative, if God did not create the world, i.e., if the world always was or came about by itself, the rest of the Torah and the whole Jewish vocation becomes pointless. Indeed, all of life is pointless without God the Creator.

> From his essay in Moment magazine, February 1999.

·✦·

If there is no God, life itself, let alone Judaism, is ultimately pointless—
and cruelly pointless for the innumerable millions who have led lives
primarily of suffering. If there is no God, we human beings are merely
chance creatures of blind, impersonal forces . . . And if there is no
God, morality, too, is make-believe, a pragmatic invention of people to
try to stop the powerful from exploiting the powerless.

Ibid.

Dennis Prager/Joseph Telushkin

CONTEMPORARY U.S. AUTHORS

The Jew introduced God into the world, and called all people to live in
brotherhood by accepting one moral standard based upon God. Each of
these ideals, a universal God, a universal moral law, and universal brotherhood, was revealed for the first time 3,200 years ago, to some ex-
slaves in the Sinai desert.

From their The Nine Questions People Ask About Judaism
(1975).

Sally Priesand

[1946–]

FIRST U.S. FEMALE RABBI

In rabbinical school I always believed in an all-powerful God, but when
you start dealing with real people who suffer, that's not the kind of God
you can believe in. I've started to believe in a God who is not all-powerful but loving, who is with us, helping us to cope, sometimes disap-
pointed in us, not able to prevent tragedies from happening to us—a
God who weeps with us.

From an interview with Judy Petsonik in Hadassah Magazine, June–July
1993.

Emanuel Rackman
[1910–]
U.S. ORTHODOX RABBI, SCHOLAR, EDUCATOR

Truth for me is God's name. His total being. It must address itself to my total being. Much I may never be able to explain, but the explanation exists. It exists in God. And to His will I deliver myself—or at least aspire to deliver myself.

From an essay in Condition of Jewish Belief (1966), compiled by the editors of Commentary magazine.

．•．

God may have His own reason for denying us certainty with regard to His existence and nature. One reason apparent to us is that man's certainty with regard to anything is poison to his soul. Who knows this better than moderns who have had to cope with dogmatic Fascists, Communists, and even scientists?

Ibid.

Rashi
[1040–1105]
FRENCH BIBLE AND TALMUD COMMENTATOR

When the heathen will forsake their idols, God will be One.

Commentary on the verse in Zechariah (14:9): "In that day God will be One and His name One."

Resh Lakish
Also known as Rabbi Shimon (Simeon)
SECOND/THIRD-CENTURY TALMUDIC SCHOLAR

Proselytes are dear to God more so than those Jews who stood at Mount Sinai, for had the latter not heard the thunder and seen the lightening and observed the mountains shaking and experienced the sounding of the shofar, they would not have accepted the sovereignty of God. But these converts experienced none of these things, and yet accepted the dominion of God. Is anyone dearer to God?

Quoted in Midrash Tanchuma, Lech Lecha 6.

· ◆ ·

The king of wild animals is the lion; the king of cattle is the ox; the king of birds is the eagle; and man is exalted over them all. But the Holy One, blessed be He, is exalted over them and over the whole world.

Quoted in the talmudic tractate Chagiga (13b).

Anne Roiphe
[1935–   ]
U.S. WRITER, NOVELIST

I cannot accept God as the Good-Surgeon-in-the-Sky. Whatever tumors He may be removing, He has also planted there.

From her Generation without Memory (1981).

Franz Rosenzweig
[1886–1929]
GERMAN PHILOSOPHER, THEOLOGIAN

As long as God is still creating, he does not in fact say "I," He says "We," an absolute, all-inclusive term which does not refer to an I outside the self but is the plural of all-encompassing majesty. It is an impersonal I, an I that does not face another Thou, that does not reveal anything but lives, like the metaphysical God of pre-creation, only in itself.

Commenting on "Let us make man . . ." in Genesis 1:26. From his Star of Redemption (1970).

Leon Roth
[1896–1963]
ENGLISH-BORN PHILOSOPHER, SCHOLAR

Monotheism means not only the positive search for unity but also, negatively, the refusal to set man in the throne of God.

From his Jewish Thought (1927).

Richard Rubenstein

[1924–]

U.S. CONSERVATIVE RABBI, AUTHOR, EDUCATOR

I believe in God as the Holy Nothingness, the Ground of all existence, the Source out of which we come and to which we ultimately return. . . . To speak of God as the Holy Nothingness, Das Heilige Nichts, the En Sof of Kabbalah, is to assert that God is beyond all limitation and finite "thinghood." Such imperfect language is not meant to suggest that God is a void. On the contrary, the holy Nothingness is a plenum so rich that all existence derives therefrom.

From his essay in Commentary, August 1966.

Israel Salanter

[1810–1883]

LITHUANIAN RABBI, MORALIST

God is called Rachmana, meaning "Merciful One." An act of mercy is a prayer, too.

Quoted in Lothar Kahn's God: What People Have Said about Him (1980).

Samuel ben Nachman

THIRD-CENTURY TALMUDIC SCHOLAR

In that hour the ministering angels wished to utter songs [of praise] to the Holy One blessed be He, but He rebuked them saying, "My own creations are drowning in the sea, and you would utter song in My presence?!"

Referring to the drowning of the Egyptians in the Red Sea when they pursued the Israelites after the Exodus. Elaborating upon the view of his teacher Rabbi Jonathan in the talmudic tractate Sanhedrin (39b).

Gershom Scholem

[1897–1982]

GERMAN-BORN HISTORIAN, AUTHORITY ON MYSTICISM

In all the numerous references to the Shekhinah in the Talmud and the Midrashim . . . there is no hint that it represents a feminine element in God.

From his Major Trends in Jewish Mysticism (1941).

Ismar Schorsch

[1925–]

U.S. CONSERVATIVE RABBI, HISTORIAN, EDUCATOR

God is a verb and not a noun, an ineffable presence that graces my life, with a daily touch of eternity.

From his essay "What Do Jews Believe?" in Commentary, August 1996.

Howard Eilberg Schwartz

CONTEMPORARY U.S. AUTHOR

A father God who has no body, or one who turns his back so that we cannot see his face, is not a father with whom some of us find it possible to be intimate. . . . I imagine a liturgy in which both male and female images are evoked, in which each of us can see God as nurturing and powerful.

From his God's Phallus: And Other Problems for Men and Monotheism (1994).

Zelda Shluker

CONTEMPORARY MAGAZINE EDITOR

God may have been declared dead in the '60s but His high profile in the '90s—in the arts, in health care and synagogues and other establishment organizations—suggests the announcement of His demise was premature.

From her Editor's Wrapup, Hadassah Magazine, November 1996.

Shneur Zalman ben Baruch of Lyadi
[1747–1813]
FOUNDER OF THE CHABAD MOVEMENT

When man completes a product, his relation to it ends; but God's power continues to permeate His creatures.
From his Tanya (1796).

All that man sees—the heaven, the earth, and all that fills it—all these things are the external garments of God, and by observing them, man recognizes the inner spirit, that is, the divine vital force which permeates them.
Ibid.

Every act of kindness that God performs for man should make him feel not proud, but more humble and loving.
Ibid.

God is totally distinct from both the upper and lower worlds and can in no way be compared to the soul of man.
From his Iggeret Ha-kodesh (1805).

Sholom Aleichem
[1859–1916]
UKRAINIAN-BORN AUTHOR, YIDDISH HUMORIST

God must hate a poor man, else why did He make him poor?
Spoken by the title character in his Tevye the Dairyman.

Abba Hillel Silver
[1893–1963]
U.S. REFORM RABBI, ZIONIST LEADER

Other nations of antiquity, when they were defeated, acknowledged that their gods had been defeated [and they converted to the victor's religion]. The Jews always show in their defeat the triumph of God.
From his World Crisis and Jewish Survival.

Simcha Bunam of Przyuscha
CHASIDIC LEADER

God created the world in a state of beginning. The universe is always in an uncompleted state, in the form of its beginning. It is not like a vessel at which the master works to finish it; it requires continuous labor and renewal by creative forces. Should these cease for only a second, the universe would return to primeval chaos.
Quoted in Louis I. Neuman's The Hasidic Anthology (1944).

Simeon ben Yochai
SECOND-CENTURY TALMUDIC SCHOLAR

A bird does not fall into a trap without the will of God.
Quoted in the Jerusalem Talmud, Sheviit (9:10).

Isaac Bashevis Singer
[1904–1991]
POLISH-BORN NOVELIST, NOBEL PRIZE WINNER

The belief in God is as necessary as sex.
Quoted in The New York Times, October 23, 1968.

．＊．

Although I came to doubt all revelation, I can never accept the idea that the universe is a physical or chemical accident, a result of blind evolution. Even though I learned to recognize the lies, the clichés, and the idolatries of the human mind, I still cling to some truths which I think all of us might accept someday. There must be a way for man to attain all possible pleasures, all the powers and knowledge that nature can grant him, and still serve God—a God who speaks in deeds, not in words, and whose vocabulary is the universe.

> From his lecture upon receiving the Nobel Prize in literature, delivered before the assembled guests at the Nobel Prize banquet in the city of Stockholm, Sweden, on December 10, 1978.

Religion is not a simple thing and neither is love. You can love a woman and still betray her. In my belief in God there's only one thing which is steady: I never say that the universe was an accident. The word "accident" should be erased from the dictionary. It has some meaning in everyday life but no meaning in philosophy.

> From Richard Burgin's Conversations with Isaac Bashevis Singer (1978).

Everything man says about God is pure guesswork. But since I believe in God's existence and since God created man and formed his brain, I believe also that there must be something of the divine in men's ideas about Him—even if they are far from being adequate.

> Ibid.

To me, nature is not a blind thing, as the modern scientists claim. That the sun and the moon and the galaxies operate with no knowledge, and that the only ones who have knowledge are a few professors in a few universities—is not what I believe. I said some time ago that if you would come to an island, and you would find there a wrist–watch, and someone would tell you that this wrist-watch made itself—there was a little metal, and a little glass, and in the course of a billion years they come together and became a wrist-watch—you would say: not even in twenty billion years. And I say: is the universe less complicated than a wrist-watch? So, you must recognize that there is some higher power, some idea, some plan. Once you recognize this, you begin to believe in the existence of God.

> From an interview with Nili Wachtel that appeared in The Jewish Spectator, spring 1975.

Joseph B. Soloveitchik

[1903–1993]

U.S. ORTHODOX RABBI, SCHOLAR, PROFESSOR

[The religious mind] views God from the aspect of His creation; and the first response to such an idea is a purified desire to penetrate the mystery of phenomenal reality. The cognition of this world is of the innermost essence of the religious experience.

> From his Lonely Man of Faith (1965), which explores the dual nature of religious man.

.•.

Who is He who trails me steadily, uninvited and unwanted, like an everlasting shadow, and vanishes into the recesses of transcendence the very instant I turn around to confront this numinous, awesome, and mysterious "He"?

> Ibid.

.•.

Most of our sages distinguished between chukim and mishpatim. They declared the compliance with chukim to be a gesture of pure obedience and subordination to God. Conversely, adherence to mishpatim is a result of an inner moral need that God implanted in man, when the latter was created in His image. The mere fact that man carries God's image within himself suggests that morality is characteristic of human nature, and that doing good is an indispensable necessity, no less than food or air.

> From a June 22, 1972 address to the Rabbinical Council of America.

Shalom Spiegel

[1889–1984]

U.S. AUTHOR, EDUCATOR

All these people [Arameans, Philistines, Ethiopians] and races had a variety of observances and practices which differed with the landscape. But all these peoples and races also were held by the biblical faith to be the children of one God, the Father of all men. It would seem inconceivable, if underneath their variety a trace or token of their common origin did not remain. Whatever their differences, the fingerprint of the

Creator should be discernible in all his creatures, stamping all as fellow-bearers of the divine image.

> From his essay "Amos vs. Amaziah," which was originally delivered as an address on September 13, 1957 at the Jewish Theological Seminary of America.

Baruch (Benedict) Spinoza
[1632–1677]
DUTCH PHILOSOPHER, AUTHOR

The existence and essence of God are one and the same.

> From his Ethics (1677).

·•·

God is without passions, neither is He affected by any emotion of pleasure or pain.

> Ibid.

·•·

God and all the attributes of God are eternal.

> Ibid.

·•·

Whatsoever is, is in God.

> Ibid.

·•·

God is the indwelling, not the transient cause, of all things.

> Ibid.

·•·

The power of nature is the power of God.

> From his Theological-Political Treatise (1670).

·•·

He is One. Nobody will dispute that this doctrine is absolutely necessary for complete devotion, admiration, and love toward God. For devotion, admiration, and love spring from the superiority of one over all else.

> Ibid.

Moses conceived the Deity as a Being who has always existed, does exist, and always will exist, and he therefore called Him Jehovah, which in Hebrew signifies these three phases.

Ibid.

Milton Steinberg
[1903–1950]
U.S. CONSERVATIVE RABBI, AUTHOR, SCHOLAR

Given the One God concept, the whole universe bursts into lucidity. The rationality of nature, the emergence of life, the phenomena of conscience and consciousness become intelligible. Deny it and the who becomes inexplicable.

From his A Believing Jew (1951).

By positing God it [Judaism] inhibits man from laying claim to being God. It prevents his becoming less than man through the arrogance of claiming to be more. In brief, it helps to keep man human.

Ibid.

If the believer has his troubles with evil, the atheist has more and graver difficulties to contend with. Reality stumps him altogether, leaving him baffled not by one consideration but by many, from the existence of natural law through the instinctual cunning of the insect to the brain of the genius and the heart of the prophet. This, then, is the intellectual reason for believing in God: that, though this belief is not free from difficulties, it stands out, head to shoulders, as the best answer to the riddle of the universe.

From his Anatomy of Faith (1960).

To believe in God maturely . . . is to believe that reality did not just happen, that it is no accident, no pointless interplay of matter and energy. It is to insist rather that things, including man's life, make sense, that they add up to something. It is to hold that the universe, physical and moral, is a cosmos, not an anarchy.

Ibid.

I. F. Stone
[1907–1989]
U.S. JOURNALIST

If God as some now say is dead, he no doubt died of trying to find an equitable solution to the Arab-Jewish problem.

Quoted in The New York Review of Books, *August 3, 1967.*

Daniel B. Syme
CONTEMPORARY U.S. REFORM RABBI

I deeply respect any Jew who has a firmly rooted Jewish theology, who embraces a particular notion of God and speaks of it proudly and assertively. But I am not prepared to dismiss other Jews whose theology may not be biblical or rabbinic but is deeply held conviction. . . . The fact is that no one knows what God is or isn't. There is no one authoritative, universally accepted, Jewish concept of God.

From his essay *"Talking to Kids about God,"* which appears in The Hadassah Magazine Jewish Parenting Book (1989), *edited by Roselyn Bell.*

Burton L. Visotzky
[1953–]
PROFESSOR OF MIDRASH, BIBLE SCHOLAR,
CONSERVATIVE RABBI

If humanity reflects God, we have to understand that God has both male and female aspects in some miraculous way.

Quoted in his Talking About Genesis *(1996).*

·◆·

No, what I actually said is that God is a *mean* son of a bitch.

When asked by a student if it is true that he called God "a son of a bitch."

He went on to explain he was trying to distinguish between biblical theology and rabbinic theology. "The latter depicts God as Nice or Good; the Bible made no such pretense." Quoted in his The Genesis of Ethics (1996).

Chaim Vital
SEVENTEENTH-CENTURY KABBALIST

The Lord God is father and mother too.

From his Etz Cha'yim, in which are recorded the mystic views of his teacher Isaac Luria, popularly known as the Ari.

Harlan J. Wechsler
CONTEMPORARY U.S. CONSERVATIVE RABBI,
PROFESSOR OF PHILOSOPHY

I believe in the God of the Bible—Who is utterly other, one, indivisible, and incorporeal, unlike all things of this world. Language cannot describe Him, but He is known through His actions in the world. His wisdom is manifest in His sublime creation, His love in the giving of the Torah, His justice and power in the redemption of His people from slavery . . .

From his essay in Commentary, August 1996.

Simone Weil
[1909–1943]
FRENCH PHILOSOPHER, AUTHOR

It is only the impossible that is possible for God.

Quoted in Selected Essays (1943), edited by Richard Rees.

·•·

Necessity is God's veil.

From her Gravity and Grace (1947).

·•·

Two prisoners whose cells adjoin communicate with each other by knocking on the wall. The wall is the thing which separates them but is also their means of communication. It is the same with us and God. Every separation is a link.

Ibid.

An atheist may be simply one whose faith and love are concentrated on the impersonal aspects of God.

Quoted in A Certain World (1970), by W. H. Auden.

We can only know one thing about God—that He is what we are not. Our wretchedness alone is an image of this. The more we contemplate it, the more we contemplate Him.

Ibid.

We must love all facts, not for their consequences, but because in each fact God is there present.

From her Notebooks of Simone Weil (1951).

Elie Wiesel
[1928–   ]
RUMANIAN-BORN U.S. AUTHOR, PROFESSOR

One has to be mad today to believe in God and in man—one has to be mad to believe. One has to be mad to want to remain human. Be mad, Rabbi, be mad!

From his play Zalmen, Or the Madness of God (1974).

Tear fear out by the root! Let it not become your night and your universe, your silence and your lie—or, what is worse, your truth, your God.

Ibid.

The Jew may love God, or he may fight God, but he may not ignore God.

Quoted in his Gates of the Forest (1982).

. •.

God created human beings because God loves stories.

Quoted in Our Share of Night, Our Share of Morning (1996), by Nancy Fuchs.

Sherwin Wine

CONTEMPORARY U.S. RABBI,
FOUNDER OF HUMANISTIC JUDAISM

If you ask the question, "Who made the world?" and your answer is "God," you can logically ask the question, "Who made God? Super-God?" And you can then logically ask, "Who made Super-God? Super-Super God?" There's an infinite regression. You might as well just stop with the world. The world is there. The point is, God isn't an answer. God is the avoidance of an answer.

Quoted in Moment Magazine, February 1999, in an interview with Hershel Shanks when asked: "Do you reject the idea of a Creator?"

. •.

"God" is an ordinary English word like "table," "chair" or "rug." It is attached to verbs: God hears, God knows, God sees. You can't escape that when you use the word "God."

Ibid.

. •.

I don't doubt that large numbers of Reform Jews and the overwhelming majority of Reconstructionist Jews subscribe to the humanistic idea. I was trained as a Reform rabbi. I left the Reform movement because of the absence of integrity. Why would you say, "Praised art thou, Lord our God, King of the Universe," if what you mean is that there is no king of the universe and there is no divine and loving providence out there? Most of the people at Hebrew Union College when I graduated in 1956 were basically humanistic. I tried to fit humanistic beliefs into theistic vocabulary.

Ibid.

Avi Winokur

CONTEMPORARY U.S. RECONSTRUCTIONIST RABBI

Reconstructionist Jews conceive of God as the ultimate cosmic force: that force which stands behind all creativity, all striving for justice, the will to love and the pursuit of harmony. God is not a being or a thing, but a force in motion; the very essence of the creative process that empowers our universe and ourselves.

Quoted in The Jewish Week, February 5, 1993.

Isaac Mayer Wise

[1819–1900]

GERMAN-BORN U.S. REFORM RABBI, EDUCATOR

An English word expressing at once "he was, he is, and he will be," would be an equivalent for Jehovah, but it would have to convey the meaning . . . also of causation. There is no such term in any language except the Hebrew, so far as I know.

Quoted in his Outlines of Judaism (1869).

Stephen S. Wise

[1874–1949]

U.S. REFORM RABBI, ZIONIST LEADER, EDUCATOR

But the truth is that we do not know the truth. Dogmatic humanists are much too sure that God is not something-or-other. We on the traditionalist side are much too ready to commit the Master of the universe in writing to one or another of our own pet projects. God is, whatever else, a Mystery, and Jews must be, whatever else they may be, humble before Him who spoke and theology came to be.

From his On God and Theology.

David J. Wolpe

CONTEMPORARY U.S. CONSERVATIVE RABBI, AUTHOR, EDUCATOR

Faith is grasped first by tones and mood. Before approaching the Jewish conception of God, we must step back to feel the world in which belief is born and nurtured. . . .

We are best touched at night. The day seems harsh and real and rational, but night—even with electric lamps and neon splitting the dark—casts a sensitizing shade over us. There are night thoughts and night imaginings. There are certainties of the night that can be shaken by nothing except the coming of the dawn. Fear is a night child. So is faith.

From his Healer of Shattered Hearts (1990).

.•.

As images of God we are given a sacred task. The task is to reflect that image in our lives each day. A mitzvah is a brushstroke; a well-lived life an invisible but indelible image. An idol is the work of our hands. An image begins in the work of one's heart.

From his essay in The Jewish Week, June 27, 1997.

Herman Wouk

[1915–]

U.S. AUTHOR, NOVELIST

Religious people tend to encounter . . . a cemented certainty that belief in God is a crutch for the weak and the fearful. It would be just as silly to assert that disbelief in God is a crutch for the immoral and the ill-read.

From his novel Inside, Outside (1985), in which self-deprecating Jewish comedians are condemned.

A. B. Yehoshua

[1936–]

ISRAELI NOVELIST

Even though I don't believe in God, I am concerned with the way humans use the word God.

From an essay by Rahel Muslech in Hadassah Magazine, January 1998.

Yochanan ben Nappacha
[190–279]
TALMUDIC SCHOLAR

The ministering angels wanted to chant their hymns, but the Holy One, blessed be He, said: "The work of My hands is drowning in the sea, and you want to chant hymns!"

> *Expressing how disturbed God is when any of his creatures suffer. Quoted in the talmudic tractate Megilla (10b) and Sanhedrin (39b), where it is attributed to Rabbi Jonathan.*

·•·

Wherever you find [in Scripture] an expression of God's might, you will also find mention of His humility [and compassion].

> *Quoted in the talmudic tractate Megilla (31a). Emphasizing that it is not beneath God to help the poor and downtrodden.*

·•·

The Holy One, blessed be He, does not rejoice at the downfall of the wicked.

> *Explaining why the words "for He is good" are omitted from the Prayer of Thanksgiving in II Chronicles 20:21. Quoted in the talmudic tractate Megilla (10b).*

·•·

For three persons does God proclaim his special approval each day: a bachelor who lives in a large town and does not sin; a poor man who returns lost property to its owner; and a wealthy man who tithes his produce secretly [unostentatiously].

> *Quoted in the talmudic tractate Pesachim (113a).*

Yossi ben Chalafta
SECOND-CENTURY TALMUDIC SCHOLAR

God is called Makom [Place], because He contains and is not contained, He is a place for all to flee to, and He is Himself the space which holds Him.

> *Quoted in Genesis Rabba (68:9).*

Israel Zangwill

[1864–1926]

BRITISH AUTHOR

There is no God but God, and Israel is His prophet; not Moses, not Christ, not Mohammed, but Israel, the race in whom God was revealed.

From an article in the North American Review, April 1895.

Zechariah

SIXTH-CENTURY B.C.E. PROPHET OF ISRAEL

Not by might, nor by power, but by my spirit, saith the Lord of hosts.

The prophet expressing, in the Book of Zechariah (4:6), the belief that man is the instrument of God, and all his achievements derive from God.

.•.

The Eternal shall reign over all the earth; on that day there shall be one Lord with one name.

From the Book of Zechariah (14:9).

Zevi Elimelech of Dinov

[1785–1841]

CHASIDIC MASTER

God, blessed be He, has brought all creatures into being. By His power and will, blessed be He, there has come into existence everything that was, is and will be and nothing exists except by His will and desire. His providence extends over all, in general and particular, so that even the natural order is the result of His desire to use nature as the garment of His providence.

From his compendium Derech Pikudecha ("The Way of Your Precepts"), no. 25. Quoted in Louis Jacobs's The Jewish Religion: A Companion (1995).

Sheldon Zimmerman

CONTEMPORARY U.S. REFORM RABBI, SEMINARY PRESIDENT,
EDUCATOR

I believe in God, the Creator of the universe and all that exists, the ongoing creative source of its unity, harmony, order, and meaning. God has established a covenantal relationship with all humankind and everything that lives (the Noahide covenant), calling all of us to an ethical life of justice and peace. We are all God's children.

From his essay in Commentary, August 1996.

(Mar) Zutra ben Tobiah

THIRD-CENTURY BABYLONIAN SCHOLAR

What does God say when He prays? He prays as follows: "May it be My will that My mercy may subdue My wrath, that My love may have supremacy over all My other qualities, so that I may deal with My children in accordance with the attribute of mercy, overlooking the rigorous demands of stern justice."

Quoted in the talmudic tractate Berachot (7a).

CHAPTER TWO

Searching For
and Experiencing God

Introduction

INDING GOD AND ALLOWING ONESELF to experience His presence on a continuous basis is for many people elusive. Even theologians and scholars who have spent a lifetime writing and lecturing about God have, in the end, found God to be an inexplicable mystery. Nonetheless, the search continues.

In 1994, in an address at Queens College, in New York City, Elie Wiesel shared how he establishes a connection with God:

> If I want to come closer to God . . . it is only by coming closer to my fellow human beings. . . . If I am your friend, I am God's friend. If not, I am the enemy of both God and His creatures.

Then, three years later, at a fall 1997 conference with Czech Republic president Vaclav Havel, Wiesel remarked:

> In all my work, fiction and nonfiction, I have been struggling with these questions. Where was God [when man was killing his fellow man]? Or the presence of God? The complexity of God? If you think I have the answer, you know me better than that.

Finding God in Truth

Andrew Johnson, the seventeenth president of the United States, was critically ill in July of 1875, not expecting to survive the cancer that had sapped his strength. Seven years earlier, he was impeached by the House of Representatives for violating the Tenure of Office Act because he had removed Secretary of War Edwin M. Stanton from office without first notifying the Senate. The Senate exonerated Johnson by one vote, which led the president to a sincere belief that he had found God in Truth. Johnson reaffirmed his conviction by making this unambiguous statement on his deathbed:

> Approaching death to me is a mere shadow of God's protecting wing . . . where the great fact will be realized that God is Truth, and gratitude is the highest attribute of man.

Finding God in truth is not a concept alien to Jews. In the first century, the Deputy High Priest, Rabbi Chanina, said, "The seal of the Holy One, blessed be He, is Truth." Noted philosopher Hermann Cohen (1842–1918) saw God in the same way: "We call God an idea, meaning the center of all ideas, the idea of truth."

Experiencing God through Observance

In traditional Jewish thought, the discovery of God through the pursuit of truth can be achieved only by traveling the two-lane highway consisting of prayer and the observance of the commandments (mitzvot). In his book Mitzvot: The Commandments and Their Rationale (1994), Rabbi Abraham Chill explains the linkage:

> The proper performance of a mitzva [commandment] is a soul-stirring experience which raises the Jew to unprecedented spiritual heights in his urge to seek out and communicate with God [through prayer].

Employing prayer as the vehicle for reaching God was neatly expressed by Rabbi Solomon B. Freehof in his Small Sanctuary (1942):

> Prayer in Israel teaches man to overcome bitterness and self-pity; to think not of what the world owes him, but what he owes the world and God. It is not primarily piteous pleading but is essentially grateful communion with the Infinite.

In his *Essence of Judaism* (1936), Rabbi Leo Baeck put it well when he wrote that engaging in prayer is an opportunity "to leave us alone with God," so as to experience His presence. Rabbi Joseph B. Soloveitchik posits in his *Lonely Man of Faith* (1992) that communion with the Infinite One is genuinely experienced when the inquiring mind "looks for the image of God not in mathematical formula or the natural law, but in every beam of light, in every bud and blossom, in the morning breeze and the stillness of a starlit evening."

To actor Elliot Gould prayer is a very personal, spiritual experience:

> I pray [to God] in my own way every day for peace and harmony, for humanity, nature, and the environment. . . . When I feel I'm being swept away by materialism, by pressures, and by stress, I will stop and pray just to get back in touch with my inner self.

Abraham Joshua put it this way in his *Man's Quest for God:*

> A search for God involves a search of our own measure, a test of our own spiritual potential.

What Heschel seems to be saying is that it is on the level of the inner self where God's presence is most purposeful, for it is the point at which conscience and reality intersect. It is where the voice of God speaks to man individually and man speaks to God through prayers. Prayer, earnestly engaged in, is the pendulum that provides us with the momentum to confront our cares and concerns, our inadequacies and our failures. Prayer is a wake-up call. It is the rapping on the door of our conscience reminding us of what is and what might have been, of what is d what should have been, what is and what can be. It is the voice of God, which says, "You can be like Me, kind and caring, merciful and compassionate . . ."

Extending a Helping Hand

Samson Raphael Hirsch, the German rabbi and theologican, in his *Nineteen Letters of Ben Uziel* (1899), believed that man can experience God through helping his fellow man:

> Whoever in his time . . . injures none and assists everyone according to his power to reach the goal marked out for it by God—he is a man!

Experiencing God, then, can be the feeling of elation that emerges from extending a helping hand to others, whether the "other" is a member of one's own group or family, or a total stranger; whether he or she is a widow, an orphan, a convert to Judaism, or a poverty-stricken, homeless individual.

Moses Maimonides expressed the concept deeply when he wrote in his *Guide of the Perplexed* (1190):

> The highest virtue to which a man can aspire to is to be holy, just as God is holy [as indicated in Leviticus 19:2], and to be gracious, kind, and merciful, just as God represents those attributes.

Most theologians would agree with Maimonides that the best and only way to understand God and draw close to Him is by emulating Him and accepting His ways as representing truth and justice. It is by following this course that we bring God out of hiding.

Martin Buber believed that by emulating God we experience God directly. It is not simply praying to God that brings about the experience of knowing Him, but it is the *doing* of godly things that brings us closer to Him. Prayers that end up as mere words are an exercise in futility.

In commenting on the verse in Jeremiah, "They have forsaken me and not kept My commandments" (16:11), Rabbi Chiya bar Abba places these words into God's mouth:

> It would have been far better to have them [Israel] forsake Me, but still be observant of My commandments (Lamentations Rabba 2).

Yehuda Halevi, the eleventh/twelfth-century Spanish Hebrew poet, found that the very act of searching for God brings God to oneself:

> Lord, where shall I find You?
> High and hidden is Your place.
> And where shall I not find You?
> The world is full of Your glory.
>
> I have sought Your nearness,
> With all my heart I called You,
> And going out to meet You
> I found You coming to meet me.

Theodore Gaster, a professor of comparative religion at Dropsie College, found in this summation by Yehuda Halevi an expression of a "central, unique and tremendous idea that is utterly original [with Judaism]—the idea that God and man are partners in the world, and that for the realization of His plan . . . God needs a committed, dedicated group of men and women."

In summary, as we shall see in this section, to experience God means to be touched by the Divine Spirit in one of a variety of ways. That experience may be of a Spirit that inspires and encourages; a Spirit that unleashes creative energy; a Spirit that feeds motivation and dedication; a Spirit that extends love and is repaid by love; a Spirit that strives for peace and welcomes reconciliation; or a Spirit that reaches for God by appreciating nature.

Spiritual satisfaction comes when one finds the unique way in which one personally feels God.

A popular story offers the answer. In this tale an adult, sitting on a park bench, is watching a child play with a kite. The kite soars upwards and disappears into the clouds.

The man approaches the child and asks, "What are you doing?"
She answers, "I am flying a kite."
"I don't see a kite," says the man.
"How do you know it's up there?"
"I know it's up there because I feel the pull of it."

Abba Mari ben Eligdor
FOURTEENTH-CENTURY FRENCH TALMUDIST, PHILOSOPHER

We need no ladders to the sky, we need only. . . observe the structure and functions of man's bodily organs . . . to know that the Creator exists. Job said, "From my flesh shall I see God."

From his Minchat Kenaot (1303). Quoted in A Treasury of Jewish Quotations (1956).

(Rabbi) Abbahu
Also known as Avahu
THIRD-CENTURY TALMUDIC SCHOLAR

Both are the words of the living God.

After a dispute between Beit Hillel and Beit Shammai as to whether or not life was worth living, a voice from heaven (Bat Kol) made this announcement. Quoted in the talmudic tractate Eruvin (13b).

God issues a decree but the Tzadik can annul it.

Asserting that the righteous have the power to move God to alter an adverse decree through prayer. Quoted in the talmudic tractate Moed Katan (16b). This led the Baal Shem Tov to assert that "the Tzadik is the messenger of the Shechina" and "the will of the Tzadik agrees with the will of God."

Abraham ben Samuel Chasdai
THIRTEENTH-CENTURY SPANISH TRANSLATOR

Where is God? In the heart of everyone who seeks Him.

From his The Prince and the Hermit.

Cyrus Adler
[1863–1940]
SCHOLAR, SEMINARY PRESIDENT

I will continue to hold my banner aloft. I find myself born into a people and a religion. The preservation of my people must be for a purpose, for God does nothing without a purpose. His reasons are unfathomable to me, but on my own reason I place little dependence; test it where I will, it fails me. The simple, the ultimate in every direction is sealed to me. It is as difficult to understand matter as mind. The courses of the planets are no harder to explain than the growth of a blade of grass. Therefore am I willing to remain a link in the great chain.

From his I Have Considered the Days (1941).

Grace Aguilar
[1816–1847]
BRITISH AUTHOR, THEOLOGIAN

Our Father rejects those who do good, trusting in their own righteousness to save them, looking to their own works to purchase redemption; but He equally rejects those who supinely sit, contented to trust in His word, and think nothing depends upon themselves. As works without faith are unacceptable, so equally is faith without works.

From her The Spirit of Judaism (1842), *widely read by Christians and Jews in the United States and England.*

Ahava ben Zera
FOURTH-CENTURY PALESTINIAN SCHOLAR

He who does not indulge in superstitious practices is brought closer to God even moreso than angels.

Quoted in the talmudic tractate Nedarim (32a).

Lisa Aiken
CONTEMPORARY AUTHOR, PSYCHOTHERAPIST

One of our fundamental obligations as Jews is to imitate God. We were not commanded to become millionaires, professionals, or politicians. We *were* commanded to imitate God. One of the primary ways that we do this is by imitating His deeds of lovingkindness. It is only by giving that we can truly exercise the divine image inside of us.

From her To Be a Jewish Woman (1992).

Akiba ben Joseph

[c. 50–135]

LEADING TALMUDIC SCHOLAR, ACTIVIST

Whatever the All Merciful does is all for the good.

Quoted in the talmudic tractate Berachot (60b).

Menachem Alon

CONTEMPORARY ISRAELI JURIST

A judge who has reached the age of retirement has to say the prayer of thanks to God, [known as] *Gomel*, that he came out of the process sound in both body and soul.

Upon completing, on November 24, 1993, sixteen years on Israel's Supreme Court and retiring at the mandatory age of seventy. From an interview with Netty C. Gross in The Jerusalem Post, February 4, 1994. A play on the Hebrew word gimla'ut, *meaning "retirement."*

Anonymous

I believe in the sun even when it is not shining. I believe in love even when not feeling it. I believe in God even when He is silent.

An inscription on the wall of a cellar in Cologne, Germany, where Jews hid from the Nazis.

·•·

A favorite saying of the Rabbis of Yavneh was: "I am God's creature and my fellow is God's creature. My work is in the town and his work is in the country. I rise early for my work and he rises early for his work. Just as he does not presume to do my work, so I do not presume to do his work." Will you say, I do much and he does little? We have learned [in Menachot 110a], "One may do much or one may do little; it is all one, provided he directs his heart to [God in] heaven."

Quoted in the talmudic tractate Berachot (17a).

·•·

A man has to toil diligently with both hands and then God will send His blessing.

Quoted in the Midrash on the sidra Va-yeitzei 13.

·•·

Have no doubt, the god you don't believe in, I don't believe in either.

Ascribed to a chasidic rebbe, addressing an apostate.

·•·

God bides his time, but pays off with interest.

A Yiddish aphorism.

·•·

A man is praying. He says, "God?"
God says, "Yes?"
The man says, "Can I ask you a question?"
God says, "Go right ahead."
The man asks, "What is a million years to you?"
"A million years is like a second."
The man thinks this over and then asks, "What's a million dollars to you?
God says, "A million dollars is like a penny."
"Then can I have a penny?"
God says, "Sure, just a second."

A humorous anecdote quoted in Larry King's Powerful Prayers (1998).

Aharon Appelfeld
[1932–]
ISRAELI AUTHOR

Today I can't imagine myself as a Jew without being religious. . . . I can't imagine any form of Jewish life without prayer and the synagogue. I came to that because after looking inside myself, I felt there is meaning to life, even after Auschwitz, and so there is the obligation to continue. If there is meaning, then there is God. Faith gives us a chance. It is up to us what to do with it.

From an article in the Baltimore Jewish Times. Quoted in Anne Roiphe's Season for Healing (1988).

Max Arzt

[1897–1975]

U.S. CONSERVATIVE RABBI, AUTHOR

We need to advance from affiliation to affirmation, from external compliance to inner conviction. Solomon Schechter, the great Anglo-American theologian, called our attention to the truism that one cannot love God with his father's heart.

From his Justice and Mercy (1963).

Israel Baal Shem Tov

[c. 1700–1760]

FOUNDER OF CHASIDISM

There is no room for God in a person who is full of himself.

By attribution.

·◆·

We must bend down [when praying to God] but not too low and not too often, for in bowing too low and too often, we may forget how to raise our heads.

A disciple explained: "When we are bent over, the shadow of God contracts, and when we stand erect, the shadow of God is extended." Quoted in Harold M. Schulweiss's For Those Who Can't Believe (1994).

·◆·

When you serve God through God's compassion, you empower yourself with greater strength, elevate your mind with higher thoughts, and soar with the angels. This is what is called "complete service."

Quoted in Miraculous Living (1996), by Shoni Labowitz.

·◆·

Man should know that in all human anguish, whether corporeal or spiritual, there is a spark of the divine, except that it is covered, but when he becomes aware of that, the cover is removed and the force of the anguish is broken.

Quoted in the work Toldot Yaakov Yosef, by Jacob Joseph Palonnoge (died 1782), a disciple of the Besht.

The world is new to us every morning—this is God's gift; and every man should believe he is reborn each day.

By attribution.

Your prayer opened the gates of heaven.

To an immigrant Jew who reported to him that although he wished to pray he could only recite the letters of the Hebrew alphabet. After doing so he said to God, "Here, God, are Your holy letters. Make them into the right words."

People should get to know what the unity of God really means. To attain a part of this indivisible unity is to attain the whole. The Torah and all its ordinances are from God. If I therefore fulfill but one commandment in and through the love of God, it is as though I have fulfilled them all.

Quoted in Solomon Schechter's Studies in Judaism (1924).

Leo Baeck
[1873–1956]
GERMAN REFORM RABBI, THEOLOGIAN

To avoid wrong and to seek good means to know God.

From his Essence of Judaism (1936).

The purpose of prayer is to leave us alone with God.

Ibid.

Man's creed is that he believes in God, and therefore in mankind. . . .

Ibid.

Service of God consists in what we do to our neighbor.

Ibid.

Bernard J. Bamberger
[1904–]
U.S. REFORM RABBI, BIBLE SCHOLAR

[Martin] Buber insists that Judaism is not merely to be understood; a concept of God is not adequate for religion. Judaism must be experienced directly. It is the confrontation of God by the individual soul. Religion is not talk about God; it is the saying of "Thou" to God.

From his The Story of Judaism (1964).

Baruch of Medzebozh
[c. 1756–1810]
CHASIDIC RABBI

Picture two children playing hide-and-seek. One hides but the other does not look for him. God is hiding and man is not seeking. Imagine His distress.

Explaining the idea of a hidden God. Quoted in Elie Wiesel's Souls on Fire (1972).

Richard Beer-Hofmann
[1866–1945]
AUSTRIAN POET, PLAYWRIGHT, NOVELIST

Lord, whate'er Thy will imposes on me
I'll bear like a crown, not like a yoke.

From his Jacob's Dream (1919).

Beit Shammai
Anyone who humbles himself, God elevates, and he who exalts himself, God humbles.

Quoted in the talmudic tractate Eruvin (13b).

Samuel Belkin

[1911–1976]

U.S. ORTHODOX RABBI, SCHOLAR, EDUCATOR

God has endowed man with two great gifts: memory and forgetfulness, differentiating him from the irrational animals in nature. If man had no memory, civilization could not continue; if man lacked forgetfulness, he could not endure the pain of life's grim experiences.

From the introduction to Understanding Bereavement and Grief (1977), edited by Norman Linzer.

Henri Bergson

[1859–1941]

FRENCH PHILOSOPHER, AUTHOR

God is love, and the object of love: herein lies the whole contribution of mysticism.

From his Two Sources of Morality and Religion (1935).

Eliezer Berkovits

[1908–1992]

U.S. ORTHODOX RABBI, SCHOLAR, AUTHOR

I believe that God did indeed speak to Moses, as the Bible says. I am, however, unable to imagine, much less to describe, the actual event. Notwithstanding the fact that the Bible does say that God "spoke to Moses face to face, as a man speaketh to his friend," I find it impossible to visualize how an infinite, incorporeal Being speaks to a man "face to face."

From his essay in The Condition of Jewish Belief (1966), a symposium compiled by the editors of Commentary magazine.

.•.

Judaism is neither ethics nor doctrine, but a life of obedience to God out of awe, and of submission to Him out of love; within this life ethics and doctrine, too, have their place.

Ibid.

Saul J. Berman

CONTEMPORARY ORTHODOX U.S. RABBI, SCHOLAR, EDUCATOR

I find belief in God to be simple; my real struggle is to achieve knowledge of the existence of God. Maimonides, in the first positive commandment in his book of the commandments, leaves uncertain whether the prime *mitzvah*, or commandment, is belief in or knowledge of His existence. I think that the real challenge of religion is to gain knowledge of God and Her [sic] will for each of us, through revelation, reason, and experience.

From his essay in Commentary, August 1996.

Beruria

WIFE OF SECOND-CENTURY TALMUDIC SCHOLAR RABBI MEIR

Our two sons haven't died, Meir. "God gives and God takes away." The Almighty has taken back only what He entrusted to us.

Breaking the news to her husband that God's gift to them has been recalled. The story appears in the Midrash, Proverbs 964.

Michael Bloomberg

CONTEMPORARY JEW

I'm not terribly religious, but I am terribly sensitive to the fact that it's my heritage. I don't spend time *davening* [praying]. If I don't call God, he won't call me.

Describing his relationship to God and Judaism. From an interview in The Jerusalem Report, March 9, 1995.

David R. Blumenthal

CONTEMPORARY CONSERVATIVE U.S. RABBI,
PROFESSOR OF JUDAIC STUDIES

I trust in God because God is a living presence in my life. I experience God in prayer—in joy, in fear, in power, and in admitting and asking for my own innermost needs. I feel God's presence as deeply personal.

I am embraced, judged, and listened to by God. . . . I also experience God in nature. . . . I also feel God's presence in moments of human contacts. . . . I sense God, too, when studying and teaching sacred texts. . . . I also sense God in history.

From his essay in Commentary, August 1996.

Ben Zion Bokser
[1907–1983]
U.S. CONSERVATIVE RABBI, SCHOLAR, AUTHOR

Prayer is the human side of an unending dialogue between God and man. In the wondrous phenomena of nature as in the inspired word of Scripture, God speaks to man. God speaks to man of His love for him, of His purposes in having fashioned life, and of the ultimate goodness of all existence. We who hear God, try to respond. Man's response to God is prayer.

From the introduction to his Prayerbook: Weekday, Sabbath, and Festival (1957).

•◆•

Prayers of praise have their origin in the emotions of awe and love. But our prayers also help to create these emotions and to deepen them. They charge us with the sensitivity to see God's providence over our lives and in the world around us.

Ibid.

•◆•

The mind is but a tiny flame
To lift the dark that veils God's name.
His work is all that mortals see,
The tokens of His sovereignty.

From his Judaism: Profile of a Faith (1963).

Ludwig Börne

[1786–1837]

GERMAN JOURNALIST, ESSAYIST

In nature I have always sought God, God only, and in art the divine; and where I did not find God, I saw nothing but miserable botch-work. History, men, and books I have judged in like manner.

Quoted in Georg Brandes' Main Currents *(1924).*

Herb Brin

CONTEMPORARY U.S. PUBLISHER, POET

A blade of grass upon a timeless land
I stand alone
Tossed by winds of eternity.

A falling leaf upon a shifting sand
I seek my God
Alone, in the Days of Awe

From his Wild Flowers *(1965).*

Ruth F. Brin

CONTEMPORARY U.S. POET

God of men and mountains,
Master of people and planets,
Creator of the universe:
I am afraid.

I am afraid of the angels
Thou hast sent to wrestle with me:

The angel of success
Who carries a two-edged sword,

The angels of darkness
Whose names I do not know,

The angel of death
For whom I have no answer.

I am afraid of the touch
Of Thy great hand on my feeble heart.

Yet must I turn to Thee and praise Thee,
Awful and great though Thou art,
For there is none else.

> From her Time to Search (1959).

Lenny Bruce
[1925–1966]
U.S. COMEDIAN, SATIRIST

Every day people are straying away from the church and going back to God.

> From one of his classic routines. From The Essential Lenny Bruce (1967), edited by John Cohen.

Martin Buber
[1878–1965]
GERMAN THEOLOGIAN, AUTHOR

Can one still speak to God after Auschwitz? Can one still, as an individual and as a people, enter at all into a dialogue relationship with Him? Dare we recommend to the survivors of Auschwitz, the Jobs of the gas chambers, "Call to Him, for He is kind, for His mercy endures forever"?

> From his essay "Dialogue Between Heaven and Earth," in Will Herberg's Four Existentialist Theologians (1958).

·◆·

After the heavenly sacred fact of being a child of God, nothing is as great in human existences as the earthly sacred fact of being a brother of men.

> From a 1952 address to the Brotherhood Movement of the Jewish Theological Seminary of America.

•◆•

Genuine religious movements do not seek to offer man the solution to the mystery of the world, they seek to equip him to live through the power of that mystery; they do not seek to teach him about the nature of God but to show him the path where he can encounter God.

From his speech at the reopening of the Frankfort Jewish Lehrhaus in 1936.

•◆•

Fear of God never means to the Jews that they ought to be afraid of God, but that, trembling, they ought to be aware of his incomprehensibility. The fear of God is the creaturely knowledge of the darkness to which none of our spiritual powers can reach, and out of which God reveals himself. Therefore, "the fear of God" is rightly called "the beginning of knowledge." (Ps. 111:10) It is the dark gate through which man must pass if he is to enter into the love of God.

From his essay "The Two Foci of the Jewish Soul," in his Israel and the World (1980).

•◆•

God is incomprehensible, but he can be known through a bond of mutual relationship. God cannot be fathomed by knowledge, but He can be imitated. The life of man who is unlike God can yet be an *imitatio Dei*. The "likeness" is not closed to the "unlike." This is exactly what is meant when the Scripture instructs man to walk in God's way and in His footsteps.

Ibid.

•◆•

We perfect our souls toward God. Being like God is then not something which is unconnected with our earthly life; it is the goal of our life, provided that our life is really a perfecting of our soul toward God. And this being so, we may well add that the perfection of a soul is called its being like God, which yet does not mean any equality, but means that this soul has translated into reality that likeness to God which was granted it.

From his essay "Imitatio Dei," in his Israel and the World (1948).

Existence will remain meaningless for you if you yourself do not penetrate into it with active love and if you do not in this way discover its meaning for yourself. Everything is waiting to be hallowed by you; it is waiting for this meaning to be disclosed and to be realized by you. . . . Meet the world with the fullness of your being and you shall meet God. If you wish to believe, love!

From his At the Turning (1952).

Art Buchwald
[1925–]
U.S. HUMORIST, COLUMNIST

Well, as you know, the stations are fighting for ratings and the kookier you are, the more chance you have of making the news. For example, if you made a statement that God doesn't hear the prayers of Jews, we could get you on all three networks.

From his collection of humorous pieces, Laid Back in Washington (1981). Referring to the 1980 statement of Reverend Baily Smith: "God Almighty does not hear the prayer of a Jew."

Ruth Calderon
[1961–]
CO-FOUNDER OF THE ELUL STUDY GROUPS

Our Jewish identity was both relaxed and profound. Our God was sweet, while our secularism was without hubris. That is the Mediterranean approach: non-dogmatic and natural. The new cultural message will come from that form of Judaism.

Describing the Jewish identity she learned growing up in a mixed Bulgarian-German family, which she hopes to achieve once again in Israel.

Nina Beth Cardin
CONTEMPORARY CONSERVATIVE U.S. RABBI

Belief in God motivates all that I do. Not that I do not wonder about the existence of God—I do. And not that I do not puzzle over the nature of God—I do that, too. But in truth, on a daily basis these wonders and doubts do not overly occupy my mind. . . .

Still I need and thrive on my belief in God. I believe in this belief because it is this belief in God, even more than the existence of God, that motivates me, that makes a claim on me. This is not blasphemy. Judaism itself realizes that "all is in the hands of God except the fear of God." It is not the existence of God alone that animates the world, but our response to that belief.

From her essay in Commentary, *August 1996.*

Abraham Isaac Carmel
CONTEMPORARY CLERGYMAN

Judaism does not and cannot offer any season tickets to Heaven at reduced prices. Every pilgrim travels under his own steam, so to speak. The Jew believes that he, as all men, has sufficient willpower, assisted by prayer, to resist any evil inclination. He does not require an extravagant sacramental system, born of human ingenuity rather than Divine revelation, to snatch him from the fires of God's anger.

From his autobiography, So Strange My Path *(1964), written after this once Roman Catholic priest converted to Judaism in 1963.*

(Rabbi) Chama
FOURTH-CENTURY BABYLONIAN TALMUDIC SCHOLAR

Just as He clothes the naked, so must you clothe the naked. Just as He visits the sick, so must you visit the sick. Just as He comforts mourners, so must you comfort mourners. Just as He buries the dead, so must you bury the dead.

Explaining the meaning of the text in Deuteronomy (13:5): "You shall walk after the Lord your God."

(Rabbi) Chanina

FIRST-CENTURY DEPUTY HIGH PRIEST, SCHOLAR

Greater is he who acts because he is commanded by God to do so than he who acts without being so commanded by Him.

Quoted in the talmudic tractate Kiddushin (31a) and Avoda Zara (3a).

Chanina ben Dosa

FIRST-CENTURY TALMUDIC SCHOLAR

When one's fellow creatures are pleased with him, God is pleased with him; when one's fellow creatures are not pleased with him, God is not pleased with him.

Quoted in the Ethics of the Fathers (3:13).

Abraham Chill

CONTEMPORARY ORTHODOX U.S. RABBI, AUTHOR

The proper performance of a *mitzvah* [commandment] is a soul-stirring experience which raises the Jew to unprecedented spiritual heights in his urge to seek out and communicate with God.

From his Mitzvot: The Commandments and Their Rationale (1994).

(Rabbi) Chisda

THIRD-CENTURY TALMUDIC SCHOLAR

God says about any person who is rude and crude: "He and I cannot coexist in this world."

Quoted in the talmudic tractate Sota (5a).

.•.

Every man who is haughty, the Holy One, blessed be He, declares: "He and I cannot both dwell in the world."

Ibid.

.•.

Of him who slanders, the Holy One, blessed be He, says: "He and I cannot live together in the world."

Quoted in the talmudic tractate Arachin (15b).

Henry Cohen
[1863–1952]
U.S. REFORM RABBI, CIVIC LEADER

I recall Abraham Cronbach, *alav ha-shalom*, once saying cryptically: "We are Jews because we want to be Jews." My wanting has to do with the radical freedom I prize when my mind searches for the meaning of God and man. I cherish the thought that almost wherever my mind roams I can find within the Jewish community someone to join me in my dissent.

My wanting has to do with feeling at home with a tradition that has usually given high marks to man and, even in the midst of despair, held out hope for mankind.

From his Why Judaism: A Search for Meaning in Jewish Identity *(1973).*

Morris Raphael Cohen
[1880–1947]
U.S. PHILOSOPHER, PROFESSOR, AUTHOR

The glory of God is not visible except to those who are profoundly moved by compassion for their fellow-men.

From his Dreamer's Journey *(1949).*

Seymour Cohen
CONTEMPORARY U.S. CONSERVATIVE RABBI, AUTHOR

God wants us to become human. . . . When we realize our potential, when we make the most of ourselves, when we live up to our resources, when we strive for a better world, when we complete ourselves, when we realize our limitations and also our strength, then we become human.

From his sermon in Best Jewish Sermons of 5713 *(1953),* edited by Saul I. Teplitz.

Paul Cowan
[1940–1988]
U.S. AUTHOR

She said that she had been thinking about the idea [of conversion] for months, ever since she discovered that worshiping as a Jew released something inside her which enabled her to think about God; to feel, at rare moments, a faith whose intensity startled her.

From his An Orphan in History (1982), *describing his wife Rachel's spiritual rebirth through conversion to Judaism.*

Abraham Cronbach
CONTEMPORARY U.S. RABBI

On June 16, 1953, the forty-seventh anniversary of my ordination, I conversed with President Dwight D. Eisenhower in the Presidential office of the White House Annex. I had been invited to join three Christian clergymen in beseeching the President for clemency toward Julius and Ethel Rosenberg, sentenced to be executed on June 18. . . . I remarked, "Mr. President, all of us are dedicated to the interests of America. All of us are solicitous that America shall suffer no harm. Would not America be adequately safeguarded if, instead of death, the penalty of the Rosenbergs would be imprisonment, no matter how long? . . . Life is full of problems that baffle our intelligence. All of us need the guidance of God. Mr. President, may you have the guidance of God!"

Quoted in Critical Studies in American Jewish History (1971).

(King) David
SECOND KING OF ISRAEL, RULED C. 1000–960 B.C.E.

Lord, who shall sojourn in thy tabernacle?
Who shall dwell upon Thy holy mountain?
He that walketh uprightly, and worketh righteousness,
And speaketh truth in his heart;
That hath no slander upon his tongue,
Nor doeth evil to his fellow,
Nor taketh up reproach against his neighbor;

95

In whose eyes a vile person is despised,
But he honoureth them that fear the Lord;
He that sweareth to his own hurt, and changeth no;
He that putteth not out his money on interest,
Nor taketh a bribe against the innocent.
He that doeth these things shall never be moved.

> Psalm 15, from the Book of Psalms.

• • •

Even in my suffering, when I spoke rashly and said "all men are deceit-ful," I still believed in God.

> From the Book of Psalms (116:10).

Alan M. Dershowitz
[1938–]
U.S. PROFESSOR, ATTORNEY, AUTHOR

What I find very hard to accept is a God that needs to be praised. I think if there is a God, he's sitting up there saying, "Stop praising me already. You're praising me for your own good, not for my good. I don't need to be praised so much."

> In answer to Larry King's question, "Do you believe there is a personal God that answers your prayers?" Quoted in Larry King's Powerful Prayers (1998).

Wayne Dosick
CONTEMPORARY CONSERVATIVE U.S. RABBI, AUTHOR

Though no one ever told us, though no one ever showed us, every-thing we want, everything we need, everything we have been search-ing for, everything that will satisfy our souls, everything that will bring us to God is not far from home. . . . All that we are seeking is right in Judaism.

> From his Dancing With God (1997).

• • •

If we feel bad about not hearing from God, just think how bad God must feel about not hearing from us.

Ibid.

Dostai ben Judah

SECOND-CENTURY TALMUDIC SCHOLAR

The ways of God are not like the ways of flesh and blood. How does flesh and blood act? If a man brings a present to a king, it may be accepted or it may not be accepted; and even if it is accepted, it is still doubtful whether he will be admitted to the presence of the king or not. Not so God. If a man gives but a farthing to a beggar, he is deemed worthy to receive the Divine Presence.

Commentng on the meaning of Psalm 17:15. Quoted in the talmudic tractate Bava Batra (10a).

Kirk Douglas

[1916–]

U.S. ACTOR

I feel the place where God hears you better than anywhere else is the Western Wall, the Wailing Wall in Jerusalem. The last time I prayed there was in 1994. I remember it as if it were yesterday. The massive stones of the Wall were bathed in the golden rays of the setting sun. The plaza beneath the Wall was crowded with worshippers—praying the afternoon Mincha prayer. The energy emanating from all the praying Jews, davening at a wild pace was overwhelming.

From his book Climbing the Mountain: My Search for Meaning (1997), describing his difficulties in reaching an accord with God.

·◆·

The Bible tells us that God created us; we can't create God. God is beyond and above us all.

From his book Young Heroes of the Bible.

Albert Einstein
[1879–1955]
GERMAN-BORN U.S. SCIENTIST

Now I know there is a God in heaven.

> After listening to child prodigy Yehudi Menuhin's violin performance in Berlin in 1928.

·◆·

Before God we are all equally wise—equally foolish.

> From his Cosmic Religion.

Ira Eisenstein
[1906–1997]
U.S. RECONSTRUCTIONIST RABBI, AUTHOR, EDUCATOR, LECTURER

We now realize that the Torah is a record of the search our People undertook and carried out for a thousand years, the search for the will of God, for the answer to the questions: What is the good life? What is the way that is pleasing in the eyes of God? How shall we worship and commune with God? How shall we perform rites that will give us the morale, the courage, the faith, the hope, the patience to keep on working for the better world, though we see the world not yet responding?

> From his Judaism under Freedom. Quoted in the Reconstructionist, October 29, 1965.

(Rabbi) Eleazar
SECOND-CENTURY TALMUDIC SCHOLAR

Prayer is more dear to God than all sacrifices.

> From Midrash Tanchuma, sidra Ki Tavo.

·◆·

Prayer is more efficacious than sacrifices. . . . Prayer is more efficacious than good deeds.

> Quoted in the talmudic tractate Berachot (32b).

Eleazar ben Judah of Worms

[c. 1160–1238]

GERMAN CODIFIER, KABBALIST, POET

The soul is filled with love [of God], bound with the bonds of love in great joy. This joy chases away all bodily pleasure and worldly delight from his heart. The powerful joy of love seizes his heart so that he continually thinks, "How can I do God's will?" . . . The love of heaven in his heart is like the flame attached to the coal. He does not gaze at women; he does not engage in frivolous talk, but he concerns himself only to do God's will, and he sings songs in order to become filled with joy in the love of God.

From his Sodei Raza ("Secret of Secrets").

.•.

"Let a man always be subtle in the fear of God." This means that a person should reflect on the subtleties and the glories of the world: how, for example, a mortal king commands his soldiers to engage in battle. Even though they know they may be killed, they are afraid of him and obey him even though they know that the fear of him is not everlasting, because he will eventually die and perish and they can escape to another country. How much more so, therefore, should men fear the King of the King of Kings, the Holy One, blessed be He, and walk in His ways, since He is everywhere and gazes at the wicked as well as the good.

Ibid.

Eleazer ben Pedat

THIRD-CENTURY TALMUDIC SCHOLAR

Even in anger, the Holy One is compassionate.

A view based upon the verse in Hosea (1:6) where compassion is mentioned in connection with retribution. Quoted in the talmudic tractate Pesachim (87b).

(Prophet) Ezekiel
SIXTH-CENTURY B.C.E. PROPHET OF ISRAEL

If a man is righteous and does what is just and right . . . if he has not wronged . . . if he has followed My laws and kept My rules and acted honestly—he is righteous. Such a man shall live, declares the Lord God.

From the Book of Ezekiel (18:5–9).

Emil L. Fackenheim
[1916–]
CONTEMPORARY U.S. RABBI, THEOLOGIAN, AUTHOR

Jews are forbidden to hand Hitler posthumous victories. They are commanded to survive as Jews, lest the Jewish People perish. . . . They are commanded to remember the victims of Auschwitz, lest their memory perish. They are forbidden to despair of man and his world, and to escape into either cynicism or otherworldliness, lest they cooperate in delivering the world over to the forces of Auschwitz. Finally, they are forbidden to despair of the God of Israel, lest Judaism perish. . . . A Jew may not respond to Hitler's attempt to destroy Judaism by himself cooperating in its destruction.

From his Jewish Return Into History (1978).

Moshe Feinstein
[1895–1986]
U.S. ORTHODOX RABBI, EDUCATOR, AUTHOR

Their [women's] motivation is fundamentally a complaint against God and His Torah. Their intention is not a truthful desire to serve Him, and their actions do not constitute a mitzvah [commandment]. Their disrespect for our Torah and our sages amounts to nothing less than blasphemy.

Commenting on women who put on talitot (prayer shawls) and tefilin (phylacteries) when they pray. Quoted in Moment magazine, April 1994.

Aaron Feuerstein

[1927–]

ENTREPRENEUR, PHILANTHROPIST

Yeshiva taught me two important lessons. First, think creatively; look beyond rote solutions. Second, Jewish values must live in the workplace as well as in the synagogue because all people, owners and workers alike, are created in the image of God.

After a fire burned down his Malden Mills in Massachusetts on December 11, 1995 and fourteen hundred workers were without jobs. He promised to rebuild the plant and, on December 14, pledged to pay his workers full salaries.

Edmond Fleg

[1874–1963]

FRENCH POET, PLAYWRIGHT, ESSAYIST

Evidence of God I have found in the existence of Israel.

From his essay "Why I Am a Jew" (1929), translated into English by Victor Gollancz (1943).

Anne Frank

[1929–1945]

HOLOCAUST VICTIM, DIARIST

The best remedy for those who are afraid, lonely, or unhappy is to go outside, somewhere where they can be quite alone with the heavens, nature, and God. Because only then does one feel that all is as it should be and that God wishes to see people happy, amidst the simple beauty of nature. As long as this exists, and it certainly always will, I know that then there will always be comfort for every sorrow. . . . And I firmly believe that nature brings solace in all troubles.

At age thirteen, addressing the diary she kept while in hiding from the Nazis, who occupied Holland in 1942. From Anne Frank: Diary of a Young Girl (1952).

·•·

I am becoming still more independent of my parents, young as I am, I face life with more courage than Mummy; my feeling for justice is immovable, and truer than hers. I know what I want, I have a goal, an opinion, I have a religion and love. Let me be myself and then I am satisfied. I know that I'm a woman, a woman with inward strength and plenty of courage.

If God lets me live, I shall attain more than Mummy ever has done, I shall not remain insignificant, I shall work for the world and for mankind.

Ibid. (entry from 1944).

Solomon B. Freehof
[1892–1990]
U.S. REFORM RABBI, SCHOLAR, AUTHOR

A man should praise God even for misfortunes as much as he praises Him for happiness [say the Rabbis in the Talmud]. Whether this lofty courage is attainable by the average Jew or not, he learns to feel and to express, or perhaps to express and thus to feel, a constant sense of gratitude to the Master of the Universe. Prayer in Israel teaches man to overcome bitterness and self-pity; to think not of what the world owes him, but what he owes the world and God. It is not primarily piteous pleading but is essentially grateful communion with the Infinite.

From his Small Sanctuary (1942).

·•·

Prayer is the search for harmony between man and God, the quest for communion between the finite and the infinite.

Ibid.

Betty Naomi Friedan
[1921–]
U.S. FEMINIST LEADER, AUTHOR

It moves me very much, in that small hotel room, to watch young Naamah Kelman, an American-born Israeli daughter of 13 generations of rabbis, in her white prayer shawl, leading us in the ancient rituals only men have been allowed to perform. And tears came to my eyes as I join the young women in prayer: "Blessed are You, O God, who has made me free. Blessed are You, O God, who has made me in Your image."

> *Referring to the fact that she had been invited to help form a minyan (quorum of ten) for morning prayers. From her article in* The New York Times Magazine, *October 28, 1984.*

David Frishman
[1865–1922]
HEBREW AUTHOR, POET

Brethren, give me a God, for I am full of prayer!

> *From his poem* Ha-yadata. *Quoted in Meyer Waxman's* History of Jewish Literature *(1930).*

Marc Gellman
[1947–   ]
CONTEMPORARY U.S. REFORM RABBI, AUTHOR

God is not some problem I constitute, but rather that mystery within which I myself am constituted. I believe that God is the author of all moral laws, and of those ritual laws that link me to the sacred rhythms of Jewish time and space. When a ritual conflicts with the ethical teachings of Judaism, that ritual must be altered or abandoned. I believe that God has implanted within us eternal life, and I am bewildered and saddened by the widespread ignorance of this ancient and authentic Jewish belief.

> *From his essay in* Commentary, *August 1996.*

·•·

There's a kind of exultation in the way we [Jews] argue, the way we use words. That's because we spent 4,000 years trying to understand an invisible and incomprehensible God.

> *Explaining why there are so many Jewish humorists. Comment made on the March 1997 PBS show "A Laugh, A Tear, and A Mitzvah," which had as its theme: What It Means to Be Jewish in America.*

Neil Gillman

CONTEMPORARY U.S. CONSERVATIVE RABBI, THEOLOGIAN

To the invariable question, "Do we then invent God?" I respond, No, we discover God and create the metaphors/myths which reflect our varied human experiences of God.

From his essay in Commentary, August 1996.

Harry Golden

[1902–1981]

U.S. NEWSPAPER PUBLISHER, AUTHOR

When I was young, I asked my father, "If you don't believe in God, why do you go to synagogue so regularly?" My father answered, "Jews go to synagogue for all kinds of reasons. My friend Garfinkle, who is Orthodox, goes to synagogue to talk to God. I go to talk to Garfinkle."

In his autobiography The Right Time (1969) Harry Golden tells a similar story about his father, Leib Goldhirsch.

Herbert Goldstein

CONTEMPORARY U.S. ORTHODOX RABBI

Prayer serves not only as a petition to God, but as an influence upon ourselves. Our Sages, centuries ago, voiced the thought echoed by the great poet George Meredith, who declared, "He who rises from his worship a better man, his prayer is answered." Prayer has the double charm of bringing God down to man, and lifting man upward to God.

From his Letter on Prayer.

Israel Goldstein

[1896–1986]

U.S. RABBI, ZIONIST LEADER, AUTHOR

We have our own preferences, our own commitments, perhaps our own prejudices as Conservative Jews. But we should be tolerant, perhaps more than a certain Episcopalian clergyman who was having an argument with a Unitarian clergyman. Finally, the Episcopalian, with a great show of expansive tolerance, said to his Unitarian colleague, "Well, my friend, you do it your way. I'll do it God's way."

> In a dialogue with Rabbi William Berkowitz at the Institute of Adult Jewish Studies in New York. Quoted in Berkowitz's Ten Vital Jewish Issues (1964).

Blu Greenberg

[1936–]

U.S. WRITER

Yes, I believe in God. I must add all the caveats: with many questions, with moments of great doubt, with moments even of anger. But yes, I believe in God. For the gift of the Sabbath alone, I believe in God; and for nature; and for daily miracles; and for beautiful music, though I well know that it was God's covenant partner who paired the notes and created the rhythm.

> From her essay in Commentary, August 1996.

Sidney Greenberg

[1917–]

CONTEMPORARY U.S. CONSERVATIVE RABBI, AUTHOR

For all the unkind things said about envy, it would only be fair to acknowledge that not all envy is destructive. If envy leads us to work hard and to improve our skills, it becomes a stimulant to self-improvement. God has given us no quality that cannot be used for good.

> From his Say Yes to Life (1982).

Joshua O. Haberman

CONTEMPORARY U.S. REFORM RABBI, AUTHOR

The relationship with God is what the Bible is all about. It is the sum and substance of Judaism. . . . I believe that God revealed to us collectively, and to some individually, truths about the universe, and guidance in the form of commandments for the conduct of life.

> From his essay in Commentary, August 1996.

Hai Gaon
[939–1038]

LAST HEAD OF THE ACADEMY IN PUMBEDITA, BABYLONIA

Delight in what comes from God, and say, "This, too, is for the best."

> From his Musar Haskel (c. 1000). Quoted in Benzion Halper's Post-Biblical Hebrew Literature (1921).

Yehuda Halevi
[1075–1141]

POET, PHILOSOPHER

The servant of God does not withdraw himself from secular contact lest he be a burden to the world and the world to him; he does not hate life, which is one of God's bounties granted to him. . . . On the contrary, he loves this world and a long life, because they afford him opportunities of deserving the world to come. The more good he does, the greater is his claim on the world to come.

> From his Kuzari (c. 1135).

· ✦ ·

Man can approach God only by doing His commands.

> Ibid.

· ✦ ·

When far from Thee, I die
while yet in life;
But if I cling to Thee, I live,
though I should die.

> From The Selected Poems of Jehuda Halevi (1924), translated from the Hebrew by Nina Salaman.

· ✦ ·

Remove lust from the midst of thee;
Thou wilt find thy God within thy bosom
Moving gently.

> Ibid.

· ✦ ·

Lord, where shall I find You?
High and hidden is Your place.
And where shall I not find You?
The world is full of Your glory.
I have sought Your nearness,
With all my heart I called You,
And going out to meet You
I found You coming to meet me.

    Ibid.

·•·

O God, Thy Name! I will exalt Thee, and
Thy righteousness I will not conceal.
I have given ear, and I have trusted; I will
Not question, I will not prove. . . .

    Ibid.

David Weiss Halivni

CONTEMPORARY U.S. PROFESSOR OF TALMUD

The truly religious Jew is awe-stricken both by the mystery of God and by the efficacy of the mitzvot to bring man closer to God. He dares not tamper with the mitzvot for he humbly acknowledges that he knows not their secret, or secrets.

    From his letter of resignation, in 1985, from the Jewish Theological Seminary faculty because of the issue of women's ordination.

David Hartman

CANADIAN-BORN CONTEMPORARY ORTHODOX RABBI, AUTHOR

God who is worshipped through the mitzvot [commandments] anchors the Jew within the historical and makes him or her understand that God's home lies within the temporal. The revealed commandments constitute a total way of life that must be implemented within the framework of human history.

    Quoted in Lewis Glinert's Joys of Hebrew (1992).

Goldie Hawn

[1945–   ]

U.S. ACTRESS

I've been praying since I was a little girl. I would have my own private moments talking to God, and I found such peace. My mother told me, "You don't have to go to a church or a synagogue to pray." I remembered that—that I could talk to God wherever I was.

Quoted in Larry King's Powerful Prayers *(1998).*

·•·

I always start with health because it's the most important thing. Money is the least of my prayers. It doesn't really enter into my prayers. I also pray to receive the light of God, the energy—the positive energy— because I know that I'm an instrument . . .

Ibid.

·•·

One of my biggest prayers is to be an instrument of God's light and give back to my family and the people I come in contact with, and on a higher level, because I've been given this life, this time, this place where I can do some good. I'm so thankful and humbled by that.

Ibid.

Heinrich Heine

[1797–1856]

GERMAN POET

The contrasts are boldly paired,
Love of pleasure in the Greek, and thought of God in the Judean,
Oh! this conflict will never end,
The true must always contend with the beautiful.

Expressing his continuing struggle to harmonize the pure morality of Judaism and the symmetrical beauty of Hellenism. Quoted in Heinrich Graetz's History of the Jews *(1894).*

Joseph H. Hertz

[1872–1946]

CHIEF RABBI OF ENGLAND, SCHOLAR, AUTHOR

That opening sentence of the Shema ["Hear, O Israel, the Lord is our God, the Lord is One" (Deuteronomy 6:4)] rightly occupies the central place in Jewish religious thought; for every other Jewish belief turns upon it; all goes back to it; all flows from it.

From his Pentateuch and Haftorahs (1961).

Arthur Hertzberg

[1921–   ]

U.S. CONSERVATIVE RABBI, SCHOLAR, AUTHOR

God seems to be replacing anti-Semitism as the hot subject of contemporary Jewish discussion; in books and on the Jewish lecture platform. He is being portrayed with astonishing certainty by theologians who tell us they know His limits or who assert, with even greater certainty, that they can tell us how to find the union of the soul with Him. . . . The supposed theological revival is not about God at all. It is mostly about the obsession with self.

From in essay in Hadassah Magazine, November 1996.

·❖·

At the center of most of this God-seeking is "the hungry" . . . The hungry self is still troubled by its own pain. It is now trying God. The old new, and supposedly most potent, mood-transforming drug. Perhaps He will make me happy. . . . If you want to feel that you are united with God, stop talking and go do a mitzva: any mitzva.

Ibid. His closing statement is a quote from the rabbinic scholar Solomon Schechter.

Abraham Joshua Heschel

[1907–1972]

U.S. RABBI, THEOLOGIAN, AUTHOR, ACTIVIST

We must insist upon loyalty to the unique and holy treasures of our own tradition and at the same time [acknowledge] that in this aeon of religious diversity may be the providence of God. . . . [The ecumenical spirit was] born of the insight that God is greater than religion, that faith is deeper than dogma . . . and that religion involves the total situation of man, his attitudes and deeds, and must therefore never be kept in isolation.

From his Insecurity of Freedom (1966).

Faith is real only when it is not one-sided but reciprocal. Man can rely on God if God can rely on man.

From his Man Is Not Alone (1951).

Let us be frank. Too often a ceremony is the homage which disbelief pays to faith. Do we want such homage? Judaism does not stand on ceremonies. . . . Jewish piety is an answer to God, expressed in the language of *mitzvot* rather than in the language of *ceremonies*. The *mitzvah* rather than the ceremony is our fundamental category. What is the difference between the two categories?

Ceremonies whether in the form of things or in the form of actions are required by custom and convention; *mitzvot* are required by Torah. Ceremonies are relevant to man; *mitzvot* are relevant to God. Ceremonies are folkways; *mitzvot* are ways to God.

From his essay "Toward an Understanding of Halacha," included in
Seymour Siegel's Conservative Judaism and Jewish Law (1977).

The problem of religious thinking is not only whether God is dead or alive, but also whether we are dead or alive to His realness. A search for God involves a search of our own measure, a test of our own spiritual potential.

From his Who Is Man? (1965).

The trouble is that some see all of Judaism reflected in its Law; in their concern for the letter of the Law they give up the Jewish spark. They make the fence more important than the tradition it is meant to protect. Such extremism and severity do us great harm; even the Creator of the world, finding that a world could not exist by justice alone, combined the quality of justice with the quality of mercy. Flexibility, not fanaticism, is needed.

From his We Cannot Force People to Believe (1959).

God may be of no concern to man, but man is of much concern to God. The only way to discover this is the ultimate way, the way of worship. For worship is a way of living, a way of seeing the world in the light of God. To worship is to rise to a higher level of existence, to see the world from the point of view of God.

From his Man's Quest for God: Studies in Prayer and Symbolism (1996).

Of all the sacred acts, first comes prayer. Religion is not what man does with his solitariness. Religion is what man does with the presence of God. And the spirit of God is present whenever we are willing to accept it. True, God is hiding His face in our time, but He is hiding because we are evading Him.

Ibid.

Great is the power of prayer. For to worship is *to expand the presence of God* in the world. God is transcendent, but our worship makes Him immanent. This is implied in the idea that God is in need of man: His being immanent depends upon us.

Ibid.

At the beginning of all action is an inner vision in which things to be are experienced as real. Prayer, too, is frequently an inner vision, an intense dreaming for God—the reflection of the Divine intentions in the soul of man. We dream of a tie "when the world will be perfected under the Kingship of God, and all the children of flesh will call upon

111

Thy name, when Thou wilt turn unto Thyself all the wicked of the earth." We anticipate the fulfillment of the hope shared by both God and man. To pray is to dream in league with God, to envision His holy visions.

Ibid.

·•·

The focus of prayer is not the self. A man may spend hours meditating about himself, or be stirred by the deepest sympathy for his fellow man, and no prayer will come to pass. Prayer comes to pass in a complete turning of the heart toward God, toward His goodness and power.

Ibid.

·•·

This is the law of life: Just as man cannot live without a soul, religion cannot survive without God. Our soul withers without prayer.

Ibid.

·•·

All mitzvoth are means of evoking in us the awareness of living in the neighborhood of God, of living in the holy dimension. . . . They are indications of our awareness of God's eternal presence, celebrating His presence in action.

From his God in Search of Man (1976).

·•·

The legitimate question concerning the forms of Jewish observance is the question: Are they spiritually meaningful? . . . To say that the mitzvot have meaning is less accurate than to say that they lead us to wells of emergent meaning, to experiences which are full of hidden brilliance of the holy, suddenly blazing in our thoughts.

Ibid.

·•·

We do not have to discover the world of faith; we only have to recover it. It is not a terra incognita, an unknown land; it is a forgotten land, and our relation to God is a palimpsest rather than a tabula rasa.

Ibid.

·•·

God is not indifferent to man's quest for Him. He is in need of man, in need of man's share in redemption. God who created the world is not at home in the world, in its dark alleys of misery, callousness, and defiance.

Ibid.

Susannah Heschel
CONTEMPORARY U.S. PROFESSOR OF JEWISH STUDIES, AUTHOR

When I was growing up, being Jewish was always associated with generosity and devotion to others, and a mitzvah meant doing something for another human being, or for God. My father [Abraham J. Heschel] use to say that a mitzvah is a prayer in the form of a deed. I also learned form him that religious life and social justice were intertwined.

From her essay in Commentary, August 1996.

Milton Himmelfarb
[1918–   ]
U.S. WRITER, RESEARCHER

Gershom Scholem, the great scholar of Jewish mysticism, believed in God but not in kashrut, unable to imagine Him closely involved with the kitchen.

From his essay in Commentary, August 1996.

Emil G. Hirsch
[1852–1923]
U.S. REFORM RABBI

The belief in God is merely the outcome of the belief in man. God is the apex of the pyramid, not the base. Man is the cornerstone; and from the true conception of man have the Jewish thinkers risen to the noblest conception of the Deity. Those are shallow who talk of their agnosticism and parade their atheism. No one is an agnostic and no one is an atheist, except he have neither pity for the weak nor charity for the erring; except he have no mercy for those who need its soothing balm.

From a sermon preached in 1893.

.·❖·.

The question fundamental for man to ask is not "What is God?" but "What is He for us as men?" What is God for man is indeed the basic inquiry of Judaism, and to it Judaism gives a clear and definite answer: God for man stands in the consciousness of man's dignity.

From his article "The Sociological Center of Religion," which appeared in The Reform Advocate, vol. 11 (1896).

.·❖·.

True worship is not a petition to God; it is a sermon to our own selves. The words which are its raiments are addressed to us. They speak of God and the divine in man, and thus make man find in himself the God that so often is forgotten when the battle rages and the batteries roar.

From his article in The Reform Advocate, vol. 14 (1897).

Samson Raphael Hirsch
[1808–1888]
GERMAN ORTHODOX RABBI, SCHOLAR, AUTHOR

Whoever in his time, with his equipment of powers and means, in his condition, fulfills the will of God toward the creatures that enter into his circle, who injures none and assists every one according to his power, to reach the goal marked out for it by God—he is a man!

From his Nineteen Letters of Ben Uziel (1899), translated by Bernard Drachman.

Lawrence A. Hoffman
CONTEMPORARY LITURGIST, AUTHOR, PROFESSOR

God can be known only in relationship and can never be adequately described outside of relationship.

Arguing that God's difference (otherness) from us is what makes possible a relationship with Him. By attribution.

(Prophet) Hosea

EIGHTH-CENTURY B.C.E. MINOR PROPHET

For I desire righteousness [chesed], not sacrifice,
And knowledge of God more than burnt offerings.

From the Book of Hosea (6:6).

.•.

I will betroth you to Me forever;
I will betroth you to Me in righteousness and justice,
In steadfast love and compassion.
I will betroth you to Me in faithfulness,
And you shall know God.

From the Book of Hosea (2:21–22).

Abraham ibn Ezra

[1089–1164]

SPANISH SCHOLAR, POET

I see Thee in the starry field,
I see Thee in the harvest's yield,
In every breath, in every sound,
An echo of Thy name is found.
The blade of grass, the simple flower,
Bear witness to Thy matchless power.

.•.

Man eats to live, he does not live to eat. . . . He was created to serve
God and to cleave to Him, not to accumulate wealth and erect buildings which he must leave behind.

From his Yesod Mora (1158).

Moses ibn Ezra

[c. 1055–1135]

SPANISH HEBREW POET

He who believes in a thing that is contrary to all logic abuses the finest
gift God gave him.

From his Shirat Yisrael ("Songs of Israel").

115

Isaac ibn Ghiyath

ELEVENTH-CENTURY SPANISH HEBREW POET

I sought You out and found You in my thoughts:
My heart has eyes within that let me see.
The soul You breathed in me clings to Your throne,
Though it resides in a battered, aching clod.

Translated by Raymond P. Scheindlin.

Bachya ibn Pakuda

[c. 1050–1120]

SPANISH PHILOSOPHER, AUTHOR

The essence of selfless service to God is to desire, whether in public or private, to serve for the sake of God rather than for the sake of winning approval of others.

From his Duties of the Heart, translated by Moses Hyamson (1962).

·•·

If one prays with his tongue, and his heart is otherwise engaged, his prayer is like a body without a spirit, or a shell without a kernel. . . . Therefore, my brother, arrange the contents of your prayer in proper form in your heart. Let it correspond with the words which you utter. Let both the words and the thought be directed to God.

Ibid.

(Rabbi) Iddi

THIRD-CENTURY TALMUDIC SCHOLAR

He who is good to Heaven [God] and good to man, he is a righteous man who is good. He who is good to Heaven but not good to man, he is a righteous man who is not good.

Quoted in the talmudic tractate Kiddushin (40a).

(Rabbi) Isaac

THIRD-CENTURY TALMUDIC SCHOLAR

Why is the prayer of the righteous compared to a pitchfork? As a pitchfork turns the sheaves of grain from one position to another, so does the prayer of the righteous turn the dispensations of God from the attribute of anger to the attribute of mercy.

Quoted in the talmudic tractate Yevamot (64a).

Louis Jacobs

[1920–]

BRITISH ORTHODOX RABBI, SCHOLAR, AUTHOR

Nowhere in the whole of the biblical record is there the faintest suggestion that God imposes upon man arbitrary rules which must be observed purely on the grounds that God so desires.

From his essay "The Relationship between Religion and Ethics in Jewish Thought," in Religion and Morality (1973), edited by Gene Outka and John P. Reeder, Jr.

Jeremiah

SIXTH-CENTURY B.C.E. PROPHET OF ISRAEL

Woe to the one who builds his house with unfairness and his upper chambers with injustice, who makes his fellow man work without pay and does not give him his wages, who thinks: I will build myself a vast palace with spacious upper chambers, provided with windows, paneled and cedar, painted with vermilion! Do you think you are more a king because you compete in cedar? Your father ate and drank [like you], but he dispensed justice and equity, then all went well with him. He defended the rights of the poor and needy and all was well. Is not this what it means to know me?—declares the Lord.

From the Book of Jeremiah (22:13–16).

Job
BIBLICAL CHARACTER

The Lord has given and the Lord has taken. Blessed be the name of God.

From the Book of Job (1:21).

(Rabbi) Jonah
FOURTH-CENTURY C.E. PALESTINIAN SCHOLAR

God's spirit does not dwell in one who does not have a happy disposition.

Quoted in the Jerusalem Talmud, tractate Sukka (5:1).

Flavius Josephus
[c. 37– c. 95 C.E.]
HISTORIAN, AUTHOR

Woman, says the Law, is in all things inferior to man. Let her accordingly be submissive, not for humiliation, but that she may be directed; for authority has been given by God to man.

From his Against Apion (2:24).

(Rabbi) Judah
A FIRST-CENTURY HIGH PRIEST

Being hospitable to the wayfarer is of higher merit than greeting the Divine Presence.

Quoting Rav in the talmudic tractate Shabbat (127a).

Judah ben Pazzi
FOURTH-CENTURY PALESTINIAN SCHOLAR

God shows mercy also to cattle and birds.

Quoted in Deuteronomy Rabba (6:1).

Judah the Prince
Also known as Yehuda Ha-nasi
[c. 135– c. 219]
PALESTINIAN PATRIARCH, TALMUDIC SCHOLAR

It is well-known to God who created the world that a son honors his mother more than his father, because she sways him by [winning] words, therefore did God command the honor of the father first. It is also well-known to Him that a son reveres his father more than his mother, because the father teaches him Torah, therefore God placed reverence of the mother before reverence of the father.

> Referring to Leviticus 19:3 where the Torah says: "Each man—his mother and father you are to revere," whereas in the Ten Commandments the fifth commandment (Exodus 20:12) reads: "Honor thy father and thy mother." Quoted in the talmudic tractate Kiddushin (30b).

Mordecai M. Kaplan
[1881–1983]
U.S. RABBI, RECONSTRUCTIONIST MOVEMENT FOUNDER

We cannot afford to wait with our health until we know the final truth about our bodies and minds. Neither can we afford to wait with our ethical and spiritual health until we know the ultimate truth about the world and God.

> From his Not So Random Thoughts (1966).

···

We shall not come to experience the reality of God unless we go in search of Him. To be seekers of God, we have to depend more upon our own thinking and less upon tradition. Instead of acquiescing passively in the traditional belief that there is a God, and deducing from that belief conclusions which are to be applied to human experience and conduct, we must accustom ourselves to find God in the complexities of our experience and behavior. . . . Only by way of participation in human affairs and strivings are we to seek God.

> From his Meaning of God in Modern Jewish Religion (1962).

···

When we believe in God, we believe that reality—the world of inner and outer being, the world of society and nature—is so constructed as to enable man to achieve salvation.

Ibid.

· ◦ ·

The moral attributes of God are holiness, justice, mercy, love and faithfulness. The knowledge of these is derived from the ideals for which men strive. In ascribing such attributes to God, we imply that God is the ideal, the pattern and inspirer of all morality.

From his Judaism as a Civilization (1934).

Gerald Kersh
[1911–1968]
BRITISH AUTHOR, JOURNALIST

I can't believe in the God of my fathers. If there is one Mind which understands all things, it will comprehend me in my unbelief. I don't know whose hand hung Hesperus in the sky, and fixed the Dog Star, and scattered the shining dust of Heaven, and fired the sun, and froze the darkness between the lonely worlds that spin in space.

From his They Die with Their Boots Clean (1941).

Larry King
[1933–]
TALK-SHOW HOST, COLUMNIST

Somewhere along the line I stopped liking the God of the Old Testament. I asked great Jewish and other religious leaders why there was a Holocaust or why Hitler lived to sixty-six and a child dies at age eight. I never got good answers.

From an interview with Elinor and Robert Slater. Quoted in their Great Jewish Men (1996).

Francine Klagsbrun
CONTEMPORARY U.S. AUTHOR, SOCIAL ACTIVIST

I live the life of a believing Jew, but always with the awareness that my belief is shadowed by doubt. On the most primitive level, I plead and bargain with the God I'm not sure exists when I or people dear to me face illness or trouble. I rage at that God when I confront suffering and injustice, but also thank God for the good that comes my way.

From her essay in Commentary, August 1996.

I envy those people whose souls are truly in love with God, and I admire those engaged in serious explorations into the nature of divinity.

Ibid.

I live with the tension of both believing and not believing, recognizing that I will probably never resolve it. I grew up in a time when Jews rarely spoke about God, and theology, it was said, was not a Jewish pursuit. That has changed now, and God-talk is everywhere.

Ibid.

Arthur Koestler
[1905–1983]
BRITISH AUTHOR

God seems to have left the receiver off the hook, and time is running out.

From his Ghost in the Machine (1967).

Alfred J. Kolatch
[1916–]
U.S. CONSERVATIVE RABBI, AUTHOR

Once upon a time,
in the very beginning,
when things were aborning
and no one knew mourning

for lost loves
or missed opportunities,
God was a Thou,
and man was a you.

Once upon a time,
at the very outset,
when the earth was unsoiled
and the world unspoiled,
God had a mind-set
to create a universe
with time unlimited
and space unbounded,
where the myriad of His creations
could flower and ripen,
mature and multiply,
reproduce and diversify.
Man was set at the helm
to be master
over land and air and sea,
as far as the eye could see;
to roam the world and explore,
to discover ever more and more,
unencumbered by trauma and stress
footloose to enjoy Heaven's largesse.
It was a time
when God was a Thou
And man was a you.

But then,
when man's adventurous spirit,
activated by his inventive genius
and inquiring mind,
began delving
deeper and deeper
to see what he could find,
he discovered the mystery of the gene
and hoped to uncover much more
yet unseen.

And with bloated ego bragged
that he was a match with God,
a partner on almost every level,
not a mere junior
in any limited sense,
but full and equal—
a team-player with whom
God could not dispense.

No longer was God addressed as Thou
or approached with a bow;
no longer did His sacred name
make man rise in awe
or revere His Law.
No longer was His majesty overwhelming
as it was in the beginning
when life was aborning
and no one knew mourning,
when the world was fresh and clean,
spotless, totally pristine,
when God was a Thou
And man was a you.

Janusz Korczak

[1879–1942]

POLISH EDUCATOR, AUTHOR, PHYSICIAN

We have not given you God because you must search for him and find
him within yourself. . . .

We give you one thing, however. We give you a longing for a better
life, based on truth and justice, which you are destined to build for
yourself.

We hope that it will be this longing that will lead you to God, to
your country, and to love.

Message given to graduates of the orphanage he ran in Warsaw. Noted In
Geoffrey Wigoder's Dictionary of Jewish Biography (1991).

Lydia Kukoff

[1942–]

U.S. REFORM LEADER, AUTHOR

The allowance, sometimes encouragement, of questions concerning belief, God, and truth is a welcome relief. One can be religious and question; in fact it is one's duty to question. Once I learned that Israel meant "to struggle with God," I felt my destiny at hand.

> From her Choosing Judaism (1981), *explaining why she converted to Judaism.*

Harold Kushner

[1935–]

U.S. CONSERVATIVE RABBI, AUTHOR

Prayer is first and foremost the experience of being in the presence of God. . . . A person who has spent an hour or two in the presence of God will be a different person for some time afterward.

> From his Who Needs God? (1989).

•◆•

You don't have to be perfect. Just do your best, and God will accept you as you are. Don't expect your children to be perfect. Love them for their faults, for their trying and stumbling, even as our Father in Heaven loves us.

> From his How Good Do We Have to Be? A New Understanding of Guilt and Forgiveness (1996).

•◆•

I don't like the notion that when we pray and don't get answers, God has considered our request and said, "No." I'd get very upset if I felt God had the power and chose not to. I don't know anything about the nature of God. But I know prayer makes life better and richer.

> Quoted in Newsweek, *March 31, 1997.*

•◆•

We experience the reality of God in our own lives, but we experience it vicariously as well when we examine the history of the Jewish people. No one who reads the story of our 3,000 years of tribulation and accomplishment can deny that God makes a difference in the world.

From his When Children Ask about God (1971).

Lawrence Kushner

CONTEMPORARY U.S. REFORM RABBI, AUTHOR

To be aware of God's presence and God's purpose sounds like a beautiful idea, but who could remember it even most of the time? There are so many distractions. . . . For this reason, ever since Abraham and Sarah, our people have invented ways to try to remain spiritually aware, every day. Our people created a tradition filled with songs, stories, legends and laws to help them remember. That tradition . . . is called Judaism.

From his Book of Miracles (1987).

Maurice Lamm

CONTEMPORARY U.S. ORTHODOX RABBI, AUTHOR

Let me say right away: When we deal with hope, we must deal with God. . . . From the womb of hope have emerged the twin blessings of faith and love to enrich all humankind.

From his The Power of Hope (1995).

Norman Lamm

[1927–   ]

U.S. ORTHODOX RABBI, UNIVERSITY PRESIDENT

It goes without saying I believe in God. But my big terrifying question is whether He believes in me.

From a symposium in Commentary, August 1996, on the question: "What Do American Jews Believe?"

Morris S. Lazaron
[1888–?]
U.S. REFORM RABBI

You cannot conquer the world for the God of love by a jihad of hate.
From his Common Ground (1938).

Yeshayahu Leibowitz
[1903–1994]
ISRAELI PROFESSOR, BIOCHEMIST, BIBLE SCHOLAR, AUTHOR

Encounter with God is the fulfillment of the mitzvot. If I washed today at half past six in the morning and went to the synagogue to fulfill the prayer duty, that was my encounter with God.
Quoted in The God I Believe In (1994), *by Joshua O. Haberman.*

Michael Lerner
[1943–]
ENVIRONMENTAL EDUCATOR, AUTHOR, RABBI

In the final analysis, then, the assertion about the possibility of over-coming cruelty is not an empirical one but a statement of faith in the God of Israel, just as its denial is a statement of faith in the religion of "cynical realism."
By attribution.

Julius Lester
[1939–]
U.S. PROFESSOR, AUTHOR

In the winter of 1974, while I was on retreat at the Trappist monastery in Spencer, Massachusetts, one of the monks told me, "When you know the name by which God knows you, you will know who you are."

I searched for that name with the passion of one seeking the Eternal Beloved. I called myself Father, Writer, Teacher, but God did not answer. Now I know the name by which God calls me. I am Yaakov Daniel ben Avraham v'Sarah.

I have become who I am. I am who I always was. I am no longer deceived by the black face which stares at me from the mirror. I am a Jew.

From his Lovesong: Becoming a Jew (1988).

Sam Levenson
[1914–1980]
U.S. COMEDIAN, AUTHOR

For me the final answer is God. God doesn't send anybody or anything to live on earth without a reason. There's a message that we all have to deliver to the human race.

Quoted in Dialogues in Judaism (1991), edited by William Berkowitz.

Levi Yitzchak of Berditchev
[1740–1809]
CHASIDIC RABBI

I have asked you to close your shops and leave your homes to come here, because I have news of great importance which cannot be delayed for even another hour. And this is my announcement: "There is a God in the world!"

Quoted in Lothar Kahn's God: What People Have Said about Him (1980).

Tehilla Lichtenstein
LEADER OF THE JEWISH SCIENCE MOVEMENT

God has given us the physical eye, a miraculous instrument, with which to behold reality, the world about us, but he has given us the still more miraculous instrument of the imagination. He has given us the power of visualization, with which to create new and greater realities, a more perfect and happier world than the one we have experienced. . . .

From her essay "Believing Is Seeing," in Jewish Science Interpreter, vol. 26, no. 5 (April 1955).

Believing in God . . . is seeing God; seeing Him in the form of those attributes that you believe Him to possess, seeing Him as strength, seeing Him as love, seeing Him as guidance, as shelter, as protection, as infinite loving kindness.

From her essay "Believing Is Seeing," in Applied Judaism: Selected Jewish Science Essays (1989).

Max Lilienthal
[1815–1882]
GERMAN-BORN REFORM RABBI, EDUCATOR

The best religion is humanity. The best divine service, love thy neighbor as thyself. The motto which we inscribe on our banner is the fatherhood of God and the brotherhood of man.

From an 1876 speech.

Jacques Lipchitz
[1891–1973]
LITHUANIAN-BORN SCULPTOR

I daven [pray] every morning. It is of great help to me. First of all, it puts me together with all my people. I am with them. And I am near to the Lord, the Almighty, I speak with Him. I cannot make any prayers individual, but I speak to Him. He gives me strength for the day. . . . I could not live any more without it.

Explaining the effect upon him of the Lubavitcher rebbe's suggestion that he start to wear tefilin every day. From a statement published after his death in The Reconstructionist, February 1974.

Judah Loew
[c. 1525–1609]
RABBI OF PRAGUE, KABBALIST

The dignity of a neighbor, who was created in the divine image, is equivalent to God's dignity.

Quoted in Ben Zion Bokser's From the World of Cabbalah (1954).

Moses Chaim Luzzatto

[1707–1746]

ITALIAN KABBALIST, HEBREW POET, AUTHOR

Man came into the world only to achieve nearness to God.

In his Messilat Yesharim (1740).

·✦·

It is fundamentally necessary both for saintliness and for the perfect worship of God to realize clearly what constitutes man's duty in this world, and what goal is worthy of his endeavors throughout all the days of his life. Our Sages have taught that man was created only to find delight in the Lord, and to bask in the radiance of His Presence. But the real place for such happiness is the world to come, which has been created for that very purpose. The present world is only a path to that goal. "This world," say our Sages, "is like a vestibule before the world to come." Therefore, has God, blessed be His name, given us the miswot [sic]. For this world is the only place where the miswot [sic] can be observed. Man is put here in order to earn with the means at his command the place that has been prepared for him in the world to come.

Ibid. Quoted in Mordecai M. Kaplan's Judaism as a Civilization (1934).

Moses Maimonides

[1135–1204]

SPANISH PHYSICIAN, SCHOLAR, PHILOSOPHER, AUTHOR

You may recite every prayer in proper order and you need not make any changes. You may pray in the same manner as every Jew by birth. . . . Moses separated us from the nations and brought us beneath the wings of the Divine presence and gave to all of us one law. Since you have also entered beneath the wings of the Divine presence, there is no difference between us and you.

In response to a letter addressed to him by Obadiah the Proselyte, who had been criticized for using the words "our God and God of our fathers" in his prayers. Maimonides comforted Obadiah by declaring that although he was not a Jew by birth, he had a right to say our God.

·✦·

129

Go tell your teacher that he owes you an apology. And tell him that he should fast and pray and ask God to forgive him for what he said to you. He must have been intoxicated, and he forgot that in thirty-six places the Torah reminds us to *respect* the convert and that in thirty-six places it admonishes us to *love* the convert. A convert is a child of Abraham, and whoever maligns him commits a great sin.

Ibid.

. •. .

Your prayer and blessing should be the same as that of any other Israelite, regardless of whether you pray in private or conduct the service. The explanation is as follows: Abraham, our father, taught mankind the true belief and the unity of God, repudiating idolatry; through him many of his own household and also others were guided "to keep the way of the Lord, to do righteousness and justice." Thus he who becomes a proselyte and confesses the unity of God, as taught in the Torah, is a disciple of Abraham, our father.

Ibid.

. •. .

The highest virtue to which a man can aspire is to become similar to God as far as this is possible: that means that we must imitate His actions, as has been indicated by our Rabbis in their comment on the words "You shall be holy" (Leviticus 19:2): As He is gracious, so shall you be gracious; as He is merciful, so shall you be merciful.

From his Guide of the Perplexed (1190).

. •. .

The worship is possible only when correct notions of God have previously been conceived.

Ibid.

. •. .

Man's love of God is identical with his knowledge of Him.

Ibid.

. •. .

Avoid lengthy repetitions [of prayers], and thus prevent the desecration of the Name, for the rumor has spread among Gentiles that Jews spit and cough and chatter during their prayers.

From a letter to his son Abraham. Contained in Letters and Responsa: Kobez Teshuboth ha-Rambam, *edited by A. Lichtenberg (1859).*

.•.

Man ought to remember his difficult days in his days of prosperity. He will thereby be inclined to thank God repeatedly, to lead a modest and humble life. Therefore, on Tabernacles we leave our houses in order to dwell in booths. We shall thereby remember that this has once been our condition.

Commenting on Leviticus 23:42 and the commandment to dwell in sukkot (huts).

.•.

The highest virtue to which a man can aspire is to be like God as far as possible. This means, we must imitate His actions.

Quoted in Lothar Kahn's God: What People Have Said about Him *(1980).*

.•.

The foundation of all foundations, the pillar supporting all wisdoms, is the recognition of the reality of God.

Ibid.

.•.

The prayer of the congregation is always hearkened to, even if sinners are among them. God does not despise the prayer of the group, hence man should always make an effort to join with the congregation in prayer. As long as he is able to pray with the congregation, he should not pray alone.

From his Mishneh Torah, Hilchot Tefila 8:1.

.•.

In that era [of the messianic age] there will be neither famine nor war, neither jealousy nor strife. Blessings will be abundant, comforts within the reach of all. The one preoccupation of the whole world will be to know the Lord. Hence Israelites will be very wise, they will know the things that are now concealed and will attain an understanding of their

Creator to the utmost capacity of the human mind, as it is written: "For the earth shall be full of the knowledge of the Lord, as the waters cover the sea" (Isaiah 11:9).

Ibid., Melachim 12:5.

·•·

He who serves God out of love, studies the Torah, observes the commandments, and walks in the paths of wisdom, not because of the ulterior motive of either punishment or reward—but *does the right thing because it is right*; he will find happiness in the end. This is a very exalted state, and not every Sage attains it.

Ibid., Hilchot Teshuva 10.

Morris Mandel

[1911–]

U.S.-BORN PSYCHOLOGIST, AUTHOR, EDUCATOR

Today is here. Breathe in the fresh cool air, enjoy the patches of sunshine. Mix with sincere friends. Exchange ideas and see the beautiful, not the ugly side of life. Beauty is God's therapy. It is there for all to enjoy—today.

From the introduction to his and Leo Gartenberg's Tomorrow Is Today (1977).

·•·

Faith is not to be confused with determination, optimism or imagination. Actually, it is simply *believing*. It is knowing there is an ocean, because you have seen a brook; a mountain, because you have seen a hill; God, because you have seen man.

Ibid.

Gil Mann

FOUNDER OF A COMPUTER COMPANY, AUTHOR

We need to openly discuss spirituality and God in new and user-friendly ways. For example, we need to actively examine how Judaism defines God, how we individually define God, and how our day-to-day lives can be enriched by what Judaism says about God and spirituality. Are there prayers that will really speak to and touch people? We need to broach these subjects in new and meaningful ways from our pulpits, prayerbooks, newsletters, weekend retreats, conventions, and in one-on-one conversations.

From an interview with Judge Norman Krivosha in the United Synagogue Review, spring 1997.

Jose Rolando Matalon

CONTEMPORARY U.S. CONSERVATIVE RABBI, ACTIVIST

Our synagogue is filling up with seekers. There's a sense that there's got to be more to life than just science and technology and money. Part of the search is to ask what happens when you're gone.

By attribution.

Daniel C. Matt

PROFESSOR OF MYSTICISM, CONSERVATIVE RABBI, AUTHOR

The world is teeming with God. Since God is in everything, we can serve God through everything. In looking for the divine spark, we discover that what is ordinary is spectacular. The holy deed is doing what needs to be done, now.

God is not some object, or a fixed destination. There is no definite way to reach God. But, then again, you don't need to reach something that's everywhere. God is not somewhere else. God is right here, hidden from us.

From an article in Moment magazine, February 1997.

(Rabbi) Meir

SECOND-CENTURY TALMUDIC SCHOLAR

God said: "Be like Me. As I repay good for evil, so should you repay good for evil."

Commenting on Exodus 17:5. Quoted in Exodus Rabba (26:2).

·◆·

Just as one blesses God for good happenings, so should he bless God for the bad things that befall him.

Quoted in the talmudic tractate Berachot (48b).

Meir ben Isaac Nehorai
[died before 1096]
GERMAN PREACHER, LITURGICAL POET

Could we with ink the ocean fill,
Were every blade of grass a quill,
Were the world of parchment made,
And every man a scribe by trade—
To write the love
of God above
Would drain the ocean dry;
Nor would the scroll
contain the whole,
Though stretched from sky to sky.

From his famous Aramaic poem "Akdamut Milin," recited on Shavuot in Ashkenazic synagogues.

Menachem Mendel of Kotzk
Also known as the Kotzker Rebbe
[1787–1859]
POLISH-BORN CHASIDIC LEADER

God dwells wherever man lets Him in.

Quoted in Martin Buber's Tales of the Hasidim (1947).

.•.

I will have to find Him [God] first for myself and only then can I speak of Him as "the God of my father."

When his father (who was an opponent of Chasidism) upbraided him for abandoning the old ways. As his defense he quoted Exodus 15:2: "This is my God and I will exalt Him, the God of my father and I will elevate Him." Quoted in Newman's The Hasidic Anthology (1963).

Moses Mendelssohn
[1729–1786]
GERMAN-BORN SCHOLAR, AUTHOR

If I were to find my reason in contradiction to the word of God, I could command reason to be silent; but the arguments, so long as they have not been refuted, will nevertheless assert themselves in the innermost recesses of my heart; the arguments will assume the form of disquieting doubts, which will resolve themselves into childlike prayers, earnest supplication for enlightenment. I should utter the words of the Psalmist: "Lord, send me Thy light, Thy truth, that they may guide me, and bring me to Thy holy mount, to Thy dwelling-place!"

Quoted in Lothar Kahn's God: What People Have Said about Him (1980).

Micah
EIGHTH-CENTURY B.C.E. PROPHET OF ISRAEL

It has been told you, O mortal, what is good,
and what the Eternal requires of you—
Only this: to do justly,
and love mercy,
and walk humbly with your God.

From the Book of Micah (6:8)

Lily (Lilian) H. Montague
[1873–1963]
BRITISH SOCIAL WORKER, LIBERAL RELIGIOUS LEADER

Whatever the creed of his father, . . . a religious man must seek and discover God for himself.

From an article in the Jewish Quarterly Review, Old Series.

.•.

Kinship with God is derived from the actual experience of prayer and from the effort after righteousness. We have no power to explain God. If we could, we should be God ourselves.

Quoted in Elinor and Robert Slater's Great Jewish Women (1994).

Claude G. Montefiore
[1858–1938]
BRITISH SCHOLAR, AUTHOR

When we are told that the Jewish God is distant, we smile with astonishment at the strange accusation. So near is He, that He needs no Son to bring Him nearer to us, no intercessor to reconcile Him with us or us with Him.

From his Liberal Judaism (1903).

Enenit Shula Mula
HEBREW UNIVERSITY STUDENT

Whereas in Ethiopia I was not encouraged to question traditional beliefs or practices, in Israel I am free to think and develop my own understanding of being Jewish. I believe that God wants us to be honest, ethical, and compassionate, and to be responsible for each other. Our goal is a society based upon Jewish ideals of justice and caring for the needs of all its citizens. And I believe that God wants us to reach beyond ourselves to a concern for humanity.

From a New York Times May 8, 1996 advertisement sponsored by the American Jewish Committee on the subject: "What Being Jewish Means to Me." She arrived in Israel in 1984.

Nachman ben Simcha of Bratzlav
[1772–1810]
CHASIDIC REBBE

Solitude is the highest stage. Only in solitude can man attain union with the eternal God. Therefore a man must seek to be alone, at least for an hour each day, especially at night, when everyone is asleep and all things are quiet. Solitude in the open air, in the forest, or in the desert is of the utmost importance.

Quoted in S. A. Horodetzky's Leaders of Hasidim *(1928).*

． ✦ ．

If the Zaddik [hasidic leader] serves God, but does not take the trouble to teach the multitude, he will descend from his rung.

From Martin Buber's Tales of the Hasidim *(1948).*

Nachman of Kosov
EIGHTEENTH-CENTURY GALICIAN RABBI

Some people think of business when they are at the synagogue. Is it too much to ask them to think of God when they are at business?

From his writings.

Nachmanides (Moses ben Nachman)
[1194–1270]
SPANISH TALMUDIST, PHYSICIAN

Humility is the first virtue, for if you are aware of God's greatness and man's lowliness, you will fear God and avoid sin.

From a letter to his son (c. 1268). Quoted in Nahum Glatzer's In Time and Eternity *(1946).*

． ✦ ．

The benefit which comes from the observance of the precepts is not to God Himself, may He be exalted, but the benefit is for man himself, to keep him far from injury or from evil beliefs or from ugly traits of character or to remind him of the miracles and wonders of the Creator, blessed be He, so that man might come to know God. This is the meaning of "to refine people," that they should be as refined silver. For the silver-refiner does not carry out his task without purpose, but does it in order to remove all the dross from the silver. So it is with regard to the precepts. Their aim is to remove every evil from our hearts, to make the truth known to us, and to remind us of it at all times.

From his Commentary to the Pentateuch (1960) on the verse in The Book of Psalms *(18:31).*

(Rabbi) Nehemiah

SECOND-CENTURY TALMUDIC SCHOLAR

Not everyone who is near to God is of necessity permanently near, nor is everyone who is far from God of necessity permanently far. There are some who are chosen and rejected and then brought near; and there are some who are chosen and cast off.

> *Quoting his teacher Samuel ben Isaac in Midrash Numbers Rabba (3:12).*

Jacob Neusner

[1932–   ]
U.S. CONSERVATIVE RABBI, SCHOLAR, AUTHOR

The power of religion is to teach us to look for God's image and likeness in the face of others, but the pathos is that beyond "the others" whom we know and differentiate lies the outsider, "the other," who is left without distinctive traits. The power of religion is to define worthy goals for the social order, setting forth components of public policy that accord with our vision of humanity "in our image, after our likeness." The pathos of religion is that, whether now or a thousand years ago, religion has proved unable to cope with difference and change.

> *From an article in* The Jewish Spectator, *winter 1990, based on his remarks of September 27, 1990 to the Fourth International Meeting for Peace, in Bari, Italy.*

.•.

In the end God governs. Each of us owes God one death, and, in the interim, bears liability also for that huge and interesting conversation with God that each one of us knows as, and calls, life.

> *From his essay in* Commentary, *August 1996.*

Moses Pava

CONTEMPORARY UNIVERSITY PROFESSOR, AUTHOR

Judaism looks to God as the ultimate source of value in our lives. From a religious perspective, the first question in ethics is always about God's values and never about man's desires.

> *From his* Business Ethics: A Jewish Perspective *(1997).*

Jan Peerce

[1904–1984]

NEW YORK-BORN OPERA SINGER

I am very thankful for the little endowment that I have, but we must have respect for our limitations. God doesn't expect us to do every-thing. What you do, do it with love and respect; love your fellow men, love your audience.

When asked to what he attributed his successful career as a singer.

Jakob Petuchowski

[1925–1991]

U.S. PROFESSOR, THEOLOGIAN

God cannot be manipulated by man. He can only be *addressed*. He may, or may not grant a specific request. But there is no mechanism of man's devising which would compel Him to do so. In addressing God, man knows that a "No" can be as much of an "answer" as a "Yes."

From an essay in The Jewish Spectator, *winter 1984.*

Philo

[*c.* 20 B.C.E.–40 C.E.]

ALEXANDRIAN PHILOSOPHER, BIBLE SCHOLAR, AUTHOR

Nothing is better than to search for the true God, even if the discovery of Him eludes human capacity, since the very wish to learn, if earnestly entertained, produces untold joys and pleasures.

From his Special Laws.

⋅◆⋅

Who can look upon statues or paintings without thinking at once of a sculptor or painter? . . . And when one enters a well-ordered city . . . what else will he suppose but that this city is directed by good rulers? So he who comes to the truly Great City, this world, and be-holds hills and plains teeming with animals and plants, . . . the yearly seasons passing into each other, . . . and the whole firmament revolv-ing in rhythmic order, must he not . . . gain the conception of the Maker and Father and Ruler also?

Ibid.

If a man practices ablutions and purifications, but defiles his mind while he cleanses his body; or if, through his wealth, he founds a temple at a large outlay and expense; or if he offers hecatombs and sacrifices oxen without number, or adorns the shrine with rich ornaments, or gives endless timber and cunningly wrought work, more precious than silver or gold—let him none the more be called religious. For he has wandered far from the path of religion, mistaking ritual for holiness, and attempting to bribe the Incorruptible, and to flatter Him whom none can flatter. God welcomes genuine service, and that is the service of a soul that offers the bare and simple sacrifice of truth, but from false service, the mere display of material wealth, He turns away.

Quoted in David Winston's Philo-Judæus of Alexandria (1981).

Wisdom is a straight high road, and it is when the mind's course is guided along that road that it reaches the goal which is the recognition and knowledge of God. Every comrade of the flesh hates and rejects this path and seeks to corrupt it. For there are no two things so utterly opposed as knowledge and pleasure of the flesh.

From his essay "That Every Good Man Is Free."

The thirsty soul knows God immediately by direct contact.

Quoted in The History of Jewish Literature (1938), by Meyer Waxman.

Judith Plaskow

[1948–   ]

FEMINIST THEOLOGIAN, EDUCATOR

I believe it is important to find ways of speaking to and about God that reflect feminist experience and makes sense in the modern world. I am convinced that a feminist Judaism can restore the viability of God-talk, within Judaism, providing the tradition with a language it has lost and sorely needs.

From her Standing Again at Sinai: Judaism from a Feminist Perspective (1990).

Marlene Post

FORMER HADASSAH PRESIDENT

When people around us start talking about spirituality, many of us are likely to shrug and ask, "What is it?" I can only say what it is to me, but I say it unabashedly. Spirituality is my connection to God. I believe there is one God, something greater than myself. Prayer is my way of reaching through time and space to those things I cannot see. While it is legitimate for prayers to be in the form of requests, I usually pray to praise God and give thanks.

From her President's Column, Hadassah Magazine, November 1996.

·•·

Longer lives don't ensure our connection with God, they just give us more years of opportunity to make contact.

Ibid.

Dennis Prager

CONTEMPORARY U.S. EDITOR, AUTHOR,

RADIO TALK-SHOW HOST

Every time a Jew sits down to eat a kosher meal he or she is reminded that the animal being eaten is a creature of God, that the death of such a creature cannot be taken lightly, that hunting for sport is forbidden, that we cannot treat any living thing irresponsibly, and that we are responsible for what happens to other beings. . . .

From Prager and Telushkin's The Nine Questions People Ask about Judaism (1986).

·•·

The most important component of happiness, by far—there isn't a close second—is gratitude. Nothing instills gratitude as much as religion and prayer done correctly. Prayer is a major vehicle to gratitude. Not request prayer, grateful prayer: Thank you, God. My favorite holiday is Thanksgiving, the day of gratitude to God.

When asked to explain the relationship between prayer and happiness. Quoted in Larry King's Powerful Prayers (1998).

Sally Priesand
[1946–   ]
FIRST U.S. FEMALE RABBI

Judaism encourages doubt even as it enjoins faith and commitment. A Jew dare not live with absolute certainty, because certainty is the hallmark of the fanatic, and Judaism abhors fanaticism, [and] because doubt is good for the human soul. . . . One apparent reason [why God denies us certainty] is that man's certainty with regard to anything is poison to his soul. Who knows this better than moderns who have had to cope with dogmatic Fascists, Communists, and even scientists?

From an essay in Condition of Jewish Belief (1966), compiled by the editors of Commentary magazine.

Raba
THIRD/FOURTH-CENTURY BABYLONIAN SCHOLAR

God asks for the heart.

Quoted in the talmudic tractate Sanhedrin (106b).

Rav
Also known as Abba Aricha
THIRD-CENTURY BABYLONIAN SCHOLAR

God loves three types of people: those who never get angry; those who never get drunk; and those who are not stubborn.

Quoted in the talmudic tractate Pesachim (113b).

····

Any blessing that does not contain the name of God is no blessing.

Quoted in the talmudic tractate Berachot (12a).

····

The precepts [mitzvot] were given for no other reason than to refine people. For what difference does it make to God whether the act of slaughtering animals for food is done at the neck or from the back of the neck?

Quoted in Genesis Rabba (44:1). Emphasizing that observing the letter of the law is less important than learning the moral and ethical teaching the commandment is intended to convey.

Jack Riemer

CONTEMPORARY CONSERVATIVE U.S. RABBI, AUTHOR

The difference between a religious and non-religious person is simply this: The religious person knows he is not God and therefore he might be wrong; the person who is not religious is likely to think that he is the "be all and end all," the possessor of wisdom.

Quoted in Moment magazine, June 1998.

Joan Rivers

[1935–]

U.S. ACTRESS, COMEDIENNE, AUTHOR

God is great and we reach Him joyfully in many equally valid ways. A belief in God and a feeling for religious rituals will help bond your marriage. I pray that you and John will always have this celestial glue.

Advice given to her daughter who was about to be married. Quoted in her From Mother to Daughter (1998).

Naomi H. Rosenblatt

CONTEMPORARY U.S. AUTHOR

If we feel deep within that we have been created in the image of God, then no matter where we are or what we are going through we never feel alone. We are never anonymous.

From her introduction to Wrestling with Angels: What Genesis Teaches Us about Our Spiritual Identity, Sexuality, and Personal Relationships (1995).

Ruth

MOABITE ANCESTOR OF KING DAVID

Entreat me not to leave thee, and to return from following after thee; for whither thou goest, I will go; and where thou lodgest, I will lodge; thy people shall be my people, and thy God, my God; where thou diest, will I die, and there will I be buried; the Lord do so to me, and more also, if aught but death part thee and me.

Imploring her mother-in-law, Naomi, to take her along to Bethlehem. From the Book of Ruth (1:16).

Saadya Gaon

[882–942]

BABYLONIAN SCHOLAR, LITURGIST

Reason has long since decided that God needs nothing, but that all things need him.

From his Emunot Ve-deot—"Book of Beliefs and Opinions" (933).

Jessie Ethel Sampter

[1883–1938]

U.S.-BORN AUTHOR, POET, ZIONIST

Each one of us alone with God,
Behind the mask of face and deed,
Each wrestles with an angel.

From her Brand Plucked From the Fire (1937).

Zalman Schachter-Shalomi

[1924–]

U.S. ORTHODOX RABBI, MYSTIC, EDUCATOR

When someone who eats in a nonkosher restaurant orders beefsteaks instead of porkchops because he keeps kosher, I can no longer laugh at him. His choice was occasioned by a sort of low-level, yet very genuine, concern not to eat [nonkosher] beasts. . . . When he refuses butter on it and milk with his coffee because of "seethe not the kid in its mother's milk," I respect him still further. And if he orders a scalebearing fish instead of meat, I see him struggling honestly to do God's will.

From his essay in Condition of Jewish Belief (1966), compiled by the editors of Commentary magazine.

.•.

The rebirth of Israel's national consciousness and the revival of Judaism are inseparable. When Israel found itself, it found its God. When Israel lost itself, or began to work at its self-effacement, it was sure to deny its God.

By attribution.

Laura Schlessinger
[1948–]
AUTHOR, RADIO TALK-SHOW HOST, FAMILY THERAPIST

I had spent my whole life trying to find meaning—in being the "good kid," in doing well in school, in being intelligent, in being successful. Though it was all important, it didn't fill some special empty space, where meaning needed to be. Realizing that I had a God-mandated responsibility to represent His character, love, and ethical will was the meaning I'd been searching for.

> After reading Exodus 19:4–6 where God calls Moses to the top of Mount Sinai and instructs him what to say to the children of Israel. From her The Ten Commandments: The Significance of God's Laws in Everyday Life (1998).

Menachem Mendel Schneerson
[1902–1994]
SPIRITUAL LEADER OF CHABAD

It's not two sides, it's one side, because we are one people in the City of New York, under one administration protected by one God, and may God protect the police and all the residents of the city.

> After Mayor David Dinkins visited him, on the Sunday following the Crown Heights riots of 1991, and expressed the hope that he could bring peace to both sides.

Gershom Scholem
[1897–1982]
GERMAN-BORN HISTORIAN, AUTHORITY ON MYSTICISM

He who has attained the highest degree of spiritual solitude, who is capable of being alone with God, is the true center of the community, because he has reached the stage at which true communion becomes possible.

> Quoted in Polish-Jewish History (1988), edited by Ulf Diederichs.

Ismar Schorsch

[1925–]

U.S. CONSERVATIVE RABBI, HISTORIAN, EDUCATOR

Shabbat imbues us with a sense of proportion. In the silence of the garden, we hear again God's voice. It comes through in the music of our prayers, the chant of the Torah reading, a walk in the park, and our immersion in the study of sacred texts. We withdraw from conquering the world to conquer ourselves.

From an article in Masoret magazine, fall 1995.

Harold Schulweiss

[1925–]

U.S. CONSERVATIVE RABBI, AUTHOR

I feel most fulfilled in and through my relationship to the community. The rabbinate is really far from an occupation or profession in the sense that medicine or law is a profession. Every talk I give is autobiographical. My struggles are expressed in lectures, sermons, comments. I have never withheld from the congregation my wrestlings with the nature of God, prayer, the chosen people. They are quite aware that these are things I have difficulty with.

From a 1982 Present Tense magazine article in which the popular California rabbi reveals his inner conflicts and aspirations.

. ◆ .

We don't pray that God will stop a catastrophe. For example, with the Holocaust, we can't say that because of our sins, one million Jewish children were killed. The logic is bad. The theology is worse. I don't believe a post-Holocaust world can think that way. . . . It turns God into what atheists make of Him—a cruel, wrathful deity. Prayer, instead, is meant to move the God within us.

Characterization of the devastating earthquake that hit Los Angeles in 1994.

. ◆ .

I now know where to look for God. I must begin with myself. You have only to look within yourself. Look into the mirror and discover the deepest part of yourself.

> *A conclusion based on the verse in the Book of Genesis (1:27), "And God created man in His own image." From a lecture delivered on December 10, 1998 at Valley Beth Shalom, in Encino, California.*

Natan Sharansky
[1948–]
RUSSIAN REFUSENIK, MEMBER OF THE KNESSET

I was lucky, I had a chance to compare both ways of life, life without God, a fully materialistic life, and the kind of life when you are doing what you feel will satisfy your sense of what ought to be. And that is how I came to God.

> *Quoted in* The God I Believe In *(1994), by Joshua O. Haberman.*

Abraham Shemtov
WASHINGTON, D.C., EMISSARY OF CHABAD

Everyone who places his faith in God finds that faith tested. You assume that if you pray God will answer you. And suppose the answer is not an evident one? How do you explain it to the nonbeliever, and how do you explain it to that part of yourself which is not a believer? Belief is constantly under attack by logic.

> *Commenting on the belief by some that the deceased Lubavitcher rebbe, Menachem Schneersohn, was the Messiah. Quoted in* New York *magazine, February 14, 1994.*

Shneur Zalman ben Baruch of Lyadi
[1747–1813]
FOUNDER OF THE CHABAD MOVEMENT

Do you know why our master went to the pond every day at dawn and stayed there for a little while before coming home again? He was learning the song with which the frogs praise God. It takes a very long time to learn that song.

In discussing with colleagues the character and greatness of their master, the chasidic rebbe Dov Ber of Mezritch. By attribution.

⋅✦⋅

The middle course [to reach perfection] is attainable by every individual; each person should try to reach it. A person who pursues the middle course . . . is called upon to depart from evil and do good through his behavior, in deed, word and thought . . . Therefore, let him delight in God, praised be He, by contemplating the greatness of the Eternal to the full extent of his capacities. Even though he recognizes that he will not reach this to its ultimate depth, but only by approximation, it is incumbent upon him to do what he can.

From his Tanya (1796).

Simeon ben Yochai
SECOND-CENTURY TALMUDIC SCHOLAR

To honor parents is more important even than to honor God.

Quoted in the Jerusalem Talmud, Mishna Peiah (1:1).

Oswald J. Simon
[1855–1932]
ENGLISH AUTHOR

Faith, love and sorrow are three elements that mysteriously blend in human experience, each having its own tale to tell of the relation which we bear to the Supreme Being.

From his Faith and Experience (1895).

Isaac Bashevis Singer
[1904–1991]
POLISH-BORN NOVELIST, NOBEL PRIZE WINNER

I was exalted; everything seemed good. There was no difference between heaven and earth, the most distant star, and my red hair. My tangled thoughts were divine. . . . The laws of nature were divine; the true sciences of God were mathematics, physics, and chemistry. My desire to learn intensified.

The conclusion of In My Father's Court (1966), a memoir of his childhood in Warsaw, where his father served as a rabbi.

Henry Slonimsky
[1884–1970]
U.S. PHILOSOPHER, PROFESSOR

We can't all pray from our own creative resources because we are not all of us religious geniuses, and prayer and religion are as truly a form of genius, a gift from God, as poetry or music or any high endowment. We can't all write Shakespeare's poetry or Bach's music but we can still make it our own: we can open our hearts to it, and enrich and expand ourselves by sharing and appropriating it. And so in prayer we must turn to the great religious geniuses, the Isaiahs and Jeremiahs and Psalmists, and make our own the visions they have seen, the communion they have established, the messages they have brought back.

From his Essays (1967).

Joseph B. Soloveitchik
[1903–1993]
U.S. ORTHODOX RABBI, SCHOLAR, PROFESSOR

We are committed to God and to observing His laws, but God also wills us to be committed to mankind in general and to the society in whose midst we live in particular. To find fulfillment, one must partake of the human endeavor.

An often expressed view that Orthodoxy can thrive in a constantly changing society.

·◦·

[The genuinely inquiring mind] looks for the image of God not in mathematical formula or the natural law but in every beam of light, in every bud and blossom, in the morning breeze and the stillness of a starlit evening.

From his Lonely Man of Faith (1992).

Aaron Spelling

[1925–   ]

U.S. TELEVISION PRODUCER

I always take them to the airport and I pray they get there safely. And the one rule we have in our family is call from the airport after you land. I pray when that plane takes off and I say, "Please God, let them arrive safely," and I repeat this about two times in my head. Then, when I get the phone call, I know my prayers have been answered.

> He promised his mother never to fly but makes sure to say a prayer when his wife and children fly. Quoted in Larry King's Powerful Prayers (1998).

Shalom Spiegel

[1889–1984]

U.S. AUTHOR, EDUCATOR

Ritual, like precedent, is a footprint left by the encounter of just and holy men with God who is holiness and justice. Footprints like these deserve to be followed, as they may lead again to the source of holiness and justice.

> From his essay "Amos vs. Amaziah," which was originally delivered as an address on September 13, 1957 at the Jewish Theological Seminary of America before a distinguished audience, including former President Harry S Truman and U.S. Supreme Court Chief Justice Earl Warren.

Baruch Benedict Spinoza

[1632–1677]

DUTCH PHILOSOPHER, AUTHOR

The more we understand individual things, the more we understand God.

> From his Ethics (1677).

· ◆ ·

The mind's highest good is the knowledge of God, and the mind's highest virtue is to know God.

> Ibid.

Milton Steinberg
[1903–1950]
U.S. CONSERVATIVE RABBI, AUTHOR, SCHOLAR

A musician must practice by pre-arranged schedule, regardless of his inclination at the moment. So with the devout soul. It may not rely on caprice or put its hope in chance. It must work. The man on the other hand who folds his hands, waiting for the spirit to move him to think of God—who postpones worship for the right mood and the perfect setting, a forest or mountain peak, for example—will do little of meditating or praying.

From his Basic Judaism (1955).

.•.

From the Jewish heritage, I have derived my world outlook, a God-centered interpretation of reality in the light of which man the individual is clothed with dignity, and the career of humanity with cosmic meaning and hope; a humane morality, elevated in its aspirations yet sensibly realistic; a system of rituals which interpenetrates my daily routines and invests them with poetry and intimations of the divine.

Ibid.

.•.

God is the only tenable explanation for the universe.

From his Anatomy of Faith (1960).

Devora Steinmetz
CONTEMPORARY RESEARCHER IN JEWISH EDUCATION

Whatever God is or is not, awareness of God means to me the awareness that there is something larger than the tiny bit of reality which I experience, and that there is something beyond the present, that the past is not forgotten, that the future must be kept in mind. I am chosen if I believe that I have a calling; the language of chosenness tells me that I have responsibilities and that my life is not lived properly if I do not work to clarify and fulfill my calling.

From her essay in Commentary, August 1996.

.•.

I don't believe that if one has to look for the Lord, one has to look to the ceiling or to the heavens. The Lord is everywhere, not just spacewise, but everywhere in every meaning of things. . . . The Gentiles say that the Lord is on high. He's sitting in heaven. We say that He is even higher because He looks down upon heaven and earth. The Lord is so infinite that He deals with the smallest physical being—with the molecule, with a germ, with a grain of wheat—in the same way that he deals with angels, with the galaxies. He is so great that all these things are in the same way insignificant, but very significant when all of them are together.

Ibid.

Abraham Sutzkever

COMPOSER OF YIDDISH MUSICALS

In cellars,
holes,
the murderous silence weeps,
so I run higher,
over roofs,
searching.
Where are You?
Where?

His Holocaust poem first sung in the Vilna ghetto in 1943. Translated by Zalmen Mlotek.

Stewart Vogel

CONTEMPORARY CONSERVATIVE RABBI, AUTHOR

To believe in God is to believe that humans are more than accidents of nature. It means that we are endowed with purpose by a higher source, and that our goal is to realize that higher purpose. If each of us creates his own meaning, we also create our own morality. I cannot believe this.

Expressing his deep belief in a personal God. From his introduction to The Ten Commandments (1998), of which he is co-author with Laura Schlessinger.

Simone Weil

[1909–1943]

FRENCH PHILOSOPHER, AUTHOR

A science that doesn't bring us nearer to God is worthless.
From her Gravity and Grace (1947).

·•·

Of two men who have no experience of God, he who denies Him is perhaps nearer to him than the other.
Ibid.

·•·

Every perfect life is a parable invented by God.
From her New York Notebook (1942).

·•·

In relation to God, we are like a thief who has burgled the house of a kindly householder and been allowed to keep some of the gold. From the point of view of the lawful owner this gold is a gift; from the point of view of the burglar it is a theft. He must go and give it back. It is the same with our existence. We have stolen a little of God's being to make it ours. God has made us a gift of it. But we have stolen it. We must return it.
Ibid.

·•·

It is not my business to think about myself. My business is to think about God. It is for God to think about me.
From her Waiting for God (1950).

Franz Werfel

CZECH-BORN POET, PLAYWRIGHT, NOVELIST

Religion is the everlasting dialogue between humanity and God. Art is its soliloquy.
From his Between Heaven and Earth (1944).

Max Wiener

[1882–1950]

CONTEMPORARY PHILOSOPHER

Religion and morality, the way to God and the way to man, coincide.

Quoted in S. Bernfeld's Foundations of Jewish Ethics (1929).

Elie Wiesel

[1928–   ]

RUMANIAN-BORN U.S. AUTHOR, PROFESSOR

I wanted to show the end, the finality of the event. Everything came to an end—history, literature, religion, God. There was nothing left. And yet we begin again with Night. Only where do we go from there? Since then, I have explored all kinds of options. To tell you that I have now found a religion, that I believe—no. I am still searching. I am still exploring. I am still protesting.

Commenting on the publication of his first book, Night (1960),
originally issued in French as La Nuit (1958), which opened up a general
discussion about the Holocaust for the first time.

..•..

If I want to come closer to God . . . it is only by coming closer to my fellow human being. . . . If I am your friend, I am God's friend. If not, I am the enemy of both God and his creatures.

In an April 1994 address at Queens College, New York, urging the rejection
of fanaticism and the embracing of tolerance and love.

..•..

In all my work—fiction or nonfiction—I have been struggling with these questions. Where was God? What about God? How does one explain the silence of God, the absence of God? Or the presence of God? The complexity of God? If you think I have the answer, you know me better than that. I do not. And it is too easy to put everything on God's shoulders. Much too easy. Where was man, where was humanity, where was civilization?

From Civilization, April–May 1998, reporting on his comments at
Forum 2000, held in Prague in the fall of 1997.

David J. Wolpe

CONTEMPORARY U.S. CONSERVATIVE RABBI, AUTHOR, EDUCATOR

God works through community. In the Jewish tradition, the synagogue is called not a house of worship, but a house of gathering. You need ten to make a *minyan*, a prayer quorum, because God is best addressed by voices that rise together in prayer.

From his When Children Ask about God (1993).

·◆·

Judaism is not an end in it itself but rather a means to an end. Judaism is a route toward God. Halacha, Jewish law, is from a word meaning "to go." Law is a path, not an end. The end is closeness to God.

From his column "Musings," in The Jewish Week, January 10, 1997.

·◆·

Moses died when he had at last seen God face to face. That is in some sense our task in life—to see God truly according to our capacity. When we have fulfilled that task, we are through.

To see God truly means to see the possibilities of this world, to work for its betterment, to grow our own souls. Could our life be a quest to see the face of God? There are worse ways to define one's life quest.

From his column "Musings," in The Jewish Week, March 6, 1998.

·◆·

Perhaps what God seeks is not request but relationship, and we must learn to redirect our hearts to seek out not the goods that God could offer but to seek God.

From his Why Be Jewish? (1995).

Yochanan ben Nappacha

[190–279]

PALESTINIAN TALMUDIC SCHOLAR

How do we know that the Holy One, blessed is He, prays? From the verse: "Even them will I bring to My holy mountain, and make them joyful in My house of prayer" (Isaiah 56:7). Scripture does not say their house of prayer, but My house of prayer. Thus we deduce that God prays.

Quoting Rabbi Yosi in the talmudic tractate Berachot (7a).

.•.

When a poor man returns a lost article to its owner, the Holy One, blessed be He, proclaims his merit daily.

Quoted in the talmudic tractate Pesachim (113a).

(Rabbi) Yosi

FIFTH-CENTURY BABYLONIAN TALMUDIC SCHOLAR

God arranges marriages.

Quoted in Genesis Rabba (68:4).

CHAPTER THREE

God, Jews, and the World-at-Large

Introduction

The battle against polytheism intensified between the third and fifth centuries C.E. when Christianity, seeking converts, began luring Jews from Judaism. The third-century scholar Rabbi Abbahu led the charge in denigrating the Christian belief in the Trinity. Commenting on the verse "I am the Lord thy God" (Exodus 20:2), he said (Exodus Rabba 29:5):

> A king of flesh and blood may be a ruler, and may be a father and brother. But God said: "I am first, for I have no father, and I am last for I have no brother, and other than myself there is no God, for I have no son."

For many centuries, however, Jews classified Christians as idolators because of their concept of the godhead as a trinity comprising the Father, the son, and the Holy Spirit. In the early Middle Ages, this attitude began to change. While eminent scholars such as Spanish-born Moses Maimonides (1135–1204), who lived under Muslim rule for most of his life, considered the Christian worship of a trinity to be pure polytheism and labeled Christians "idolators" and "heathens" (*Mishneh Torah*, Hilchot Teshuva 3:7), other scholars living in a Christian-dominated society were more conciliatory.

Prominent among this latter group was the French-born Rabbenu Tam (1100–1171), the grandson of Rashi, who spent his life in Christian Europe. He accepted the view of Christian theologians who viewed the Trinity concept as consistent with the belief in one God. The three elements that are part of the one God are not, explained these theologians, to be thought of as individual gods. Just as spokes of a wheel are not in themselves wheels but components that are integral to the actual wheel, so the three aspects of the Trinity are not gods, although together they do compose the one God. (See his commentary in Tosafot, Sanhedrin 63b and Bechorot 2b.)

The outstanding German rabbinic scholar Jacob Israel Emden (1697–1776) agreed with Rabbenu Tam and wrote that Christians cannot be considered idol worshipers. Moreover, he believed that it is incumbent upon every Jew to befriend Christians in their hour of need, as was taught by the Sages of the Talmud (Gittin 61a).

Oddly enough, while Jews accepted the views of Rabbenu Tam and Jacob Emden, many Christians themselves continued to reject the idea of a trinity. John Adams, elected second president of the United States in 1796, was among those who rejected the concept. "To say that three is one and one is three is sheer mystical gimmickry," he said.

The initial rejection by Jews of the basic Christian concept of a trinity in which God is manifest in three different forms countered the Church's rejection of the biblical assertion that the Jews alone were God's Chosen People.

In actuality, in the Covenant at Sinai God promises Israel that it can be His Chosen People "if you will hearken to my voice and keep My commandments" (Exodus 19:5). Israel's chosenness was conditional. In fact, Rabbis in later generations asserted, "The righteous people among all nations [and creeds] can have a share in the world-to-come" (Tosefta, Sanhedrin 13). One does not have to be one of the Chosen People to merit a place in paradise.

The concept of Israel's chosenness dates back to a covenant between God and Abraham in which God, in effect, promised Abraham that if he would spread God's name throughout the world, Abraham and his descendants would be blessed forever (Genesis 12:1–3).

The significance of this covenant was emphasized by the prophet Isaiah who, when speaking for God, says, "You are my witnesses and I am the Lord" (Isaiah 43:12). To the Rabbis of the Midrash (Genesis Rabba 30:10), this meant that God needs man just as man needs God. Man and God are partners in the enterprise called life. Or, as Abraham Joshua Heschel put it, "God is a partner and partisan in man's struggle for justice, peace, and holiness, and that is why He entered into a covenant with man."

Martin Buber, in his I and Thou, framed the concept this way:

> That you and I need God more than anything, you know at times in your heart. But don't you know also that God needs you? . . . How would God exist if man did not need him, and how would you exist? You need God in order to be, and God needs you—for that is the meaning of your life.

American scholar Theodore H. Gaster summed up these views when he commented: "God needs a committed people to articulate His glory on earth." However, the idea of Israel being God's Chosen People did not sit well with all Jews, even in earliest times. Some Rabbis of the Talmud took offense and rejected the idea that a special partnership existed between man and God. They presented this view in answer to the question, "Why was Adam the last of all God's creations?" If, as Judaism believes, all of the world was created for man, why was Adam not the first of God's creations? The answer of the Rabbis is, "Man was created on the eve of the Sabbath [making him the last of all creations] so that the Sadducees should not say, 'Man was God's partner in creating the world'" (Sanhedrin 38a).

Despite the initial aversion of the Rabbis to the idea of linking God to man as partners, this view was, and still is, subscribed to by most traditional theologians. This partnership, they say, is an expression of God's immanence, of God's concern for man, the crown of all His creations. Man, by his faith and actions, contributes to the perfection of the world. The Jew, in particular, makes his contribution toward creating an improved world (Tikun Ha-olam) through prayer and study and the observance of the commandments (mitzvot).

·•·

In this chapter, we shall find many views expressed on the above issues as well as comments on Israel's mission to be a "light to the nations," the acceptance and treatment of converts, and how the profanation of God's name militates against peace while the sanctification of God's name promotes peace and amity.

Finally, the question of how far the State should be involved in Church matters is discussed. Taking their cue from Thomas Jefferson, the third president of the United States, mainstream Jews have supported the view that there must be an impenetrable wall that separates Church from State, as is called for in the First Amendment to the Constitution of the United States. The amendment implies very clearly that the government shall in no way impinge upon the religious practices of the individual, establish a state religion, or allow the religious views or practices of any one group to become associated with governmental institutions.

Mainstream Jews have repeatedly made it a point to strengthen this separation, for its breach may place democracy itself at risk. As Rabbi Morris Kertzer said in a dialogue with Rabbi William Berkowitz in 1964, "We Jews worry about the separation of Church and State more than any other group."

The significance of the First Amendment to the U.S. Constitution, known as the Establishment Clause, was summed up in a statement by Stephen S. Breyer, on July 13, 1994. In responding to a question posed by the Senate Judiciary Committee, which was inquiring into his fitness to serve as a Supreme Court justice, he said:

> . . . persons who are agnostic, persons who are Jewish, persons who are Catholic, persons who are Presbyterian, all religions, and nonreligions too, are on an equal footing as far as the Government is concerned. That's the basic principle.

This chapter also includes quotations regarding the responsibility of the Jew to improve and enhance the world and thus uphold God's Name. In Judaism, the behavior of an individual is of far more importance than his beliefs. When one battles against evil and stands for what is right, that person is on God's side, a true believer. Even when alone in the struggle, the individual's voice is important. Judaism believes in the Arthurian legend that one man can create a peaceable kingdom. Even a lone voice can make a difference in eradicating evil and creating a better world.

Abbaye

[c. 230–339]

TALMUDIC SCHOLAR

Miracles were performed for our ancestors because they sacrificed their lives for the sanctification of the Name.

Quoted in the talmudic tractate Berachot (20a).

·•·

What is the Sanctification of the Name? Conduct which leads to people to love the name of Heaven.

Quoted in the talmudic tractate Yoma (86a).

Akiba ben Joseph

[c. 50–135]

LEADING TALMUDIC SCHOLAR, ACTIVIST

Israel is beloved, for they were called God's children.

Quoted in the Ethics of the Fathers (3:18). The reference is to Deuteronomy 14:1.

·•·

He who sheds blood is regarded as though he had defaced God's likeness.

Commenting on Genesis 9:6. Quoted in Genesis Rabba (34:14).

Anonymous

Art thou a Jew, one of God's Chosen People? . . . May I examine thee? . . . Hmpf! Thou art no different from us.

Observation of a Quaker woman after examining the first Jew she ever met. Quoted in Max Dimont's Jews in America (1978).

·•·

One should expose hypocrites to prevent the profanation of God's name.

Quoted in the talmudic tractate Yoma (86b).

·•·

There are three partners in man, the Holy One, blessed be He, the father, and the mother. When a man honors his father and his mother, the Holy One, blessed be He, says, I ascribe [merit] to them as though I had dwelt among them and they had honored Me.

Quoted in the tractate Kiddushin (30b).

⋅◆⋅

Everyone who issues a just verdict is considered by Scripture to be a partner with God in Creation.

Quoted in the Midrash Mechilta d'Rabbi Ishmael, Yitro 2.

⋅◆⋅

One should always live in the Land of Israel. . . . A person who dwells in the Diaspora may be regarded as one who has no God.

Quoted in the talmudic tractate Ketubot (110b).

⋅◆⋅

There is nothing more detestable and abominable to God than a person who appears naked in public. Rabbi Yochanan said: "This refers to the Parsees [who practice a Zoroastrian ritual]."

Quoted in the tractate Yevamot (63b).

⋅◆⋅

One must act properly in his association with his fellowman even as he does with God.

Quoted in the talmudic tractate Shekalim (3:2).

⋅◆⋅

The Holy One, blessed be He, said: "The land of Israel is more precious to Me than everything."

Quoted in the Midrash Be-midbar Rabba (23:7).

⋅◆⋅

God hates one who says one thing with his mouth, and another in his heart, and he who possesses evidence concerning a neighbor and does not testify for him.

Quoted in the talmudic tractate Pesachim (113b).

.◆.

Stealing from a non-Jew is worse than stealing from a Jew because it is a profanation of God's name.

Quoted in the Tosefta, Bava Kamma (10:15).

Mary Antin
[1881–1949]
RUSSIAN-BORN U.S. AUTHOR, ZIONIST

He [God] who had brought my ancestors safe through a thousand perils was guiding my feet as well. God needed me and I needed Him, for we two together had work to do, according to an ancient covenant between Him and my forefathers.

From her The Promised Land (1912).

Bradley Shavit Artson
CONTEMPORARY U.S. CONSERVATIVE RABBI, AUTHOR

We Jews are notoriously uncomfortable discussing God. We prefer to leave that to Christians. . . . For the sake of Jewish survival, and to make that survival worthwhile, it is time to transcend our discomfort with God.

From an essay in Women's League Outlook, winter 1996.

Israel Baal Shem Tov
[c. 1700–1760]
FOUNDER OF CHASIDISM

Every Jew is an organ of the Shechina [Divine presence]. As long as the organ is joined to the body, no matter how loosely, there is still hope that it will become healthy. But, when the organ is cut off, there is no hope for it.

From his Shivchei Ha-Besht (1903). Lamenting over the fact that Jacob Frank (1726–1791), the false Messiah, and his followers converted to Christianity.

Isaac Babel

[1894–1941]

RUSSIAN AUTHOR

If you need my life you may have it, but all make mistakes, God included. A terrible mistake has been made, Aunt Pesya. But wasn't it a mistake on the part of God to settle Jews in Russia, for them to be tormented worse than in Hell? How would it hurt if the Jews lived in Switzerland, where they would be surrounded by first-class lakes, mountain air, and nothing but Frenchies? All make mistakes, God not excepted.

> Words spoken by Benya Krik, the gangster boss of Jewish Odessa, in Babel's
> story, "How It Was Done in Odessa."

Leo Baeck

[1873–1956]

GERMAN REFORM RABBI, THEOLOGIAN

In the language of the Bible the word *berit* became a characteristically religious word, one of these words in which the idea of great interrelatedness, the great unity of all, of mystery and ordered certainty, seeks to express itself. The God-given order was to find expression in this term. . . . The Old Aramaic translation of the Bible translated *berit* as *ka'yama* [that which is established], indicating that which is above all change, above all that comes and goes.

> From his People of Israel (1965).

·•·

If our life is to be filled with devoutness, we must from time to time abandon the ways of the world so that we may enjoy the peace of God.

> From his The Essence of Judaism (1948).

Eliyahu Bakshi-Doron

SEPHARDIC CHIEF RABBI OF ISRAEL

The situation in Israel is terrible and we pray that God should give peace. . . . When I speak of peace, they [the PLO] want war. There is not a single Jew who does not want peace. We have had enough wars. Jews want to serve God. We are never out to conquer.

From a speech delivered in New York during his visit to the United States in April–May 1994.

·•·

We have to do whatever we can to stop violence and the only way to do that is through dialogue. I am full of hope that Sheikh Yassin can solve this problem. I call on him as a [fellow] believer in God.

A message by the Sephardic Chief Rabbi of Israel sent to Sheikh Ahmand Yassin, head of Hamas, after his release from an Israeli prison in October 1997.

Menachem Begin

[1913–1992]
ISRAELI PRIME MINISTER (1977–1983)

My generation, dear Ron, swore on the Altar of God that whoever proclaims the intent of destroying the Jewish state or the Jewish people, or both, seals his fate.

From a letter to U.S. President Ronald Reagan. Quoted in London's Observer, January 2, 1983.

Ely Ben-Gal

MUSEUM OF THE DIASPORA HISTORIAN

Perhaps now we can accept in a certain way that we were chosen: not God's chosen people, but the exact opposite, the people selected to be backed against the wall. So perhaps it is because of what we need—for ourselves, and using you as intermediary—to have a ceremony and a medal. We need it to be able to say to our children that they must not lose faith in humanity, that in our worst moments of abjection, we were not alone.

Speaking to fellow historians in 1990 at the Diaspora Museum in Tel Aviv.

Eliezer Berkovits

[1908–1992]

U.S. ORTHODOX RABBI, SCHOLAR, AUTHOR

God's chosen people is the suffering servant of God. The majestic fifty-third chapter of Isaiah is the description of Israel's martyrology through the centuries [and] the way Christianity treated Israel through the ages only made Isaiah's description fit Israel all the more tragically and truly.

From his Faith After the Holocaust (1973), *in which he disputes the Christian claim that the suffering servant in Isaiah refers to Jesus.*

···

The humanization of the Word of God requires that in applying the Torah to the human condition, one takes into consideration human nature and all its needs, human character and its problems, the human condition in its forever-fluctuating dimension, the Jew and the Jewish people in their unique historical reality.

From his Not in Heaven: The Nature and Function of Halakha (1984).

···

God, as He has made Himself known to man, is a caring God. God is our surety that nothing that has value, in accordance with His desire for man, ever perishes. He is the Preserver. Because He Is we know that no good deed and no kind word, no noble thought and no sincere striving for the good, are ever in vain. Because He Is God nothing worth preserving is ever so lost in history as not to be found again—be it even beyond history.

From his God, Man, and History (1959).

Eugene Borowitz

[1924–]

U.S. REFORM RABBI, THEOLOGIAN

In my experience, what God gives most people hour by hour, generously, exceeds what as a simple matter of justice they deserve. When one lives in gratitude, the absence of justice stands out primarily in the astonishing benevolence showered on most people.

From his Renewing the Covenant (1991).

Shmuel Boteach

[1967–]

DIRECTOR OF THE L'CHAIM SOCIETY, RABBI

Yisrael, the name of the Jewish people, means "wrestle with God." A Jew is someone who is in constant dialogue with God, protesting vociferously against human suffering and perceived miscarriages of justice.

From his essay "If God Is Good, Why Do People Suffer?" which appears in his Moses of Oxford (1994).

The real question which should be posed to God upon witnessing a child with leukemia, or a collective Holocaust, is not "Please God, explain to us why this happens and how it fits into Your overall plan for creation," but rather, "Master of the universe, how could You allow this to happen! We are not interested in any rationalizations. Was it not You who taught us in Your Torah that life is sacred and must be preserved at all costs? So where is that life now?

Ibid.

Mel Brooks

[1926–]

U.S. MOTION PICTURE PRODUCER, DIRECTOR, WRITER, ACTOR

Look at Jewish history. Unrelieved lamenting would be intolerable. So, for every ten Jews beating their breasts, God designated one to be crazy and amuse the breast-beaters. By the time I was five I knew I was that one.

Quoted by Stuart Schoffman in The Jerusalem Report, December 30, 1993.

I may be angry at God or at the world, and I'm sure that a lot of my comedy is based on anger and hostility. . . . It comes from a feeling that, as a Jew and as a person, [I] don't fit into the mainstream of American society.

Quoted in Darryl Lyman's Jewish Comedy Catalog (1989).

Cecil Brown

CONTEMPORARY U.S. WRITER

But not so odd
As those who choose
A Jewish God,
But spurn the Jews.

> In response to William Norman Ewer's verse "How odd of God to choose the Jews."

Martin Buber

[1878–1965]

GERMAN THEOLOGIAN, AUTHOR

The yearning of Judaism for God is the yearning to prepare a resting place for Him in genuine community. Judaism's understanding of Israel is that genuine community will spring from that people. Its messianic expectation is the expectation of genuine community fully realized.

> From M. Friedman's Martin Buber's Life and Work (1981–83).

· ◆ ·

The God of history and the God of nature cannot be separated, and the land of Israel is a token of their unity.

> Ibid.

· ◆ ·

There is no opposition between the truth of God and the salvation of Israel.

> Ibid.

· ◆ ·

Israel is not a nation like other nations, no matter how much its representatives have wished it during certain eras. Israel is a people like no other, for it is the only people in the world which, from its earliest beginnings, has been both a nation and a religious community. In the historical hour in which its tribes grew together to form a people, it became the carrier of a revelation. The covenant which the tribes made with one another and through which they became "Israel" takes the form of a common covenant with the God of Israel. . . . He who serves this bond serves the life of Israel.

From his essay "Hebrew Humanism," in his Israel and the World (1948).

Shlomo Carlebach
[1926–1994]
U.S. ORTHODOX RABBI, FOLKSINGER

The [Lubavitcher] *rebbe* told me to go out into the world. He called me in one day, when he became the *rebbe* in 1951 and said, "God gave you so much talent to talk to people, you have to go out and talk to young people today."

From his last interview, on October 20, 1994, describing what launched his career as a peripatetic singer looking for lost souls all over the world.

. ◆ .

The most important thing my parents gave me [was] that we're responsible for the whole world. We have to become God's messengers to the world—and the message is that there is one God, we're one world, and we're all brothers and sisters.

By attribution.

Chiya bar Abba
THIRD-CENTURY TALMUDIC SCHOLAR

Where do we find that the Holy One is actually identified as the heart of Israel? In the verse "God is the rock, my heart, and my portion forever." (Psalm 73:26)

Quoted in the tractate Chulin (91b).

. ◆ .

The hatred of heathen nations toward the Jews—to what can this be compared? To a person who hated the king and wished to harm him, but could not harm him. So what did he do? He approached a statue of the king and was about to demolish it, but was suddenly overcome by fear, realizing if he were caught he would be executed for treason. So, instead, he took an iron stake and began to strike the base to undermine its foundation, feeling confident that in time the statue would collapse. In like manner do heathens plan to provoke God, but finding that they cannot accomplish this, they attack and persecute the Jews instead.

Quoted in Midrash Exodus Rabba (51:5).

Chiya ben Rav of Difti

THIRD-CENTURY BABYLONIAN SCHOLAR

Every judge who judges with complete fairness even for a single hour, Scripture considers him to be God's partner in the world's creation.

Quoted in the talmudic tractate Shabbat (10a).

Rachel Cowan

CONTEMPORARY U.S. REFORM RABBI

We need to make our community more joyful, educated, creative and welcoming. Let's make our synagogues spiritually deeper, our commitment to social justice more active. Let's bring new ideas into our Jewish world: women's perspectives on ritual, theology and leadership; outreach to Jews who are struggling with illness, grief and loneliness; awareness that our environment is God's creation and needs our action to protect it; authentic Jewish traditions of meditation to deepen our spiritual life. And let's see in the phenomenon of intermarriage an opportunity to bring new Jews into our community.

Quoted in Hadassah Magazine, June–July 1993, in answer to the question: "What is the most important thing we can do to ensure Jewish survival in America?"

· ❖ ·

God's love for the Jewish people will inspire an evolution of the religion and the community that will bring this ancient prophetic and wisdom tradition to bear on the issues and challenges that face the world, the Jewish people, and the individual soul. Our great-great-grandchildren will continue to bring light to the world.

Anticipating the structure and content of Jewish life in America in the year 2100. Quoted in Moment magazine, December 1997.

David D. Dalin

[1949–]

U.S. CONSERVATIVE RABBI, HISTORIAN

Over the years, I have always considered (and continue to regard) the Hebrew blessing thanking God "Who has chosen us from all peoples by giving us His Torah" a profoundly important and meaningful part of our traditional Jewish liturgy, and one that should never be deleted from the worship service.

From his essay in Commentary, August 1996.

Max I. Dimont

CONTEMPORARY U.S. AUTHOR, HISTORIAN

In the Mosaic code, there is the beginning of democracy, the separation of church and state. The Torah sets down the basic relations between humans and God and between citizens and state. . . .

With the prophets we find the beginning of the universalization of God—that God was not a fragmentary thing, the possession of only one people or only one nation. God was universal in scope, and He was God of all people on earth. Here we begin to find the concept of human brotherhood.

Quoted in Dialogues in Judaism (1991), edited by William Berkowitz.

Kirk Douglas

[1916–]

U.S. ACTOR

We were chosen to bring conscience into the world, to hold up the lessons of the Torah, like a mirror, to the face of humanity. . . . Some [of us] don't even know what the Torah is. I was guilty of that most of my adult life. I am sorry that it took me so long to get around to learning. I must be the oldest Torah student in the world. But I also learned that it's never too late. God is a forgiving God. There is hope for all of us—always.

From his Climbing the Mountain: My Search for Meaning (1997).

Albert Einstein
[1879–1955]
GERMAN-BORN U.S. SCIENTIST

A conviction, akin to religious feeling, of the rationality or intelligibility of the world lies behind all scientific work of a higher order. This firm belief, a belief bound up with deep feeling, in a superior mind that reveals itself in the world of experience, represents my conception of God.

Quoted in The American Weekly (1948).

My religiosity consists in a humble admiration of the infinitely superior spirit that reveals itself in the little [things] that, with our weak and transitory understanding, we can comprehend of reality. Morality is of the highest importance—but for us not for God.

Quoted in Geoffrey Wigoder's Dictionary of Jewish Biography (1991).

It suffices that we [Jews] form a social body of people which stand out more or less distinctly from the rest of humanity, and the reality of which is not doubted by anyone.

Quoted in Ronald W. Clark's Einstein: The Life and Times (1971).

A man who can stand before the Eternal Sources of this amazing universe without reverent awe, is blind.

By attribution.

Ira Eisenstein
[1906–1997]
U.S. RECONSTRUCTIONIST RABBI, AUTHOR, EDUCATOR, LECTURER

Here are hundreds of men and women like myself. They are praying for peace. They all have the same idea that I have. They hate war. So do I. They are my brothers. Hundreds of us, with one heart and one mind, are pledging allegiance to this ideal. We will win out in the end. We must win out. We will change the world and make the world give up the madness of war. God is with us.

From his What We Mean by Religion (1938).

.•.

Some of these ideas and values [peculiar to Judaism]—that man is created in the image of the divine, that life is sacred, that man is his brother's
keeper, that society must be ruled by law, that justice and compassion are
the highest virtues, that moral responsibility is the most authentic form
of ethics, that man must serve as a "partner to God" in perfecting this
world, etc.—have exerted a tremendous influence upon Western civilization. I do not, however, infer from this fact that the Jews are the chosen
people.

From his essay in The Condition of Jewish Belief (1966), a
symposium organized by the editors of Commentary magazine.

Elazar of Berotha

Give to God what is His, for you and yours are His.

Quoted in the Ethics of the Fathers (3:8).

(Rabbi) Eleazar

SECOND-CENTURY TALMUDIC SCHOLAR

God exiled the Jews from their homeland for one reason: to increase
the number of converts who would join them.

Quoted in the talmudic tractate Pesachim (87b). Reinforcing the view of
Isaiah (42:6–7) that Israel was destined to be "a light to the nations."

.•.

Anyone who brings a non-Jew closer to God is like one who is his
creator.

Quoted in the Midrash Genesis Rabba (39:14).

Eleazar ben Pedat

THIRD-CENTURY TALMUDIC SCHOLAR

Why did God fashion human fingers in their present shape? It was done
so that one can plug his ears when hearing improperly spoken words.

By attribution.

Harvey J. Fields

CONTEMPORARY U.S. REFORM RABBI, AUTHOR

We are a people that encounters God's echo in community. We approach the Holy One through the dissonance of disagreement and the harmony of agreement, and Torah discussion with others. God talk can be dangerous for Jews. It is a cul-de-sac of hot air. We have been taught to approach God not through clever, fancy talk, but through mitzvot and the sanctity of prayer.

From his article in Reform Judaism, spring 1984.

Anne Frank

[1929–1945]

HOLOCAUST VICTIM, DIARIST

Who has made us Jews different from all other people? Who has allowed us to suffer so terribly up till now? It is God that has made us as we are, but it will be God too who will raise us up again. If we bear all this suffering and if there are still Jews left, when it is over, then Jews, instead of being doomed, will be held up as an example. Who knows, it might even be our religion from which the world and all people learn good, and for that reason and that reason only do we have to suffer now. We cannot become just Netherlanders, or just English, or just representatives of any other country for that matter, we will always remain Jews, but we want to, too.

From an April 11, 1944 entry in Anne Frank: Diary of a Young Girl (1952).

Sigmund Freud

[1856–1939]

AUSTRIAN-BORN ORIGINATOR OF PSYCHOANALYSIS

[The Jewish people] has met misfortune and ill-treatment with an unexampled capacity for resistance, it has developed special character-traits and incidentally has earned the hearty dislike of every other people. . . .

We know the reason for this behaviour and what their secret treasure is. They really regard themselves as God's chosen people, they believe that they stand especially close to Him and this makes them proud and confident.

From his last book, Moses and Monotheism (1939).

Theodore H. Gaster

[1906–1992]

U.S. FOLKLORIST, AUTHOR

Judaism has a central, unique and tremendous idea that is utterly original—the idea that God and man are partners in the world and that, for the realization of His plan and the complete articulation of this glory upon earth, God needs a committed, dedicated group of men and women.

From an address to the American Council for Judaism, April 30, 1954.

Neil Gillman

CONTEMPORARY U.S. CONSERVATIVE RABBI, THEOLOGIAN

I affirm that God is unique, personal, transcendent; that God cares deeply about human life and history; that God has entered into a special relationship with the Jewish people; and that God creates, reveals, and will ultimately redeem.

From his essay in Commentary, August 1996.

Robert Gordis

[1908–1992]

U.S. CONSERVATIVE RABBI, PROFESSOR, AUTHOR

All animal life and all growing and life-giving things have rights in the cosmos that man must consider, even as he strives to ensure his own survival. The war against the spoliation of nature and the pollution of the environment is therefore the command of the hour and the call of the ages.

From an article in Congress Biweekly, April 1971.

Hayim (Chaim) Greenberg

[1889–1953]

RUSSIAN-BORN JOURNALIST, ZIONIST LEADER

Perhaps the Jewish doctrine of the chosen people may be interpreted in this way: Jews are not a chosen people, but a choosing people. According to the Haggada God went around to nation after nation with the Torah, speaking to each in its own language, offering the Torah to each of them, but without success, till the Jews said that they would accept the Torah and keep it. The Jews chose the One God, and the Jews chose the one and only true Torah. How can we apply the usual standards to a people with such an aristocratic choosiness?

From his essay "A Glance into the Future." Reprinted in Joseph Leftwich's The Way We Think (1969).

David Weiss Halivni

CONTEMPORARY U.S. RABBI, PROFESSOR OF TALMUD

Prayer accentuates the distance between God and humankind. The study of Torah brings us closer to God. There are two places in the Talmud where it is said that by keeping the Sabbath or judging with righteousness we may become partners with God in creation. By fulfilling certain commandments we may become partners in God's activity. But in learning we become part of God's very being. One cannot cleave unto God physically, as the rabbis said, for God is "a consuming fire," but one can cleave unto God spiritually through learning.

Quoted in Hadassah Magazine, October 1997.

Heinrich Heine

[1797–1856]

GERMAN POET

Formerly, I felt no special affection for Moses, probably because the Hellenic spirit was paramount in me, and I could not pardon the legislator of the Jews his hatred against the plastic arts. I did not see that, notwithstanding his hostility to art, Moses was a great artist, and possessed the true artistic spirit. But this spirit was directed by him, as by

his Egyptian compatriots, to colossal and indestructible undertak-
ings. . . . However, he built human pyramids, carved human obelisks;
he took a poor shepherd family and created a nation from it, a great,
eternal holy people, a people of God, destined to outlive the centuries,
and to serve as a pattern to all other nations, even as a prototype to the
whole of mankind: he created Israel.

> From his Confessions (1854).

·•·

How strange! The very people who had given the world a God, and
whose whole life was inspired by devotion to God, were stigmatized
as deicides!

> Ibid.

·•·

Jews are of the stuff of which Gods are made; today trampled under
foot, tomorrow worshipped on the knees. While some of them crawl
in the filthy mire of commerce, others rise to the loftiest peaks of
humanity. . . . You will find among them every possible caricature of
vulgarity, and also the ideas of purest humanity.

> From his Ludwig Börne (1840). Quoted in F. Eiven's Poetry and
> Prose of Henrich Heine (1948).

·•·

Now I perceive that the Greeks were only handsome youths, but the
Jews have always been men, powerful, stubborn men, not only in days
of yore, but even at present, in spite of eighteen centuries of persecu-
tion and misery. I have since learned to know them better, and to value
them more highly, and if pride of descent were not always a foolish
contradiction, I might feel proud of the fact that my progenitors were
members of the noble house of Israel, that I am a descendant of those
martyrs who have given a God and morality to the world, and who
have fought and suffered on all the battle-fields of thought.

> Ibid. Expressing pride in belonging to an ancient aristocracy toward the end
> of a life in which he struggled with a love-hate relationship to Judaism.

Arthur Hertzberg

[1921–]

U.S. CONSERVATIVE RABBI, SCHOLAR, AUTHOR

The Catholics have great difficulty admitting the Jewish nature of the Holocaust because of the basic tenets of their theology. At the center of the unknowable mystery, the mystical heart of Catholicism, is the belief that God sacrificed one third of the Holy Trinity. The concept of suffering as both a quality of God's and a sign of redemption is at the core of Catholic belief. When the Jews lost one third of their living body to the cross of Auschwitz, it reawakened the question that maybe they really are God's chosen people.

Quoted in Anne Roiphe's Season for Healing (1988).

There is some God-talk today that does point toward the work of perfecting the world so that it might become God's kingdom. . . . But too much of today's God-talk is self-involved and self-indulgent. To those who are, again, in quest of "peace of mind," one should quote again the profound insight of the 19th-century moralist, Israel of Salant: "If you want to save your soul, save somebody else's body."

From an essay in The Jewish Week, May 17, 1996.

The chosenness of the Jews is a mystery. Only God knows the purpose of setting apart an obscure tribe to suffer and to achieve more than could be expected from so small a band on so stormy a journey. All that we Jews can know about ourselves is that after every tragedy we have always made new beginnings.

From his Jews: The Essence and Character of a People (1998).

There is no quiet life for Jews anywhere, at least not for long. The only question is whether one lives among the tempests with purpose and dignity. We Jews know why we suffer. Society resents anyone who challenges its fundamental beliefs, behavior, and prejudices. The ruling class does not like to be told that morality overrules power. The claim to chosenness guarantees that Jews will live unquiet lives.

Ibid.

There is no personal God, but He chose the Jews and He promised them the Holy Land.

Ibid. *Suggesting to Ben-Gurion what Hertzberg believed.*

Abraham Joshua Heschel
[1907–1972]

U.S. RABBI, THEOLOGIAN, AUTHOR, ACTIVIST

We are God's stake in human history. We are the dawn and the dusk, the challenge and the test.

From his Earth Is the Lord's (1950).

Judaism is the track of God in the wilderness of oblivion. By being what we are, namely Jews . . . we will aid humanity more than by any particular service we may render.

Ibid.

Israel's experience of God has not evolved from search. Israel did not discover God. Israel was discovered by God. Judaism is *God's quest for man.* The Bible is a record of God's approach to His people. More statements are found in the Bible about God's love for Israel than about Israel's love for God. We have not chosen God; He has chosen us.

From his article in The Zionist Quarterly, summer 1951.

The Jew does not stand alone before God, it is as a member of the community that he stands before God. Our relationship to Him is not as an I to a Thou, but as a We to a Thou.

From his Man's Quest for God (1954).

Living is not a private affair of the individual. Living is what man does with God's time, what man does with God's world.

From his God in Search of Man (1955).

God's participation in human history . . . finds its deepest expression in the fact that God can actually suffer.

> From his The Prophets (1962). Philosophers such as Eliezer Berkovits rebutted this as an objectionable Jewish idea since it implies that God—a God of pathos—"is a God shaped in the image of man." See Tradition: A Journal of Orthodox Thought, spring-summer, 1964.

.•.

Pluralism is the will of God.

> Overheard saying to a startled group of Roman Catholics. Quoted in Emil Fackenheim's What Is Judaism? (1987).

.•.

I don't believe in a monopoly. I think God loves all men. He has given many nations. He has given all men an awareness of His greatness and of His love. And God is to be found in many hearts all over the world. Not limited to one nation or to one people, to one religion.

> From his Moral Grandeur.

Richard G. Hirsch
CONTEMPORARY U.S. REFORM RABBI

Jews can't simply be led to the slaughter for they have the means to defend themselves. The Jewish people will not permit themselves to be destroyed. I think God will not be God without the Jewish people. This doesn't mean that either God or the Jewish people is linked for all time inextricably to the State of Israel. But as I now look at the plight of Jews around the world, the survival of the Jewish people is at this moment inextricable from the survival of the Jewish State.

> From an article in The Christian Century magazine, December 11, 1974.

Isaiah Horowitz
[1565–1630]
POLISH-BORN KABBALIST, AUTHOR

The Torah says, "Love your neighbor like yourself." It means that what is dear and precious to you, do it also to your neighbor. If anyone has sinned against you, forgive him immediately. The whole community is one body, and will one hand strike the other hand?

The whole world is dependent on the commandment "Love your neighbor." Through his love for his fellow, man attains the love of God, for both loves flow together into the Divine Unity.

From his Shnei Luchot Ha-berit. Quoted in Arnold Posy's Mystic Trends in Judaism (1994).

(Rabbi) Huna
THIRD-CENTURY TALMUDIC SCHOLAR

Why is the epithet "Place" [Makom in Hebrew] used as a synonym for the name of the Holy One, blessed be He? Because He is the place of the world but the world is not His place.

Implying that without God there could be no world. Quoted in Genesis Rabba (68:9) and Exodus Rabba (45:6).

Chasdai ibn Crescas
[1340–1410]
SPANISH PHILOSOPHER, AUTHOR

God's justice must embrace all his children.

From his Or Adonai (1400).

Ila'i the Elder
THIRD–CENTURY TALMUDIC SCHOLAR

When a man sees that his impulse [to do evil] is about to overcome him, let him go to a place where he is not known, put on black garments and do what his heart desire, but let him not openly profane God's name.

Quoted in the tractate Chagiga (16a). Advice to one who is unable to master his sexual urges, recommending that he sin in secret. Some scholars suggest that donning dark clothing may cool his passion and he will not sin.

Walter Isaacson

CONTEMPORARY U.S. BIOGRAPHER

For Kissinger, the Holocaust destroyed the connection between God's will and the progress of history—a tenet that is at the heart of the Jewish faith. . . . After witnessing the Nazi horror, Kissinger would abandon the practice of Judaism.

From his biography entitled Kissinger (1993).

Isaiah

EIGHTH-CENTURY B.C.E. PROPHET OF ISRAEL

Grass withers and flowers fade,
But our God's word holds good forever.

From the Book of Isaiah (40:8).

.•.

[I] made you a covenant people,
a light to the nations.

Ibid (42:6).

.•.

You are My witnesses, says the Eternal One,
My servant whom I have chosen.

Ibid (43:10).

Louis Jacobs

[1920–]

BRITISH ORTHODOX RABBI, SCHOLAR, AUTHOR

It becomes obvious that we are not discussing a dogma incapable of verification, but the recognition of sober historical fact. The world owes Israel the idea of the One God of righteousness and holiness. . . . Clearly, God used Israel for this great purpose.

From his Jewish Theology (1975).

Jeremiah

SIXTH-CENTURY B.C.E. PROPHET OF ISRAEL

Israel is holy to the Eternal, the first fruit of God's harvest.
From the Book of Jeremiah (2:3).

Morris Joseph

[1848–1930]

BRITISH REFORM RABBI, THEOLOGIAN

Judaism is something more than a badge, something more than a birth-mark; it is a life. To be born a Jew does not declare any of us to be of the elect; it only designates us for enrollment among the elect. God signs the covenant, but we have to seal it—to seal it by a life of service.
In his Judaism as Creed and Life (1903).

Joshua ben Karcha

SECOND-CENTURY TALMUDIC SCHOLAR

A Jew submits first to the sovereignty of God, then to that of the Law.
Quoted in the talmudic tractate Berachot (13a).

Joshua ben Levi

THIRD-CENTURY TALMUDIC SCHOLAR

Even an iron curtain will not cause a divide between Israel and their Father in Heaven.
Expressing Israel's devotion to God even when oppressed by the Roman conqueror. Quoted in the talmudic tractate Pesachim (85b).

Zvi Hirsch Kalischer

[1795–1874]

RABBI, AUTHOR, ZIONIST PIONEER

Let no one think that God will suddenly descend from heaven to earth to say to His people, "Go out," or that He will send His Messiah from heaven to blow with a big shofar and to summon the scattered remnants of Israel and gather them into Jerusalem. . . . Not so, for the beginning of redemption will be through the awakening of the spirit of individuals and through concessions granted by governments which will lead to the ingathering of Jewish people in the Holy Land.

Cited in Jacob Bernard Agus's, High Priest of Rebirth: The Life, Times and Thought of Abraham Isaac Kook (1972).

Kalonymos ben Yehuda

TWELFTH/THIRTEENTH-CENTURY GERMAN POET

Yea, they slay us and they smite,
Vex our souls with sore affright;
All the closer cleave we, Lord,
To thine everlasting word.
Not a line of all their Mass
Shall our lips in homage pass;

Though they curse, and bind, and kill,
The living God is with us still.
We still are Thine, though limbs are torn;
Better death than life forsworn.

From dying lips the accents swell,
"Thy God is One, O Israel";
And bridegroom answers unto bride,
"The Lord is God, and none beside,"
And, knit with bonds of holiest faith,
They pass to endless life through death.

Composed after the Crusader massacre of the Jews of Xanten, near the Rhine, on June 27, 1096. Quoted in J. H. Hertz's Pentateuch and Haftorahs (1961).

Louis Kaplan

[1905–   ]

U.S. EDUCATOR

Our historic experience is long enough to *disabuse* us of the illusion of continuous, uninterrupted progress. It also should immunize us against the views of defeatism. Naive optimism and/or despair are not what Jewish history and especially our present situation demand of us. We must be realists whose faith in man and in God the Creator of all will enable us to cope with the evil in the world and with our own frailties. The world needs the leverage our fate and faith can provide.

From The Jewish Spectator, winter 1978.

Abraham Isaac Kook

[1865–1935]

ASHKENAZIC CHIEF RABBI OF PALESTINE AFTER 1919

Those who rebuild the land are as favored in the sight of God as the ritually observant.

Stating an unorthodox view.

·◆·

The world unites and reconciles all contradictions: all souls and all spirits, all events and all things, all desires, drives and enthusiasms; everything is part of a larger order and kingdom. God is King.

From his Orot Ha-kodesh (1938). Quoted in Harvey Lutske's History in Their Hands (1996).

Lydia Kukoff

[1942–   ]

REFORM LEADER, AUTHOR

Judaism never asked that things be accepted purely on faith. It gave each person an active role to play in the world as a genuine partner of God.

From her Choosing Judaism (1981).

Harold Kushner
[1935–]
U.S. CONSERVATIVE RABBI, AUTHOR

People are not afraid of dying; they are afraid of not having lived. We can handle mortality. What we cannot accept is anonymity, insignificance. If people would realize that Judaism is not a matter of obeying or pleasing God, it is a matter of changing the world by investing ordinary moments with holiness and making our lives matter in the process, then living Jewishly would no longer be an obligation. It would be an irresistible answer to one of life's most pressing questions.

When asked: "What is the most important thing we can do to ensure Jewish survival in America?" Quoted in Hadassah Magazine, June–July 1993.

·•·

The ultimate goal is to transform the world into the kind of world God had in mind when He created it.

From his To Life! (1993).

Lawrence Kushner
CONTEMPORARY REFORM RABBI, AUTHOR

The goal of spirituality is the bringing together of seeing, hearing, and doing into one whole person. It is to see yourself mirrored in the heavens above and to realize that [God] the Holy One created you personally to help complete the work of repairing the world.

From his The Book of Miracles: A Young Person's Guide to Spirituality (1987).

Maurice Lamm
CONTEMPORARY ORTHODOX U.S. RABBI, AUTHOR

The Jewish religion is not simply a calling; conversion is not simply a profession of faith. It is a network of profound ideas and rich insights, which during its long history has generated the fundamental beliefs of all Western religion. It has contributed to the civilized world its crowning ideals and its most glorious convictions—among them the idea of one God, a system of jurisprudence, a structure of ethics and morals . . . and numerous ideas, ideals, and institutions.

From the preface to his Becoming a Jew *(1991).*

．◆．

For Judaism, the value in human sexuality comes only when the relationship involves two people who have committed themselves to one another and have made that commitment in a binding covenant recognized by God and society. The act of sexual union, the deepest personal statement that any human being can make, must be reserved for the moment of total oneness.

From his Jewish Way in Love and Marriage *(1980).*

Morris S. Lazaron

[1888–?]

U.S. REFORM RABBI

In the nationalism of our times, we must cry out the universal message of Israel: Not the blood cult, state cult, hate cult, war cult of nationalism, but on humanity on earth as there is one God in heaven.

From his Common Ground *(1938).*

James M. Lebeau

CONTEMPORARY U.S. CONSERVATIVE RABBI

Israel's uniqueness is that it is a Jewish state and not just a state for Jews. Traditional Jewish ethical and moral principles must influence every governmental decision and serve as a guide to daily life. It is not enough that Israelis live by the Jewish calendar; we must live by Jewish values. I believe that God gave Israel to the Jewish people as a gift, but a gift with duties and requirements. The government and society of Israel should be a model for other nations in fulfillment of Isaiah's charge that Israel be a "light unto the nations."

From a statement in the United Synagogue Review, *fall 1997.*

Herbert H. Lehman

[1878–1963]

U.S. SENATOR FROM NEW YORK (1949–1957)

I believe that all religions play a useful and very necessary part in people's lives, and I respect all religions that teach belief and faith in God.

> Responding to a young Jew who asked whether being Jewish affected the senator's career. The letter was read at Lehman's funeral in New York City on December 8, 1963.

Gotthold E. Lessing

[1729–1781]

GERMAN POET, CRITIC

God selected a people for His special education, and precisely the rudest and unruliest, in order to begin with it from the very beginning. . . . He was bringing up in them the future teachers of the human race.

> From his Education of the Human Race (1778).

(Rabbi) Levi

THIRD-CENTURY TALMUDIC SCHOLAR

Great is peace, for all the blessings and supplications we invoke before God conclude with shalom. The (evening) Shema is concluded with "He who spreads a canopy of peace," the priestly benediction closes with shalom; and the Tefilah concludes with oseh ha-shalom ("the Maker of peace").

> Commenting on the frequency with which the word shalom appears in the liturgy. Quoted in Leviticus Rabba (9:9).

Levi Yitzchak of Berditchev

[1740–1809]

CHASIDIC RABBI

All the worlds above and below, God created only for the sake of Israel.

> By attribution.

·•·

You are always making demands on your people. Why not help them in their troubles?

Ibid.

Uriah P. Levy

[1792–1862]

U.S. NAVY COMMANDER

I am a Jew. I will not insult the Source of the authority of this court and of this nation, nor will I demean my conscience, by defending or explaining my form of worship. The decision as to the faith into which I was born was God's. I believe the same is true of you. I suggest that it is not within the province of the Navy to alter that fact or to place penalties upon His judgment.

Addressing the naval court before which he was brought on charges of insubordination because of his relentless campaign against the Navy's practice of flogging sailors as a means of punishment. He refuses to defend his position and instead accuses his superiors of discriminating against him by refusing to give him good assignments worthy of his proven ability.

David L. Lieber

[1925–   ]

U.S. CONSERVATIVE RABBI, SCHOLAR, EDUCATOR

The enduring nature of Israel's covenant with God remains central to Judaism today, and holding on to it, I believe, is critical to our survival as a people. It offers a reason for that survival—to be "light unto the nations"—and a method, a way of life which seeks to make God manifest in the world.

From his essay in Commentary, *August 1996.*

Saul Lieberman

[1898–1983]

BYELORUSSIAN-BORN U.S. TALMUDIC AUTHORITY

The most tragic character in the Bible is God.

His response to the question he asked of Professor Mufts, his colleague at the Jewish Theological Seminary, who had first suggested Jeremiah, then Ezekiel. Quoted in Burton L. Visotzky's The Genesis of Ethics *(1996).*

Eugene Lipman

CONTEMPORARY U.S. REFORM RABBI, SCHOLAR, AUTHOR

Judaism begins with God and the covenant. The date, place, and circumstances of its beginning are unclear because more than one covenant situation is mentioned in the Bible.

God entered into a covenant with Noah. . . . God also entered a covenant with Abraham, with Isaac, and with Jacob. . . . Then God entered into a covenant relationship with the entire Jewish people. At Mount Sinai He covenanted with that people, present and future. Down through the centuries, the Jewish people have considered themselves a covenant people, in sacred relationship to God.

From his The Mishnah: Oral Traditions of Judaism *(1974).*

·◆·

The Sabbath is the greatest symbol of the spirit of Judaism. More than any other concept in the Jewish religious system, it raises the individual to his proper stature as the child and partner of God, co-creator of the world, being "but little lower than the angels." It is Judaism's prime statement about the uniqueness of the individual and his essential freedom of will.

Ibid.

190

Moses Chaim Luzzatto
[1707–1746]
ITALIAN KABBALIST, HEBREW POET, AUTHOR

When a man is convinced that, wherever he is, he always stands in the presence of God, blessed be He, he is spontaneously imbued with fear lest he do anything wrong, and so detract from the exalted glory of God.

> Quoted in Lothar Kahn's God: What People Have Said about Him (1980).

Moses Maimonides
[1135–1204]
SPANISH RABBI, PHYSICIAN, SCHOLAR, PHILOSOPHER, AUTHOR

I believe with complete faith that the prophecy of Moses our teacher, peace upon him, was true, and that he was the father of all the prophets—both those who preceded him and those who followed him. All are below him in rank, for he was chosen by God.

> Based upon his commentary to the Mishna Sanhedrin (10), in which he presents Thirteen Principles (Articles) of Faith, every Jew must believe in order to be assured a place in the world-to-come.

. .

"The heavens are the heavens of the Lord; but the earth hath He given to the children of men" (Psalm 115:16). This is to say, only God knows in a perfect way the true nature of the heavens, their essence, their formations, their motions, and their origins. But in the terrestrial sphere He gave man the faculty of knowledge. It is man's world; the realm assigned to him, and of which he himself is a part.

> From his Guide of the Perplexed (II: 24).

. .

To avoid transgression or to perform a precept, not from fear or ambition but purely out of love of God, is to sanctify His name in public.

> Quoted in his Mishneh Torah, Yesodei ha-Torah (5:10).

Menachem Mendel of Vitebsk
[1730–1788]
CHASIDIC RABBI

All my life I have struggled in vain to know what man is. Now I know.
Man is the language of God.

By attribution.

Mendele Mocher Seforim
Né Shalom Jacob Abramowitsch
[1835–1917]
BYELORUSSIAN-BORN HEBREW-YIDDISH AUTHOR

Israel is the Diogones of the nations; while his head towers in the heavens and is occupied with a deep meditation concerning God and His wonders, he himself lives in a barrel.

Quoted in the introduction to Irving Howe's A Treasury of Yiddish Stories *(1954).*

Julian Morgenstern
[1881–1977]
U.S. REFORM RABBI, BIBLE SCHOLAR, EDUCATOR

In rabbinical tradition Esau and Edom came to symbolize Rome, the colossal, temporal, material power, which sought to crush nations, which overran the earth with warfare and bloodshed, and found its highest pleasure in murderous gladiatorial combats. And Jacob continued to represent Israel, the spiritual people, the servant of the Lord, whose mission was to bind up the bleeding wounds of cruelty and oppression and to bring law and order, peace and brotherhood, and the knowledge of God unto all mankind.

From his Book of Genesis *(1965).*

Moses ben Jacob of Coucy
THIRTEENTH-CENTURY FRENCH SCHOLAR, CODIFIER

We have already explained concerning the remnants of Israel that they are not to deceive anyone whether Christian or Muslim. God has scattered Israel among the nations so that proselytes shall be gathered unto them; so long as they behave deceitfully toward them [non-Jews], who will cleave to them? Jews should not lie either to a Jew or Gentile, nor mislead them in any matter.

> Urging his fellow Jews to live exemplary lives despite the atmosphere of hate for Jews that was prevalent in thirteenth-century Spain and France.

Moshe Lieb of Sassov
[1744–1807]
CHASIDIC RABBI

Even atheism can be uplifted through charity. If someone seeks your aid, act as if there were no God, as if you alone can help.

> Quoted in Martin Buber's Tales of the Hasidim (1947).

Herbert J. Muller
CONTEMPORARY AUTHOR

Altogether, both the glory and tragedy of Israel may be traced to the singular idea cherished by its people—the exalted, conceited, preposterous idea that they alone were God's chosen people.

> From his Freedom in the Ancient World (1961).

Nachman ben Chisda
FOURTH-CENTURY BABYLONIAN SCHOLAR

When God created man He created him with two impulses: the good impulse (yeitzer ha-tov) and the evil impulse (yeitzer ha-ra).

> Quoted in the talmudic tractate Berachot (61a). Commenting on the spelling of vayitzer, with two yuds, in Genesis 2:7.

Nachman ben Simcha of Bratzlav

[1772–1810]

CHASIDIC RABBI

God is present whenever a peace treaty is signed.

One of many aphorisms transmitted through his disciples.

Nachmanides (Moses ben Nachman)

[1194–1270]

SPANISH TALMUDIST, PHYSICIAN

Let no man consider sex as something ugly or repulsive, for to do so is to blaspheme God. . . . God did not create anything that is ugly or shameful.

From the introduction to his Torah commentary.

Jacob Neusner

[1932–]

U.S. CONSERVATIVE RABBI, SCHOLAR, AUTHOR

I do believe in God, I do believe the Torah to convey God's will, I do believe that the commandments represent that will, I do believe that Israel is God's first love, and that Israel, then, now, and always, accepts God's dominion and bears witness to God in the world.

From his essay in Commentary, August 1996.

David Novak

CONTEMPORARY PROFESSOR OF JUDAIC STUDIES, AUTHOR

My faith is in the God of Abraham, Isaac, and Jacob, with Whom the Jewish people exists in a unique covenantal relationship. Expression of that faith can only be defined and specified within this covenant between God and His people, into which I have been born and in which I choose to abide.

From his essay in Commentary, August 1996.

. ◆ .

I believe that God has chosen the Jewish people for a unique relationship with Himself, one whose meaning is primarily understood within the covenant itself. The only meaning of this election for the world here and now is that the elected community should live a life of covenantal faithfulness that testifies to the kingship of God.

Ibid.

Levi Olan
[?–1984]
U.S. REFORM RABBI, AUTHOR

Celebrations of historic occasions are incumbent upon us because they represent, preserve, and keep alive chunks of Jewish history. Passover and freedom are obligatory upon a Jew. If all Jews were to cease celebrating Passover, a [vital portion] of Jewish experience would be lost. No Jew has a right to do that! . . . To be a Jew is to act to preserve the historic experience of the people with God.

From a letter to Rabbi Henry Cohen, author of Why Judaism? (1973).

(Rabbi) Osha'ya
THIRD-CENTURY PALESTINIAN SCHOLAR

God did the Jews a favor by scattering them among the nations.

Quoted in the talmud tractate Pesachim (87b) as an explanation for their continued survival.

Norman Podhoretz
[1930–   ]
U.S. AUTHOR, EDITOR

In thinking about the Jews I have often wondered whether their survival as a distinct group was worth one hair on the head of a single infant. Did the Jews have to survive so that six million innocent people should one day be burned in the ovens of Auschwitz? It is a terrible question, and no one, not God Himself, could ever answer it to my satisfaction.

From an offensive remark he made in a Commentary magazine essay entitle "My Negro Problem—and Ours." Quoted in his Ex-Friends (1999).

Ruth W. Popkin
PRESIDENT OF THE JEWISH NATIONAL FUND (1993)

Zionism, like the faith from which it sprang, has room for all who share the vision of a fair and just Jewish nation, founded upon faith in God and human struggle, and built with inspired toil.

From a 1985 statement.

Dennis Prager
CONTEMPORARY U.S. EDITOR, AUTHOR,
RADIO TALK-SHOW HOST

If I did not believe that the Jews were chosen by God, I would not raise my children as Jews. . . . Being a messenger is what chosenness is about. We are here to bring the world to ethical monotheism, i.e., the one God and His one universal moral law.

From his essay in Commentary, *August 1996.*

.•.

Our role in the universe—it's not original to me—is completing God's work by using our free will to be good and holy, to make a better world than we have inherited, to appreciate what we've been given, and to enjoy it. I am absolutely convinced it is a sin to be unhappy. A big sin. It's a statement to God that he blew it.

Quoted in Larry King's Powerful Prayers *(1998). Expressing his understanding of our role in the universe.*

Raba
THIRD/FOURTH-CENTURY BABYLONIAN SCHOLAR

God provides the cure before the trauma is produced.

Referred to in the tractate Megilla *(13b) and based on* Song of Songs Rabba *(4:12).*

Emanuel Rackman
[1910–]
U.S. ORTHODOX RABBI, SCHOLAR, EDUCATOR

The sum-total of all that I have written is that I want you to perform the mitzvah [commandment] of *kiddush ha-Shem*—sanctifying God's name in everything that you do. The essence of that *mitzvah* is not martyrdom, although it sometimes calls for that. However, our sages define it differently. "So act," they enjoin us, "that all who behold you will say: 'Blessed is that man's God.'"

It is thus that I pray you will act. And you and we shall rejoice.

From a letter to his son upon his leaving for college. Quoted in This I Believe: Documents of American Jewish Life *(1990), edited by Jacob R. Marcus.*

Rav
Also known as Abba Aricha
THIRD-CENTURY BABYLONIAN SCHOLAR

What is a profanation of the Name? For example, not to pay the butcher at once where it is customary to pay in cash.

Quoted in the talmudic tractate Yoma *(86a).*

Anne Roiphe
[1935–]
U.S. WRITER, NOVELIST

There is a collective destiny, a historical experience that is Judaism but I, you, we, they do or do not choose to be a part of it. One can be a Jewish atheist, a Jewish Socialist, a Jewish Zionist, a Jewish farmer without believing in the Jewish God. The odd and special part of the Jewish experience is just this nationhood that existed without nation—this sense of historical purpose that is moving forward in some mysterious but necessary condition.

From her Generation without Memory *(1981).*

Aryeh Rubenstein
CONTEMPORARY HISTORIAN, AUTHOR

There can be no doubt whatsoever that the re-establishment of the State of Israel in 1948 is one of the most important events in Jewish history. That a nation cut off—in the main—from its land for nearly two thousand years should regain its sovereignty is amazing enough. That it should do so immediately after suffering the worst disaster any people in recorded history has ever suffered and, from a military point of view, against overwhelming odds, compounds the astonishment and, indeed, awe that any spectator must feel. With good reason, many people, both Jews and gentiles, saw the hand of God in the miracle of 1948.

From the introduction to his Hasidism *(1975).*

Richard Rubenstein
[1924–   ]
U.S. CONSERVATIVE RABBI, AUTHOR, PROFESSOR

In no sense do I believe that Jews or any other people are the chosen of God, nor do I believe the Jewish people has a more distinctive role in the world than any other. . . . Some of what we have learned may be instructive to others, but there is nothing theologically or morally privileged about our experience or the values that derive from it.

From his essay in Commentary, *August 1966.*

• ◦ •

I believe the greatest single challenge to modern Judaism arises out of the question of God and the death camps. . . . How can Jews believe in an omnipotent, beneficent God after Auschwitz? Traditional Jewish theology maintains that God is the ultimate, omnipotent actor in the historical drama. It has interpreted every major catastrophe in Jewish history as God's punishment of a sinful Israel. I fail to see how this position can be maintained without regarding Hitler and the SS as instruments of God's will. . . . The idea is simply too obscene for me to accept.

From an essay in Condition of Jewish Belief *(1966), compiled by the editors of* Commentary *magazine.*

·◆·

[The greatest obstacle to Jewish-Christian understanding] is that the true dialogue, the genuine meeting of persons, is impossible so long as Jew and Christian are committed to the religion-historic myths of their respective communities. [The Jew must release his hold on the] doctrine of the election of Israel and the Torah as the sole content of God's revelation to mankind [while the Christian, in turn, must de-emphasize] the decisive character of the Christ event in human history [a myth] that must be at best an error and at worst blasphemy.

From his After Auschwitz: Radical Theology and Contemporary Judaism (1966).

·◆·

We learned in the crisis that we were totally and nakedly alone, that we could expect neither support nor succor from God nor from our fellow creatures. Therefore, the world will forever remain a place of pain, suffering, alienation and ultimate defeat.

Ibid.

·◆·

No Jewish theology will possess even a remote degree of relevance to contemporary Jewish life if it ignores the question of God and the death camps.

Ibid.

Saadya Gaon
[882–942]
BABYLONIAN SCHOLAR, LITURGIST

God does not leave His people at any period without a scholar whom He inspires and enlightens, that he in turn may instruct and teach it, so that thereby its condition may be bettered.

From his Sefer Ha-galui. Quoted in Robert Gordis's essay on Saadya in the American Jewish Yearbook, No. 44, 1942–43.

Jonathan Sacks

[1948–]

CHIEF RABBI OF GREAT BRITAIN (1991–)

Once the presence of God was believed to make peace between Jews.
Now peace is believed to require his absence.

From his One People: Tradition, Modernity, and Jewish Unity
(1993).

Laura Schlessinger

[1948–]

AUTHOR, RADIO TALK-SHOW HOST, FAMILY THERAPIST

Rather than as metaphor, I take the covenant at Sinai as real and true.
This does put me at odds with some contemporary Jews, for whom
Judaism is more a people and a culture than a people of "the cov-
enant." However, without my firm faith and belief of a whole people expe-
riencing God directly, I wouldn't be able to believe in God at all or accept
God's authority over the world and me.

From her The Ten Commandments: The Significance of God's
Laws in Everyday Life (1998).

Moses Seixas

WARDEN OF THE HEBREW CONGREGATION
OF NEWPORT, RHODE ISLAND (1790)

Sir:—Permit the children of the stock of Abraham to approach you
with the most cordial affection and esteem for your person and merit,
and to join with our fellow-citizens in welcoming you to Newport.

With pleasure we reflect on those days of difficulty and danger when
the God of Israel, who delivered David from the peril of the sword,
shielded your head in the day of battle; and we rejoice to think that the
same spirit which rested in the bosom of the greatly beloved Daniel,
enabling him to preside over the provinces of the Babylonian Empire,
rests and ever will rest upon you, enabling you to discharge the ardu-
ous duties of the Chief Magistrate of these States.

Upon the visit of President George Washington to the synagogue on
August 17, 1790.

200

Constantine Shapiro

[1841–1900]

RUSSIAN-BORN HEBREW POET

A golden harp is Israel,
    Its strings
Are heaven's own rays,
That trembling, pour a melody
    that sings
Of holiness when poet plays.
Alas, the melody is sad and
    low,
For God has tuned the harp
    strings so.

From her Collected Poems. *Quoted in Meyer Waxman's* History of
Jewish Literature *(1941).*

Natan Sharansky

[1948–]

RUSSIAN REFUSENIK, MEMBER OF THE KNESSET

[History] is made by God through those who are ready to fight. Jackson was a man of noble principles who believed that principles do not contradict practicalities. . . . Jackson lived at a time when there were clear-cut choices between good and evil. In today's confused world, it's good to look back at those romantic times and to return to the realities of today equipped with the truths and legacies of heroes like Senator Jackson.

Commenting on the 1975 Congressional bill sponsored by Senator Henry "Scoop" Jackson from the State of Washington that denied favored-nation status to any country that did not allow free emigration. This was a boon to Soviet refuseniks and other dissidents. Reported in The Jerusalem Post, *January 14, 1995.*

Shneur Zalman ben Baruch of Lyadi
[1747–1813]
FOUNDER OF THE CHABAD MOVEMENT

Ha-teva ["nature"] has the same numerical value [gematria] as Elohim ["God"].

Both add up to 86. From his Likutei Amarim.

Abba Hillel Silver
[1893–1963]
U.S. REFORM RABBI, ZIONIST LEADER

Other nations of antiquity, when they were defeated, acknowledged that their gods had been defeated. The Jews always saw in their defeat the triumph of their God.

From his World Crisis & Jewish Survival (1941).

William B. Silverman
[1914–   ]
U.S. REFORM RABBI, AUTHOR

God needs man for a sublime purpose: God needs an Antonio Stradivari to make violins, a Michelangelo for a masterpiece of painting, a Louis Pasteur, a Lister, a Fleming, and a Jonas Salk as the instrumentalities for bringing healing to mankind—but God also needs an instrument, a means to bring spiritual healing to mankind. God needs a Moses, an Amos, a Micah, a Jeremiah, a Jesus through whom to channel divine revelation. God needs dedicated men and women of every faith, race, and nationality, dedicated and covenanted to fulfill a divine destiny.

Quoted in Lothar Kahn's God: What People Have Said about Him (1980).

Simeon ben Eleazar
SECOND-CENTURY TALMUDIC SCHOLAR

When Jews do the will of God, the Name is glorified; when they do not, the Name is desecrated.

From the Midrash Mechilta on Exodus (15:2).

Simeon ben Gamaliel II
SECOND-CENTURY TALMUDIC SCHOLAR

He who shows pity for mankind, God will show him mercy, while he who is not merciful to others will not be shown mercy.

Quoted in the talmudic tractate Shabbat (151b).

Simeon ben Yochai
SECOND-CENTURY TALMUDIC SCHOLAR

If you are My witnesses, I am God; if you are not My witnesses it is as if I am not God.

Interpreting the words of Isaiah (43:12): "You are My witnesses and I am God." Quoted in the Midrash Sifri (Deuteronomy), paragraph 346.

Simon the Righteous
FOURTH-CENTURY B.C.E. HIGH PRIEST

The world rests on three things: Torah, service to God, and acts of love.

Quoted in the Ethics of the Fathers (1:2).

George Steiner
[1929–]
AUTHOR, LITERARY CRITIC

Though the thought must, like the ritual name of God, be unspeakable, the greater verity is that Judaism would survive the ruin of the state of Israel. It would do so if its "election" is indeed one of wandering, of the teaching of welcome among men, without which we shall extinguish ourselves on this minor planet. Concepts, ideas, which exceed in strength any weapons, any *imperium*, need no passports. It is hatred and fear which issue or deny visas.

From his Errata (1998).

Moshe David Tendler

CONTEMPORARY U.S. SCIENTIST, ORTHODOX RABBI

Judaism is a world religion. It is not a compilation of local tribal customs. It speaks to Jew and non-Jew. It is a Torah—a code of conduct for all humanity. It is the only "true" religion.

God promulgated different obligatory behavior for Jew and non-Jew. . . . The seven Noahide laws are binding on all humanity. They have served as the basis for all civilized codes of conduct. They are the Torah of the non-Jew. In this sense there is but one true religion. There is one true record of the responsibilities demanded by God of man created in His image.

From an essay in Condition of Jewish Belief (1966), compiled by the editors of Commentary magazine.

Harlan J. Wechsler

CONTEMPORARY U.S. CONSERVATIVE RABBI,
PROFESSOR OF PHILOSOPHY

The saga of Jewish life is the romance between God and the people of Israel. Thus are we chosen. Not that others do not have their stories, too, or that we are better, larger, more powerful or more worthy than they. But our story, our romance, our life with God is embodied in our covenant with Him.

From his essay in Commentary, August 1996.

Avi Weiss

CONTEMPORARY U.S. ORTHODOX RABBI, SOCIAL ACTIVIST

The assassination of Prime Minister Rabin is the single greatest chilul ha-Shem [desecration of God's name] in all Jewish history. In one act, not only was a man murdered, but the people of Israel and Torah was also shot.

From a speech in November 1996 at Congregation Kehilath Jeshurun in New York City, commemorating the first anniversary of the murder of Yitzhak Rabin.

Chaim Weizmann
[1874–1952]
RUSSIAN-BORN CHEMIST, ZIONIST LEADER

God has always chosen small countries through which to convey his messages.

From his autobiography, Trial and Error (1949).

Franz Werfel
[1890–1945]
CZECH-BORN POET, PLAYWRIGHT, NOVELIST

Believe not thy foes when they say thou art forsaken like a useless slave, an old outworn servant who is summarily driven out of the house. Do not believe it, Israel! Between thy God and thee there is an unsettled reckoning that will one day be settled in thy favor, when grace will have struck the balance.

From his Between Heaven and Earth (1944).

Elie Wiesel
[1928–   ]
RUMANIAN-BORN U.S. AUTHOR, PROFESSOR

I am not at peace. I never said I lost my faith in God. I was angry. I still don't understand God's ways. If He was going to explain the Holocaust, I would say no, I want the wound to remain open. And it is.

Commenting in 1995 on his ongoing personal struggle with making sense out of the Holocaust.

···

Yes. After the Holocaust I must believe in God, I can't not believe in God. But I am angry with God and I feel that I have the right to express any anger. To demand of Him that He treat us better, that He prevent such evil occurrences from ever happening again.

In response to a questioner after a luncheon in March 1990 at the Oxford University L'Chaim Society, who asked: "After the Holocaust, do you believe in God?"

···

God is involved in man's destiny—good or bad. To thank Him for Jerusalem and not question Him for Treblinka is hypocrisy.

Quoted in the Rabbi Joseph H. Lookstein Memorial Volume (1980).

Isaac Mayer Wise
[1819–1900]
GERMAN-BORN U.S. REFORM RABBI, EDUCATOR

Moses was the greatest of all artists . . . and he left to posterity that imperishable statue of truth . . . its pedestal is the earth, its head reaches heaven's dome; the name of that inimitable colossus is Israel, the immortal, a nation graced by the choice of God.

From his essay "Moses" in Selected Writings (1889).

. •. •.

Legalism is not Judaism. Judaism is the fear of the Lord and the love of man in harmony with the dictates of reason.

Taking issue with Orthodoxy and asserting that rabbinic legislation was not binding and could be changed; only the Decalogue was binding.

Stephen S. Wise
[1874–1949]
U.S. REFORM RABBI, ZIONIST LEADER, EDUCATOR

Jesus was not a being come down from heaven, but one who attained to heavenly heights. He was not a God who walked on earth like a man but a man who walked with God on earth. He was not a God who lived humanly, but a man who lived divinely. . . . To us he belongs—not his Church, but he—the man, the Jew, the prophet.

Quoted in I. Landman's Christian and Jew (1929).

David J. Wolpe

CONTEMPORARY U.S. CONSERVATIVE RABBI, AUTHOR, EDUCATOR

Judaism without God was unthinkable to an earlier age. Through all the meetings and estrangements of history, in every medium the Jew understood—text, life, and land—God was assigned a role. In joy He was praised; in agony, blamed or supplicated.

From his Healer of Shattered Hearts (1990).

..•..

The human quest, wherever and however defined in Jewish thought, is a joint quest, with humanity and God participating together. . . . God must be prodded by the prayers of human beings to effect His own salvation! If God cannot seek salvation alone, surely human beings cannot.

Ibid.

Yochanan ben Nappacha
[190–279]
PALESTINIAN TALMUDIC SCHOLAR

Whenever God enters a synagogue and does not find ten persons there, He becomes angry immediately.

Since a full service cannot be held without a minyan. Quoted in the talmudic tractate Berachot (6b).

..•..

Concerning three types of people does God announce His approval every day: a bachelor who lives in a large city and does not sin, a poor man who returns lost property, and a wealthy man who tithes his produce secretly.

Quoted in the talmudic tractate Pesachim (113a).

..•..

These [Gentiles] are My handiwork, and those [Israelites] are My handiwork. How can I destroy the Gentiles in favor of Israel?

Quoted in the talmudic tractate Sanhedrin (19b).

Yochanan ben Zakkai

FIRST-CENTURY TALMUDIC SCHOLAR

God's voice, as it was uttered [at Sinai], exploded into seventy languages so that all nations could understand Him.

Quoted in Midrash Exodus Rabba (5:9).

Israel Zangwill

[1864–1926]

BRITISH AUTHOR

We are proud and happy in that the dread Unknown God of the infinite universe has chosen our race as the medium by which to reveal His will to the world. . . . Our miraculous survival through the cataclysms of ancient and modern dynasties is a proof that our mission is not yet over.

Quoted by Joseph Leftwich in The Jewish Spectator, May 1952.

America is God's crucible, the Great Melting Pot, where all races of Europe are melting and reforming . . . Celt and Latin, Slav and Teuton, Greek and Syrian, black and yellow, Jew and Gentile . . . How the great Alchemist melts and fuses them with his purging flame! . . . Here shall they all unite to build the Republic of Man and the Kingdom of God. Peace, peace unto ye unborn millions fated to fill this giant continent— the God of our children give you peace.

From his play The Melting Pot (1909), in which he describes how a new nation is being forged.

Sheldon Zimmerman

RABBI, SEMINARY PRESIDENT, EDUCATOR

God entered history as a redemptive force at the time of the exodus from Egypt and as guarantor of an age of justice and peace for all humankind at the end of history. We humans are called to work together cooperatively and with God to bring this ultimate time into being. Interfaith activity for social justice is a divine requirement. Tikkun olam— the obligation to repair the brokenness of the world—is ours to work for as Jews and together with other human beings.

From his essay in Commentary, August 1996.

CHAPTER FOUR

Miracles, Messianism, and the World-to-Come

Introduction

A GREAT DEBATE RAGED throughout the academies of learning in Palestine during the first century C.E. This was a time when the country was under the control of Rome, a time when Jewish political and religious freedom was slowly eroding. A point came, beginning in 66 C.E., when Jews were no longer willing to submit to oppressive Roman domination and winds of rebellion began to sweep the country. But by the year 70, the rebellion was crushed, Jerusalem lay in ruins, the Temple totally demolished.

The debate that festered during those stressful years was whether life was worth living under such adverse conditions. As reported in the Talmud (Eruvin 13b), two schools of thought, disciples of the learned Shammai (Beit Shammai) and disciples of Hillel (Beit Hillel), president of the Sanhedrin, were engaged in a prolonged dialogue that lasted two and one-half years. The core of this extended philosophical debate was whether the suffering and misery that Jews had to endure was all part of God's plan. Was God trying to send a message? Were Jews being punished for wrongdoing? Was there any rationale for what was happening?

The disciples of Shammai took the position that it would have been far better had God never created man, that the gain is not worth the pain. The disciples of Hillel, however, argued that life is indeed worth living.

Surprisingly, the Rabbis of the Talmud considered both views and reached a conclusion supporting Beit Shammai: it would have been far better had man never been born. However, they added, since man was created by God and is alive here on earth, it behooves man to examine his actions and make sure that he is living a life in keeping with God's commandments.

In this chapter we shall see the three primary methods by which the Rabbis of old buoyed the spirits of the Jews in their despair and depression. For one, they attempted to instill a strong belief that God is on their side and that they can expect that He will miraculously save them even as he did when He split the Sea of Reeds to save the Israelites from Pharaoh and his pursuing army; even as He did for Joshua by making the sun stand still so that there would be enough daylight for the Israelites to vanquish the enemy; and even as He did by providing manna in the desert to feed the malcontented Israelites who wished they had never left Egypt.

The second hope held out by the Rabbis to the masses was that a day would come when the Messiah (*Mashiach*) would appear and deliver them from all travails. The Messiah would be a scion of the House of David, a person who would usher in a period of universal peace, a time, as Isaiah put it, "When nation shall not lift up sword against nation, neither will there be war any more" (Isaiah 2:4).

All mainstream Jewish theologians, past and present, rejected the belief that the Messiah will be an actual person. The contemporary scholar Ahad Ha-Am articulated this position in his essay "Jewish and Christian Ethics":

> Jewish teachers pay much more attention to "the days of the Messiah" than to the Messiah himself. One of them even disbelieved altogether in a personal Messiah, and looked forward to a redemption effected by God Himself without an intermediary; and he was not therefore regarded as a heretic.

Finally, the concept of a world-to-come was propagated to give distressed and depressed Jews hope that a brighter future awaits them. This world, the concept maintains, is only a "corridor" leading to a better, more just world. It is in the next world that good people will be rewarded for adhering to God's commandments and the performance of good deeds. This was predicated on the acceptance by Jews and non-Jews of the Ten Commandments during the Revelation on Mount Sinai. In addition, Jews were expected to live up to all 365 positive and negative commandments scattered throughout the Torah, as listed by Maimonides and other scholars. Non-Jews were expected to enjoy the benefits of the world-to-come by adhering to the Seven Noahide Laws.

The Babylonian scholar Avdimi bar Chama laid down the condition expected of Jews if they were to gain entry into the world-to-come. He placed these words in God's mouth:

> "If you accept my Torah, it will be well with you. If not, this spot [under the mountain] will be your burial place" (Shabbat 88a).

What kind of world could the righteous be expected to inherit as a reward for following God's commandments? Rav, the third-century Babylonian scholar, envisioned the following:

> In the world-to-come there will be no eating or drinking, no propagating or business activity, no envy or hatred or contention. The righteous will be sitting on thrones with crowns on their heads, enjoying the brilliance of God's splendor (Berachot 17a).

Most scholars—Orthodox and non-Orthodox—however, were not able to subscribe to such fantastic hyperbole, agreeing instead with the English theologian Rabbi Morris Joseph, who in his *Judaism as Creed and Life* (1903) wrote:

> Heaven is not a place, for the liberated soul knows neither place nor time. It is a state of being. Its joys are not the sordid joys of the senses, for the senses perish with the body. They are the joys of the spirit. The bliss of being near God . . . that is heaven.

Contemporary Conservative theologian Rabbi Neil Gilman discusses the question of life after death (*Masoret* magazine, fall 1993):

> No more than anyone else do I know beyond question what will happen to me after I die. What I do know, however, is that what I believe about those events will decisively affect how I deal with my one and only life here on earth. And that, ultimately, is what religion is all about.

These important concepts—and others that relate to God in the realm of the natural and supernatural—are represented by the quotations introduced in this chapter.

(Rabbi) Abbahu
Also known as Avahu
THIRD-CENTURY TALMUDIC SCHOLAR

When God gave the Torah no bird sang, no fowl flew, no ox lowed, the sea ceased to roar, and all creatures were silent. The entire world was hushed into stillness and the Voice spoke forth: "I am the Lord thy God . . ."

Quoting his teacher Rabbi Yochanan in Exodus Rabba (29:9).

Jacob B. Agus
[1911–1986]
U.S. CONSERVATIVE RABBI, AUTHOR, SCHOLAR

So paradoxical is the Messianic idea that it glows as the brightest of stars on the horizon when seen in perspective from the distance, and it turns into dust and ashes, like a glowing ember, if it is brought too close and grasped too tightly. As in the case of the God-idea itself, we must beware to resist the popular temptation to fashion earthly images of the Messiah, who is the symbol of the goal of life.

From Jewish Frontier magazine, July 1952.

Ahad Ha-Am
Né Asher Ginsberg
[1856–1927]
UKRAINIAN-BORN ESSAYIST, PHILOSOPHER

His [the Messiah's] importance lies not in himself, but in his being the messenger of God for the bringing of redemption to Israel and the world. Jewish teachers pay much more attention to "the days of the Messiah" than to the Messiah himself. One of them even disbelieved altogether in a personal Messiah, and looked forward to a redemption effected by God Himself without an intermediary; and he was not therefore regarded as a heretic.

From his essay entitled "Jewish and Christian Ethics."

Anonymous
It is Thee, O God, that I desire, not the world-to-come.

Attributed to an unnamed chasidic rabbi.

Mary Antin
[1881–1949]
RUSSIAN-BORN U.S. AUTHOR, ZIONIST

I was fed on dreams, instructed by means of prophecies, trained to hear and see mystical things that callous senses could not perceive. I was taught to call myself a princess, in memory of my forefathers who had ruled a nation. . . . God needed me and I needed Him, for we two together had a work to do, according to an ancient covenant between Him and my forefathers.

From her paean to America, The Promised Land (1912).

Judah Arieh
CONTEMPORARY ISRAELI AUTHOR

His [God's] revelation is continuous. New aspects of the Torah unfold constantly. The more we study it, the more it expands.

From his Sefat Emet (1926).

Bradley Shavit Artson
CONTEMPORARY U.S. CONSERVATIVE RABBI, AUTHOR

Any Jewish discussion of God begins, as it must, with revelation—whether and how God reaches out to us. Jewish traditions generally respect God's privacy, choosing to think about God only insofar as God relates to people. What God does when humanity is not looking or involved is God's business, not ours.

From an essay in Women's League Outlook, winter 1996.

Since the Torah represents the response of the Jews to a heightened experience of God, it is patently impossible and fruitless to argue about whether the Torah is divine or human. It is inseparably both.

Ibid.

Sholem Asch
[1880–1957]
POLISH-BORN YIDDISH NOVELIST

It [the Revelation] lasted an eternity, it lasted an instant. It was an incident in human history not to be measured with the limited apprehension of man, but belonging to the province of the Eternal and the infinite of Divinity. And therefore it is impossible to speak of the duration of the exalted episode. Only when the voice of God ceased from speaking did the world fall back into its framework of time and space; and only then did Israel experience the fullness of fear. It was a peculiar dread of the ungraspable. They did not know where they were, whether on the earth or still hovering in space with God, held by an invisible power to the flying mountain.

From his Moses (1951), translated by Maurice Samuel.

Avdimi ben Chama
BABYLONIAN TALMUDIC SCHOLAR

This teaches that if you accept the Torah it will be well with you, if not there [under the mountain] will be your burial place.

Commenting on the significance of the verse: "And they [the Israelites] stood under the mountain" (Exodus 19:17). Avdimi said: "It teaches that God inverted the mountain and made this declaration while holding it over the heads of the assembled Israelites."

Quoted in the talmudic tractate Shabbat (88a).

Israel Baal Shem Tov
[c. 1700–1760]
FOUNDER OF CHASIDISM

Every man should know that since creation no other man ever was like him. Had there been such another, there would be no need for him to be. Each is called on to perfect his unique qualities. And it is his failure to heed this call which delays the Messiah.

Quoted in Martin Buber's Die chassidishen Bücher (1927), noted in Gunther Plaut's The Torah (1985).

Leo Baeck
[1873–1956]
GERMAN REFORM RABBI, THEOLOGIAN

The thought underlying the Messianic conception is that the soul must not allow itself to be subjugated to anyone but God.

From his Essence of Judaism (1936).

Bar Kappara
THIRD-CENTURY TALMUDIC SCHOLAR

If one sheds tears for a virtuous man, God counts them and places them in His treasure house.

Quoted in the talmudic tractate Shabbat (105b).

David Baumgardt
[1890–1963]

GERMAN-BORN LIBRARY CONSULTANT

The ineffable, which is the object of religion, cannot be grasped in the rational, philosophical statement. It can only be intimated¾and only by the artist and the poet.

> Quoted in his essay "Maimonides: Religion as Poetic Truth," in Commentary, November 1954.

Ben Azzai (Simeon ben Azzai)

SECOND-CENTURY TALMUDIC SCHOLAR

The greatest principle [in the Torah] is Genesis 5:1 [which says]: "This is the record of Adam's line. When God created man, He made him in the likeness of God [b'tzelem Elohim]."

> In contrast to Rabbi Akiba's choice of Leviticus 19:18. Quoted in the Jerusalem talmudic tractate Nedarim (9:4, 41c).

David Ben-Gurion
[1886–1973]

FIRST ISRAELI PRIME MINISTER (1948–1953; 1955–1963)

My concept of the messianic ideal and vision is not a metaphysical one but a socio-cultural-moral one. . . . I believe in our moral and intellectual superiority, in our capacity to serve as a model for the redemption of the human race. This belief of mine is based on my knowledge of the Jewish people, and not on some mystical faith; the glory of the Divine Presence is within us, in our hearts, and not outside us.

> A comment made toward the end of his life. Quoted in Arthur Hertzberg's The Zionist Idea (1997).

(Rabbi) Berechya

FOURTH-CENTURY PALESTINIAN SCHOLAR

If God didn't hide from all people the date of their death, nobody would build a home, nobody would plant a vineyard, because everyone would say, "I'm going to die tomorrow, so of what purpose is it for me to work today?" For this reason, God denies us the knowledge of our day of death in the hope that we will build and plant. And if we will not enjoy the fruits of our labor, others will.

Quoting his teacher Rabbi Nathan in the Midrash Yalkut Shimoni, Ecclesiastes 968.

Eliezer Berkovits
[1908–1992]
U.S. ORTHODOX RABBI, SCHOLAR, AUTHOR

The divine revelation of the Bible is the mysterious contact between God and man by which God communicated His truth and His law to Israel through Moses in a manner that excluded every possibility of doubt. . . .

From his essay in The Condition of Jewish Belief (1966), a symposium compiled by the editors of Commentary magazine.

Saul Berman
CONTEMPORARY U.S. ORTHODOX RABBI, SCHOLAR, EDUCATOR

The more I study the Torah the more I am convinced that it is the revealed word of God. . . . Torah was God's weapon in the war against idolatrous culture; and war it was.

From an essay in Commentary, August 1996.

Chaim Nachman Bialik
[1873–1934]
HEBREW POET

There are abandoned corners of our exile,
Remote, forgotten cities of dispersion,
Where still in secret burns our ancient light,
Where God has saved a remnant from disaster.
There, brands that glimmer in a ruin of ashes.

From his famous poem "Ha-matmid" (The Dedicated Student), which expresses the ultimate in Jewish idealism and hope for the future of Judaism.

Nathan Birnbaum

[1864–1937]

U.S. JOURNALIST, POLITICAL PHILOSOPHER

The pious of the Gentiles will inherit the world-to-come. The Jew is not the Almighty's only child, for whom alone the world to come is open. He is a child whom God has chosen for priority in religion, giving him the Holy Torah. Judaism is not the appointed guardian of the world-to-come. It is therefore not a recruiting religion among the peoples.

From an essay by an early collaborator of Theodor Herzl, the man who coined the word "Zionism."

David Blumenthal

PROFESSOR OF JUDAIC STUDIES

The Torah is God's communication to us. It is the structure of God's relationship to us, and ours to God; that is the meaning of covenant. . . . Perhaps that is what it means to be a "chosen people."

From his essay in Commentary, *August 1996.*

Ben Zion Bokser

[1907–1983]

U.S. CONSERVATIVE RABBI, SCHOLAR, AUTHOR

Cabbalah [Kabbala] was an exploration of the mystical way. It was the quest for God as an object of direct experience, without the mediating services of metaphysics.

From his The Maharal *(1954).*

Isaac Breuer

[1883–1946]

GERMAN ORTHODOX RABBI

The attempt of Zionism to lead Israel, nation and land, into the "normalcy" of the other nations, has no future. It is only God's kingly will, God's revealed Torah, that can shelter Israel, the people and the land, in Jerusalem's two-fold peace.

Quoted in Leo Jung's Judaism in a Changing World *(1939).*

Joseph Caro

[1488–1575]

CODIFIER OF JEWISH LAW

Let it be known that wherever [in this *Code of Jewish Law*] the words *akum*, *goy* and *nachri* are used, the reference is to those who did not recognize the true God, who did not believe in His revelation, and were far from morality; but the people on whose land we live and whose government protects us believe in God and in revelation and in ethics.

An introductory statement in the Vilna edition of his Code of Jewish Law.

Marc Chagall

[1887–1985]

RUSSIAN-BORN ARTIST

When I am finishing a picture I hold some God-made object up to it— a rock, a flower, the branch of a tree or my hand—as a kind of final test. If the painting stands up beside a thing man cannot make, the painting is authentic. If there's a clash between the two, it is bad art.

Quoted in The Saturday Evening Post, *December 1962.*

Chanina ben Chama

SECOND/THIRD-CENTURY TALMUDIC SCHOLAR

No person ever bruises a finger here on earth unless it has been so decreed [by God] in Heaven.

Quoted in the talmudic tractate Chulin (7b).

Hermann Cohen

[1842–1918]

GERMAN PHILOSOPHER, AUTHOR

This is the most general sense of revelation: that God comes into relation with man.

From his Religion of Reason Out of the Sources of Judaism (1972).

Jacob Culi

[*c.* 1685–1732]

PALESTINIAN-BORN RABBI, BIBLE COMMENTATOR

Four Torah laws cannot be explained by human reason but, being divine, demand implicit obedience: to marry one's brother's widow (Deut. 25:5); not to mingle wool and linen in a garment (Deut. 22:11); to perform the rites of the scapegoat (Lev. 16:26, 34); and the red cow. Satan comes and criticizes these statutes as irrational. Know therefore that it was the Creator of the world, the One and Only, who instituted them.

From his eighteenth-century Ladino Bible commentary, Mei-am Lo'ez (1730).

Elliot N. Dorff

CONTEMPORARY U.S. CONSERVATIVE RABBI,
PROFESSOR OF PHILOSOPHY

For Judaism, God owns everything, including our bodies. God lends our bodies to us for the duration of our lives, and we return them to God when we die.

From his Matters of Life and Death (1998).

Arnold Eisen

CONTEMPORARY U.S. AUTHOR

I treasure the plurality of voices emanating from Sinai, as I welcome the revival of serious God-talk which has taken place in recent years among American Jews. Feminists, naturalists, mystics, rational theists and learned atheists are once more sharing the benefit of their thought and experience more widely. . . . Now, as ever, there is no purpose in seeking consensus in this endeavor, and no possibility of achieving it. The point remains the conversation.

Writing about God's Revelation at Sinai and the meaning of Jewish commitment. From his Taking Hold of Torah.

Eleazar Ha-kappar
THIRD-CENTURY TALMUDIC SCHOLAR

Know, that all that happens is in accordance with a plan. Do not be deceived into thinking that the grave is a place of refuge for you. Contrary to your wishes you were born; and contrary to your wishes you will die; and contrary to your wishes you will have to give an accounting of your life before the King of Kings, the Holy One, blessed be He.

Quoted in the Ethics of the Fathers (4:22).

(Rabbi) Eliezer
FIFTH-CENTURY TALMUDIC SCHOLAR

The days of the Messiah will last forty years.

Quoted in the talmudic tractate Sanhedrin (99a), where Rabbi Eleazar ben Azariah differed and suggested 70 years. Rabbi Dosa suggested 400 years, and Rabbi Judah the Prince suggested 365 years, to match one year of the solar calendar.

. •. .

When you pray, know before whom you are standing, and in this way you will win entry into the future world.

Quoted in the talmudic tractate Berachot (28b).

Ari Elon
CONTEMPORARY AUTHOR

There are two Torahs: The Torah that commands and the Torah that is studied. The first is the source of authority and reflects the male God. The second is the source of inspiration and reflects the female goddess. The first is directed to the entire people, the second to the small exclusive group of talmidei hakhamim who isolate themselves in the Olympus of the beit midrash. Some of them are perpetually on the verge of addiction to their love goddess and on the verge of abandoning their obligation to the God who commands.

From his From Jerusalem to the Edge of Heaven: Reflections on the Soul of Israel (1996).

(Prophet) Ezekiel

SIXTH-CENTURY B.C.E. PROPHET OF ISRAEL

The hand of the Lord came upon me and brought me out in the Spirit of the Lord, and set me down in the midst of the valley; and it was full of [dry] bones. . . .

And He said to me, "Son of man, can these bones live?" I answered, "O Lord God, You know."

Again He said to me, "Prophesy to these bones, and say to them, 'O dry bones, hear the word of the Lord! Thus says the Lord God to these bones: Surely I will cause breath to enter into you, and you shall live. I will put sinews on you and bring flesh upon you, cover you with skin and put breath in you; and you shall live. Then you shall know that I am the Lord.'"

Quoted in the Book of Ezekiel (37:1–6).

. . .

I will take the people of Israel from the nations among whom they have gone and will gather them from all sides, and bring them to their own land. . . . They shall not defile themselves any more with idols . . . and they shall be My people and I will be their God. My servant David shall be king over them. . . . I will make a covenant of peace with them. . . . My dwelling place shall be with them; and I will be their God and they shall be My people.

Ibid (37:21–27).

Louis Finkelstein

[1895–1991]

U.S. CONSERVATIVE RABBI, SCHOLAR, AUTHOR, EDUCATOR

The fundamental concept of the Jewish ceremonial system is that God continually reveals Himself in nature, in history, and in man's daily life. Each ceremony seeks to emphasize some aspect of this Divine revelation, and thus becomes a means for communion between man and God.

From the essay "Jewish Religion: Its Beliefs and Practices," in his book The Jews: Their History, Culture and Religion *(1949).*

Marvin Fox

CONTEMPORARY U.S. CONSERVATIVE RABBI, SCHOLAR

I believe, because I cannot afford not to believe. I believe as a Jew, in the divinity of Torah, because without God's Torah I have lost the ground for making my own life intelligible and purposeful.

From an essay in Condition of Jewish Belief (1966), compiled by the editors of Commentary magazine.

Israel Friedlaender

[1877–1922]

U.S. ORIENTALIST, EDUCATOR

What human being can claim a right to abolish laws given by the Almighty?

From his Jewish Religion (1922).

Marc Gellman

[1947–]

CONTEMPORARY U.S. REFORM RABBI, AUTHOR

The World-to-Come is not an addition to but an essential part of my belief in God. It is the way the moral equilibrium of existence is restored, the way God's ultimate goodness is affirmed, and the way I am able to sustain the hope that I will not be separated forever from those I have loved.

From his essay in Commentary, August 1996.

David Golovensky

CONTEMPORARY U.S. ORTHODOX RABBI

The Torah is not static. It develops, but it develops according to the pattern and the formula of the halakha. . . . The Will of God cannot be compromised. We believe that compromise does not strengthen but weakens. One compromise inevitably introduces another and leads to a third.

You remember the story of the man who willed his home to a charity with the provisos that he live in it during the rest of his life, that he would pay for the minor repairs, and that the major repairs be handled by the beneficiary.

After a few years a friend of his asked how the arrangement has worked out. The donor said, "Wonderful. I didn't have to pay for a single repair, because when the minor repairs came along, I waited until they became major."

So too with compromise; you may start with a minor compromise, but the minor leads to a major. We believe that the more complex life becomes, and it is becoming more and more complex all the time, the more do we need the disciplines of religion.

In a 1960 dialogue with Rabbi William Berkowitz at the Institute of Adult Jewish Studies in New York. Reported in Berkowitz's Ten Vital Jewish Issues *(1964).*

Robert Gordis

[1908–1992]

U.S. CONSERVATIVE RABBI, PROFESSOR, AUTHOR

We accept as fundamental to a vital Jewish religion the principle of *Torah min Ha-shamayim,* "The Torah as a revelation from God." . . . This conception need not mean that the process of revelation consisted of the dictation of the Torah by God, and its passive acceptance by men. . . . Hence the idea of a progressive and growing revelation is not merely compatible with faith in its divine origin, but is the only view that reckons with the nature of the human participant in the process.

From his Judaism for the Modern Age *(1955).*

David Weiss Halivni

CONTEMPORARY U.S. RABBI, PROFESSOR OF TALMUD

The belief that there is a God, and that this God broke into human history, and that the Torah is the result of that meeting, is something I believe in, and such belief is essential to anyone who regards the Bible as the source of divine information.

From his essay in Commentary, August 1996.

·◆·

There will always be an abyss beyond which will be God and across which humankind will always try to reach out but never fully succeed. That unresolved, constant desire is what defines humankind and sets up the relationship between humankind and God.

> Ibid.

·•·

We believe that God gave the Torah, but we believe the Torah we have is a maculate edition.

> When asked how he could teach at the Jewish Theological Seminary, where they don't believe the Torah is the word of God. Quoted in an essay by Jack Riemer in Moment magazine, June 1998.

Abraham Hecht

CONTEMPORARY U.S. ORTHODOX RABBI

We religious Jews must emphasize and reiterate that this entire scenario was directed and controlled by the hand of God! The Almighty in His Infinite Mercy showed His compassion for the Jewish people and the State of Israel by causing this political upheaval, thus saving the Jewish people from the Hellenization efforts of the godless government.

> Commenting on the victory of Netanyahu over Peres in the 1996 election for Prime Minister of Israel, and considering it to be a beneficent act of God.

Will Herberg

[1901–1977]

U.S. THEOLOGIAN, SOCIAL CRITIC

These three festivals [Passover, Sukkot and Shavuot] are for us the living re-enactment of the formative events in the redemptive history of Israel. Just as Israel became Israel through the events to which they refer, so the individual Jew becomes a Jew-in-faith by "repeating" these events in his own life. It is neither past time nor timeless eternity in which we live in faith; but contemporaneity. "He who does not himself remember that God led him out of Egypt," says Martin Buber, "he who does not himself await the Messiah, is no longer a true Jew."

> From his essay "Torah: Teaching, Law and Way," in Conservative Judaism and Jewish Law, edited by Seymour Siegel (1977).

Arthur Hertzberg

[1921–]

U.S. CONSERVATIVE RABBI, SCHOLAR, AUTHOR

God left something of the primal chaos and charged mankind with the task of making order and bringing justice to finish Creation itself. The blueprint for that task was prepared before Creation. It was a book, the Torah, which God rolled out before Him, and made the world according to its prescriptions. Later, he gave this book to Moses and his people at Mount Sinai.

From the foreword to Joseph Gikatilla's Gates of Light (1994).

．＊．

He [Spinoza] has taught me that it is difficult to believe the image that God sat on Mount Sinai and dictated to Moses, who then acted as scribe and messenger. Spinoza has made his argument all the more powerful by insisting that God could not possibly have commanded, literally and verbatim, some of the cruelties that have been committed "in His name." And yet, I persist in believing that something unexplainable and mystical has guided our passage through history. Our existence is not merely the sum of our rational choices; it is rooted in the most hidden recesses of the Jewish soul.

From his Jews: The Essence and Character of a People (1998).

Abraham Joshua Heschel

[1907–1972]

U.S. RABBI, THEOLOGIAN, AUTHOR, ACTIVIST

Revelation means that the thick silence which fills the endless distance between God and the human mind was pierced, and man was told that God is concerned with the affairs of man; that not only does man need God, God is also in need of man.

From his Man Is Not Alone (1951).

．＊．

God is either of no importance or of supreme importance. God is He whose regard for me is more precious than life. Otherwise, He is not God. God is the meaning beyond the mystery.

Ibid.

＊

We must, of course, give up hope of ever attaining a valid concept of the supernatural in an objective sense, yet since for practical reasons it is useful to cherish the idea of God, let us retain that idea and claim that while our knowledge of God is not objectively true, it is still symbolically true [as Kant taught].

From his essay "Toward an Understanding of Halacha," included in
Seymour Siegel's Conservative Judaism and Jewish Law (1977).

＊

To me, religion included the insights of the Torah, which is a vision of man from the point of view of God.

Ibid.

＊

What is unique about Jewish existence? The fact that ours is not a free association with the Bible. We are her offspring, her outcome. Her spirit is our destiny. What is our destiny? To be a community in whom the Bible lives on. . . . "Ye are my witnesses, says the Lord, and I am God" (Isaiah 43:12).

From his Israel: An Echo of Eternity (1967).

＊

How embarrassing for man to be the greatest miracle on earth and not to understand it! How embarrassing for man to live in the shadow of greatness and to ignore it, to be a contemporary of God and not to sense it!

From his Who Is Man? (1965).

＊

Man's walled mind has no access to a ladder upon which he can, on his own initiative, rise to a knowledge of God. Yet his soul is endowed with translucent windows that open to the beyond. And if he wishes to reach up to Him it is a reflection of the divine light in him that gives him the power for such yearning . . . for God is not always silent and man is not always blind.

From his God in Search of Man (1955).

＊

[God's] revelation *to* Israel continues as revelation *through* Israel.
From his article "No Religion is an Island" in the Union Seminary
Quarterly Review *(January 1966).*

Susannah Heschel
PROFESSOR OF JEWISH STUDIES, AUTHOR

I do believe there have been events of divine revelation, and that my
soul was present at Sinai, but I also realize the crucial distinction between the word of God and the word of men. I have always firmly
believed that God would never forbid me to be counted in a *minyan*, a
prayer quorum, or to lead the prayers, but rather that such prohibitions
express the will of some human beings. What we have may be the Judaism of men; we need the Judaism of God.

From her essay in Commentary, *August 1996.*

Milton Himmelfarb
[1918–]
U.S. WRITER, RESEARCHER

I accept God. I hope He accepts me . . . without maintaining the photo-
graphic accuracy of Exodus 19-20 and Deuteronomy 4–5, I believe that
a law was revealed—a numinous word—to our ancestors and transmitted to us.

From his essay in Commentary, *August 1996.*

Samson Raphael Hirsch
[1808–1888]
GERMAN ORTHODOX RABBI, SCHOLAR, AUTHOR

Do we mean what we say when, in the circle of fellow-worshippers, we
point to the written word of the Torah and declare that God gave us
these teachings, that these are his teachings, the teachings of truth and
that he thereby implanted in us everlasting life? Is all this a mere mouth-
ing of high sounding phrases? If not, then we must keep those commandments, fulfill them in their original and unabbreviated form. We

must observe them under all circumstances and at all times. This word of God must be accepted by us as an eternal standard, transcending all human judgment.

From an essay in Jeschurun (1854–55).

.•.

There is no symbol for the Torah for the same reason that there is no symbol for God: the Torah is One and Unique, like God its Creator. It has nothing in common with other laws, teachings, systems and institutions. It is so unique that it can be compared only to itself, it is something sui generis.

From his Judaism Eternal (1956).

.•.

The catechism of the Jew consists of his calendar. On the pinions of time which bear us through life, God has inscribed the eternal words of His soul-inspiring doctrine, making days and weeks, months and years the heralds to proclaim His truths.

Ibid.

(Rabbi) Hoshiya

THIRD-CENTURY PALESTINIAN SCHOLAR

The Holy One looked in the Torah as He created the world.

Quoted in Genesis Rabba (1:1).

Meir ben Ezekiel ibn Gabbai

SPANISH-BORN FIFTEENTH-CENTURY KABBALIST, AUTHOR

All the designations through which God is known and called upon are no more than human linguistic terms that man uses to convey his idea of matters that are hidden and higher than his understanding. God's Name is therefore One with the divinity, co-eternal and incomprehensible, like the Prime Cause itself, which, too, is beyond comprehension.

And the unmentioned and incomprehensible, ineffable Name contains in itself all Ten Sephirot, which are not born and not created, but are emanations from God—since they, the Sephirot, are the various manifestations revealing God's Being. God's Being does not alter or change. He creates nothing new—He only emanates, radiates—and the Divinely concealed forces are revealed through the Sephirot and are brought from the potential to reality. The Sephirot are the intermediaries, the links between the Cause and the Creature. They are the tools with which the world came to be and exists.

Quoted in Arnold Posy's Mystic Trends in Judaism *(1994).*

Isaiah
EIGHTH-CENTURY B.C.E. PROPHET OF ISRAEL

Out of Zion will come the Torah and the word of God from Jerusalem.

From the Book of Isaiah (2:3).

Morris Joseph
[1848–1930]
BRITISH REFORM RABBI, THEOLOGIAN

Heaven is not a place, for the liberated soul knows neither place nor time. It is a state of being. Its joys are not the sordid joys of the senses, for the senses perish with the body. They are the joys of the spirit. The bliss of being near God . . . that is heaven!

In his Judaism as Creed and Life *(1903).*

Judah ben Chiya
THIRD-CENTURY PALESTINIAN SCHOLAR

When a man administers a drug, it may be beneficial to one limb, but harmful to another. But with God it is not so. He gave a Torah to Israel, and it is a drug of life for all his body.

Quoted in the talmudic tractate Eruvin (54a).

Aryeh Kaplan

CONTEMPORARY U.S. ORTHODOX RABBI, AUTHOR

As you continue to explore what is most meaningful to you, you may come to a point where you feel that you are reaching a new threshold. You may find yourself pondering not only the meaning of your own life, but the very meaning of existence in general.

At this point, you will have discovered God.

From his Jewish Meditation: A Practical Guide (1985).

.•.

We often think of God as being "out there," far away from the world. But it is important to realize that God is also "in there"—in the deepest recesses of the soul.

Ibid.

Marty Kaplan

POLITICAL SPEECHWRITER AND AUTHOR

The God I have found is common to Moses and Muhammad, to Buddha and Jesus. It is known to every mystic tradition. In mine, it is the Tetragrammaton, the Name so holy that those who know it dare not say it. It is what the Kabbala calls *Ayin*, Nothingness, No-Thingness. It is Spirit, Being, the All.

From his essay in Hadassah Magazine, November 1996. Reprinted from Time magazine.

Mordecai M. Kaplan

[1881–1983]

U.S. RABBI, RECONSTRUCTIONIST MOVEMENT FOUNDER

Nothing can be more repugnant to the thinking man of today than the fundamental doctrine of Orthodoxy which is that tradition is infallible. Such infallibility could be believed in as long as the human mind thought of God and revelation as semi-mythological terms.

From a 1920 article in The Menorah Journal.

Peter Knobel

CONTEMPORARY U.S. REFORM RABBI

I resonate to the Lurianic myth of God's brokenness which produced a world in need of repair. I accept as the mission of my life and as the mission of the Jewish people the responsibility to repair the divine by performing *mitzvot* which heal the world (*tikkun olam*). God is a reality Who affects my life and is to be found in the Torah.

From his essay in Commentary, *August 1996.*

Janusz Korczak

[1879–1942]

POLISH EDUCATOR, AUTHOR, PHYSICIAN

The physical immortality of man lies in his children. His spiritual existence lies in radiating the idea of brotherhood, not only his brotherhood with men, but with the stars and God in search of the magic fact—eternity.

A man thinks of, and looks upon, death as the end of everything. But in fact it is only a continuation of life in a different form. If you don't believe in soul, you must admit that your body will continue to live as green grass or a little cloud. You are, after all, dust and water.

From his ghetto diary.

David Kraemer

CONTEMPORARY U.S. WRITER

I think it would be fair to say that the insistence on future resurrection represents a response to the grave injustices and the bitter realities of Jewish history. These authors [of the apocryphal writings such as the Book of Baruch] believed in a just and caring God, but when they looked at the world around them—at the sufferings of Jews at the hands of people far less righteous than they—they could not understand how their God could permit such horrors. They then concluded that what lay before them was an incomplete picture and that perfect justice would be realized only in a future world.

From an essay in Masoret *magazine, fall 1993.*

Shoni Labowitz

RABBI, AUTHOR

In the mystical Jewish tradition, we understand and experience sexuality as a divine act. Sex is the ultimate gift of reciprocity between the male, female, and God.

From her Miraculous Living (1996).

. .•.

Within you is a godspark waiting to be freed. It is encased in a shell, called klippah. A klippah is a veil that hides your potential yet to be born, aspects of your life yet to be lived. . . . As you dismantle the klippot [plural] your godspark is released, your soul soars, and you open to new ways of being. Then you are ready to step into the unknown with faith and trust that God will lead the way.

Ibid.

. .•.

Even if someone has wronged you, consider carefully how you speak to him, for all souls are one. Your soul and another's soul originated as sparks from the Divine soul. When you diminish from the glory of another's soul, you are diminishing from the glory of your own soul.

Ibid.

Maurice Lamm

CONTEMPORARY U.S. ORTHODOX RABBI, AUTHOR

The belief in a bodily resurrection appears, at first sight, to be incredible to the contemporary mind. But when approached from the God's-eye view, why is rebirth more miraculous than birth? . . . Surely resurrection is not beyond the capacity of an omnipotent God.

From his The Jewish Way in Death and Mourning (1969).

Norman Lamm

[1927–   ]

U.S. ORTHODOX RABBI, UNIVERSITY PRESIDENT

The Torah is divine revelation in two ways: It is God-given and it is Godly. By "God-given," I mean that He willed that man abide by His commandments and that will was communicated in discreet words and letters. . . . Hence, I accept unapologetically the idea of the verbal revelation of the Torah. . . . *How God spoke is a mystery; how Moses received this message is an irrelevancy. That God spoke is of the utmost significance.*

> Explaining the Orthodox position in an essay presented in The Condition of Jewish Belief (1966), compiled by the editors of Commentary magazine.

·❖·

The idea of man's creation in the image of God would not be contradicted in any way by the non-centrality of man in the universe—since God is much bigger than we think. If we ever make contact with another, extraterrestrial civilization, which I doubt because of the distance between Earth and the nearest star, it would not threaten or challenge our fundamental Jewish outlook.

> Commenting on the discovery in August 1996 of what may turn out to be primitive life on Mars.

Jiri Langer

[1894–1943]

CZECH-BORN POET, AUTHOR

The most beautiful chasidic doctrine is that of the spiritual nature of all matter. Chasidim believe all matter is full of supernatural sparks of the holiness of God, and such purely mundane function as eating, drinking, bathing, sleeping, dancing and lovemaking are the most sublime actions in the service of God.

> From his Nine Gates to Chasidic Mysteries (1937).

Emma Lazarus

[1849–1887]

U.S. POET

No signs of life are here: the very prayers
Inscribed around are in a language dead;
The light of the "perpetual lamp" is spent
That an undying radiance was to shed. . . .
Nathless, the sacred shrine is holy yet,
With its lone floor where reverent feet once trod.
Take off your shoes as by the burning bush,
Before the mystery of death and God.

> Written in July 1867, the subject of the poem is the Jewish synagogue of
> Newport, Rhode Island. From her second volume of poems, Admetus and
> Other Poems (1871), published when she was twenty-two. It was
> dedicated "To my friend, Ralph Waldo Emerson," who had encouraged her to
> continue writing.

Yeshayahu Leibowitz

[1903–1994]

ISRAELI PROFESSOR, BIOCHEMIST, BIBLE SCHOLAR, AUTHOR

It is my firm and clearly expressed view that the meaning of Revelation
is the demand made of man and the obligation imposed on him to serve
God. Neither the Sinai Revelation nor the Revelation in the words and
deeds of the prophets succeeded in making the demand obeyed and the
obligation fulfilled.

> From an article in The Jerusalem Post, November 10, 1984.

·◆·

[The Gush Emunim movement was comprised of] messianic fools
. . . who are so presumptuous as to think they know God's will.

> From a 1990 interview with journalist Matthew Nesvisky. Reported in
> The Jewish Week, September 30–October 6, 1994.

Moses (ben Shem Tov) de Leon
[1250–1305]
SPANISH KABBALIST

It is the path taken by man in this world that determines the path of the soul on its departure. Thus, if a man is drawn towards the Holy One, and is filled with longing towards Him in this world, the soul in departing is carried upward toward the higher realms by the impetus given each day in this world.

From the Zohar, which at one time was ascribed to the authorship of the second-century scholar Simeon ben Yochai.

Julius Lester
[1939–]
U.S. PROFESSOR, AUTHOR

Even if Torah is directly from God, I believe that God changes. Every word of Torah given at Sinai is not to be understood today as it was then. Neither is every word to be understood literally. Torah is also metaphor, and metaphors by their nature are permeable and complex. Literalism leads to the cheap high of religious absolutism, and too often absolutism is presented as the model of authentic Judaism. This leaves all other expressions of Judaism prey to the accusation of being Judaisms of convenience.

From his essay in Commentary, August 1996.

(Rabbi) Levi
THIRD-CENTURY TALMUDIC SCHOLAR

The Holy One appeared [to Israel at Sinai] as though He were a statue with faces on every side. A thousand people might be looking at the statue, but it would appear to each to be looking directly at him. So, too, when the Holy One spoke each person in Israel could say, "The Divine Word is addressing me." . . . The Divine Word spoke to each and every person according to his particular capacity.

Quoted in Pesikta d'Rav Kahana (12:25).

Joshua Loth Liebman

[1907–1948]

U.S. REFORM RABBI, AUTHOR

I have come to see over the span of years that the wider world just cannot be dismissed and that man considered independent of his cosmic setting can lead only to provincial pride and defiant despair. Man is not alone and neither his mind nor his conscience nor his creative powers can be truly understood if they are regarded as orphans without some universal Parent.

> Quoted in Lothar Kahn's God: What People Have Said about Him (1980).

·•·

We can love God best by loving His letters best. Just as a child learns the alphabet one letter at a time and then combines the letters into words and the words into sentences, until at last he is able to read a book, so should we regard every human being as but one letter in the alphabet of God. The more letters we come to understand and to treasure, the more we can read the Book of God and love its Author.

> Ibid.

Moses Chaim Luzzatto

[1707–1746]

ITALIAN KABBALIST, HEBREW POET, AUTHOR

Our sages of blessed memory have taught us that man was created to find delight in the Lord and to bask in the radiance of His presence, for this is true happiness and the greatest of all possible delight. . . . This world is like a vestibule before the world-to-come. . . . Man is put here in order to earn the place which has been prepared for him in the world-to-come.

> From his Messilat Yesharim (1740).

Moses Maimonides

[1135–1204]

SPANISH RABBI, PHYSICIAN, SCHOLAR, PHILOSOPHER, AUTHOR

I believe with complete faith that the entire Torah which is found in our hands today comes from Heaven and is the same one that was given through Moses.

> From his commentary to the Mishna Sanhedrin (10), in which he presents Thirteen Principles (Articles) of Faith every Jew must believe in order to be assured a place in the world-to-come.

·◆·

I believe with complete faith that this Torah will not be abrogated and that no other Torah will come from God. One may not add to it or delete any part of it. This applies to the Written Torah and the Oral Torah.

> Ibid.

·◆·

I believe with complete faith in the coming of the Messiah, and even though he may tarry, nevertheless I do look forward to his coming every day.

> Twelfth fundamental principle.

·◆·

I believe with complete faith that there will be a resurrection of the dead.

> Thirteenth fundamental principle.

·◆·

No one should ever occupy himself with the legendary themes or spend much time on midrashic statements bearing on [the advent of the Messiah] and like subjects. He should not deem them of prime importance, since they lead neither to the fear of God nor to the love of Him. Nor should one calculate the end.

> From his Kings and Wars 12:1 and 12:2, in the Code of Maimonides, Book Fourteen, The Book of Judges (1949).

·◆·

The sages and prophets did not long for the messiah that Israel might exercise dominion over the world, or rule over the heathens, or be exalted by the nations, or that it might eat and drink and rejoice. Their aspiration was that Israel be free to devote itself to the law and its wisdom, with no one to oppress or disturb it, and thus be worthy of life in the world-to-come.

From his Mishneh Torah, Melachim 12:5.

(Rabbi) Meir
SECOND-CENTURY TALMUDIC SCHOLAR

He who devotes himself to Torah study for its own sake . . . is called beloved friend, lover of God, lover of humanity.

Quoted in the Ethics of the Fathers (6:1).

Leone Modena
[1571–1648]
ITALIAN RABBI, AUTHOR

How can we say that the creature who, by dint of his intellect, builds cities and moves mountains, changes the course of rivers, knows the paths of the high heavens, and can recognize his God—that this creature should come in the end to perish entirely like a horse, or a dog, or a fly?

Quoted in Nahum Glatzer's In Time and Eternity (1946).

Moses de Leon
[1250–1305]
SPANISH KABBALIST

In the beginning there issued forth from the impenetrable recesses of the Hidden One (God: the Ein Sof, the Infinite One) a shapely colorless nucleus, enclosed in a ring. A heavenly flame shot forth in a host of brilliant colors from a mysterious, untraceable point, which is called Reishit ("beginning"). Here was the starting point of all creation.

Commenting on the first verse word in the Book of Genesis.

Nachmanides (Moses ben Nachman)

[1194–1270]

SPANISH TALMUDIST, PHYSICIAN

The whole Torah consists of nothing but names of God.

From the introduction to his Torah commentary.

Jacob Neusner

[1932–]

U.S. CONSERVATIVE RABBI, SCHOLAR, AUTHOR

When upon entering the Jewish Theological seminary in 1954 I first met a page of the Talmud, my life commenced. In Torah study I encounter sublimity. Through Torah study I explore the mind of God. This quest takes place through the inner workings of the language God used through our Sages, of blessed memory.

Quoted in Hadassah Magazine, October 1997.

Menachem Perlmutter

[1928–]

ISRAELI SOLDIER, ENGINEER

Although I come from an Orthodox family, I'm not religious now, but I never lost my faith in God. I believe in God because so many miracles happened to me. So many times I thought, "Is this the last second I will see the blue sky?" Yet, I am still here. How else can I explain it?

Quoted in Aaron Levin's Testament (1998).

Judy Petsonk

[1946–]

TEACHER, NEWSPAPER REPORTER, AUTHOR

Each word [of the Torah] has the potential to teach one how to live in the image of God. Jewish tradition says God is in the details. Each fragment of the universe is holy and reflects the whole.

From her Taking Judaism Personally (1996).

.•.

Judaism's great sages could see the Torah as the word of God and still look at it critically. They noticed the contradictions—two passages that seem to say opposite things, an apparently needless repetition, even places where a noun and verb don't agree in number and gender. But unlike modern scholars who ascribe Scripture's unevenness to multiple authors or mistakes by the editors, the rabbis believed that every contradiction has a higher purpose.

> Ibid.

Pinchas of Koretz
Also known as Pinchas ben Abraham Abba Shapiro
[1726–1791]
UKRAINIAN CHASIDIC RABBI

How is it possible to know God in *all* ways? It is, because when God gave the Torah, the whole world was filled with the Torah. Thus there is nothing which did not contain Torah. . . . Since the beginnings of Hasidism this doctrine has always been regarded as one of its basic principles.

> Quoted in Gershom Scholem's Major Trends in Jewish Mysticism (1933).

.•.

I thank God everyday that I was not born before the Zohar was revealed, for it was the Zohar which sustained me in my faith as a Jew.

> Quoted in Ben Zion Bokser's The Maharal (1954).

W. Gunther Plaut
[1912–]
GERMAN-BORN REFORM RABBI, AUTHOR, BIBLE SCHOLAR

While God is not the author of the Torah in the fundamentalist sense, the Torah is a book about humanity's understanding of and experience with God. This understanding has varied over the centuries as have human experiences.

> From the general introduction to his The Torah: A Modern Commentary (1985).

241

The Torah tradition testifies to a people of extraordinary spiritual sensitivity. God is not the author of the text, the people are; but God's voice may be heard through theirs if we listen with open minds.

Ibid.

Arnold Posy
[1894–1976]
U.S. AUTHOR

The essential thesis of Kabbala turns on the belief in the Unity of Creation, from which derives the unity and harmony of the universe. The Unity of the Godhead unites the transcendental, spiritual world with the immanent, physical world. According to Kabbala God is the Great Deep Sense, the Great Incomprehensible, the Mystery of Mysteries, Secret of Secrets. God is beyond human power of pictorial representation. The depth of Divine Wisdom is too high for human understanding to penetrate. God is the Original of Originality, the Secret of Secrecy, the Consciousness of Super-Consciousness.

From the introduction to his Mystic Trends in Judaism (1994).

According to the Ari [Isaac Luria] before God created the world, the Infinite (En-Sof) filled the whole of infinite space. When God came to create the world, so that His (the Infinités) attributes should emerge and manifest themselves and develop their perfection, space was needed for this innovation. What did God do? He contracted Himself . . . and left an empty space [for the creation of the world].

Ibid.

Raba bar Rav Huna
FOURTH-CENTURY BABYLONIAN SCHOLAR

Any person who is knowledgeable in Torah study but does not stand in awe of God is much like a treasurer who has been entrusted with the keys to the inner vault, but was not given the keys to the outer vault.

Quoted in the talmudic tractate Shabbat (31a).

Rashi

[1040–1105]

FRENCH BIBLE AND TALMUD COMMENTATOR

If a great man from whom people learn is not careful in his actions, lesser people will denigrate the Torah because of his behavior. They will say: "This one understands that there is nothing worthwhile in the Torah and its commandments." In this manner the name of God is profaned.

> From a comment regarding the concept of chilul ha-shem (*desecration of God's name*) in the talmudic tractate Shabbat (33a).

Rav Also known as Abba Aricha

THIRD-CENTURY BABYLONIAN SCHOLAR

The future world [olam ha-ba] is not like this world. In the future world there is no eating nor drinking nor propagation nor business nor jealousy nor hatred nor competition, but the righteous sit with their crowns on their heads feasting on the brightness of the divine presence, as it says, "And they beheld God, and did eat and drink" (Exodus 24:11).

> Quoted in the talmudic tractate Berachot (17a).

Resh Lakish

Also known as Rabbi Shimon (Simeon)

SECOND/THIRD-CENTURY TALMUDIC SCHOLAR

When God created the world, He made an agreement with all of Creation that if Israel accepts the Torah, all will be well and good, but if not, He will cause the whole world to revert to a state of primeval chaos.

> Quoted in the talmudic tractate Avoda Zara (3a).

Yissachar Dov Rokach
CONTEMPORARY LEADER OF THE BELZER CHASIDIC SECT

The day will come, and that day is not far off, when the Jewish people will, heaven forbid, be split into two poles. Not left or right, not Ashkenazim and Sephardim; but on one side believers in God and Torah, and on the other, heretics who hate the Torah and the commandments.

At a rally of the ultra-Orthodox Shas movement in Israel. Quoted in The Jerusalem Report, July 10, 1997.

Laura Schlessinger
[1948–   ]
AUTHOR, RADIO TALK-SHOW HOST, FAMILY THERAPIST

The Ten Commandments are the first direct communication between a people and God. . . . God's moral laws are still binding. They are the blueprint of God's expectations upon us and His plan for a meaningful, just, loving, holy life.

From her The Ten Commandments: The Significance of God's Laws in Everyday Life (1998).

Gershom Scholem
[1897–1982]
GERMAN-BORN HISTORIAN, AUTHORITY ON MYSTICISM

Hasidism is practical mysticism at its highest. Almost all the kabbalistic ideas are now placed in relation to values peculiar to the individual life, and those which are not remain empty and ineffective. Particular emphasis is laid on ideas and concepts concerning the relation of the individual to God.

From his Major Trends in Jewish Mysticism (1941), *in which he points out the emphasis of Chabad Chasidism on psychology over theosophy.*

Harold Schulweiss

[1925–   ]

U.S. CONSERVATIVE RABBI, AUTHOR

The idea of a progressive and growing revelation is not merely compatible with faith in its divine origin, but is the only view that reckons with the nature of the human participant in the process.

From an article entitled "Restructuring the Synagogue," in Conservative Judaism, summer 1973.

Seymour Siegel

[1927–1988]

U.S. CONSERVATIVE RABBI, AUTHOR, PROFESSOR

Franz Rosenzweig argued that a revelation is not the transmittal of concrete directives. Revelations means that man and God have met each other. Revelation means the self-uncovering of the Divine in relation to man. It is the transmission to man of God's love and concern.

Assessing the German philosopher's conception of revelation. Quoted in Conservative Judaism and Jewish Law (1977).

Solomon ben Yerucham

TENTH-CENTURY FUNDAMENTALIST SCHOLAR

Woe to him who leaves the Book of God and seeks others! Woe to him who passes his time with strange sciences, and who turns his back upon the pure truth of God! The wisdom of philosophy is vain and worthless, for we do not find two who agree upon a single point. They propound doctrines which directly contradict the Law. Amongst them there are some who study Arabic literature instead of always having the word of God in their mouths.

Attacking scholars, such as Saadya Gaon, who studied philosophy and used it in the service of Judaism. Quoted in Heinrich Heine's History of the Jews (1894).

Theodore Steinberg

CONTEMPORARY U.S. CONSERVATIVE RABBI, AUTHOR

"Normal mysticism" is one of [Max] Kadushin's most felicitous terms. This remarkable and seemingly paradoxical phrase captures the spirit and style of rabbinic religion. It was "mystical" through its power to stimulate an awareness of the Divine which was private, non-conceptual and non-verbal. At the same time, because one's God-awareness was mediated through the value-concepts, it was, to that extent, public, communicable, and, therefore, "normal."

From his "Max Kadushin: An Appreciation" in Conservative Judaism, summer 1982.

Yoel Teitelbaum

[1888–1979]

SATMER REBBE, ULTRA-ORTHODOX CHASIDIC LEADER

It is clear beyond any doubt that all the buildings and institutions the misbelievers and atheists have erected and established in our Holy Land will be destroyed by the Mashiach [Messiah]. . . . God will build holy structures without any infusion of alien culture. . . . We, the few Jews whose eyes are not blinded, must gird ourselves mighty not to get swept along with the popular currents.

From his Divrei Yoel. Quoted in Harvey Lutske's History in Their Hands (1996).

Moshe David Tendler

CONTEMPORARY U.S. SCIENTIST, ORTHODOX RABBI

I would say it's impressive for God to have Martians on Mars. I would be perturbed if He gave them a different Torah, one with different commandments. . . . If on Mars there are people who have a mind and free will, then the exact same values should apply.

When asked if the existence of intelligent alien life on Mars would contradict the basic tenets of Judaism. Quoted in The Jerusalem Report, September 19, 1996.

Burton L. Visotzky

[1953–]

PROFESSOR OF MIDRASH, BIBLE SCHOLAR, RABBI

The commandment to study Torah is a life-long commitment. This is good, since the Torah seems to transform year by year as it is revealed in small doses. Depending on where I may be on my life journey, Torah-study not only teaches me about my ancestors, it teaches me about myself. I return daily to study for the opportunity to hear God's still small voice. At that rare and awesome moment of revelation, my labors in Torah are richly rewarded: I stand with my people at Sinai.

Quoted in Hadassah Magazine, October 1997.

Herbert Weiner

CONTEMPORARY U.S. AUTHOR

The full nature of the revelation at Sinai is relegated by Judaism to that category of "hidden things which are reserved to God." It is the "revealed matters that are given to man," and by "revealed" Judaism refers mainly to the mitzvot—the commandments. Deeply Jewish is the startling invitation which the Talmud attributes to God. "Abandon Me, if you will, but keep My commandments." The implication later suggested is that the keeping of the commandments will in its turn "sensitize" the eyes so that they will be better able to "see" God.

From an essay in Condition of Jewish Belief (1966), compiled by the editors of Commentary magazine.

Trude Weiss-Rosmarin

[1908–1989]

GERMAN-BORN U.S. PUBLISHER, AUTHOR, LECTURER

I am not "turned off" by the linguistic gender of God because—the Torah is feminine in Hebrew linguistic gender and in Jewish life. The Torah is "the bride" of Israel, whom we honor and adorn with silver and velvet and silk, whom we tenderly enfold in our arms, and of whom God, according to a profound symbolism said: "Would that they [Israel] had forsaken Me and clung to the Torah."

From her Jewish Survival (1949).

Elie Wiesel

[1928–]

RUMANIAN-BORN U.S. AUTHOR, PROFESSOR

If I told you that I believe in God, I would be lying. If I told you that I did not believe in God, I would be lying. If I told you that I believed in man, I would be lying. If I told you I did not believe in man, I would be lying. But one thing I do know: the Messiah has not come yet.

From his Shadows of Auschwitz.

Man, as long as he lives, is immortal. One minute before his death he shall be immortal. But one minute later, God wins.

From an interview in Writers at Work (1988), edited by George Plimpton.

Isaac Mayer Wise

[1819–1900]

GERMAN-BORN U.S. REFORM RABBI, EDUCATOR

God gives us a thousand joys for each affliction, a thousand smiles for each tear.

Quoted in the American Israelite, August 31, 1866.

Ruth Wisse

CONTEMPORARY AUTHOR, PROFESSOR

The more human beings believed in their own power, the greater the evil they would commit. Bashevis Singer ceased to believe that God had revealed himself to the Jews at Sinai, but he never stopped believing in the devil. The devil's Torah was to persuade man that he was God.

Commenting on the death of Isaac Bashevis Singer in the Forward, August 8, 1991.

David J. Wolpe
CONTEMPORARY U.S. CONSERVATIVE RABBI, AUTHOR, EDUCATOR

The corridors of eternity, however they wind, are open to all who live in a way that honors the spark of God inside them.

From his Healer of Shattered Hearts (1990).

Belief in an omnipotent God means that God could create life in whatever form He chose. . . . Ultimately, all that this discovery shows that we've only begun to glimpse the slightest corner of God's creation—only a tiny part of the curtain has been lifted. Judaism is not based on the assumption that this is God's only world; therefore no re-evaluation is needed.

Commenting on the August 1996 discovery of what may turn out to be primitive life on Mars.

Yehuda ben (bar) Simon
Also known as Yehuda ben Pazzi
FOURTH-CENTURY TALMUDIC SCHOLAR

God almost decided to give the Torah through Adam, and He thought: "This man whom I created and who is not of woman born, should I not give the Torah through him?" But he immediately decided otherwise and said: "I gave one commandment to this man that he should not eat of the fruit of the Tree of Knowledge, and he failed to obey Me. How, then, can I give him the Torah with its 613 commandments?"

Quoted in the Midrash Genesis Rabba (24:5) and Kohelet Rabba (3:14).

Anzia Yezierska
[1885–1970]
RUSSIAN-BORN U.S. NOVELIST

God didn't listen to women. . . . Women could get into Heaven because they were wives and daughters of men. Women had no brains for study of God's Torah, but they could be the servants of men who studied the Torah. Only if they cooked for the men, and washed for the men, and didn't nag or curse the men out of their homes; only if they let the men study the Torah in peace, then, maybe, they could push themselves into Heaven with the men, to wait on them there.

From her novel The Bread Givers (1925), subtitled "A struggle between a father of the Old World and a daughter of the New."

Yochanan ben Nappacha

[190–279]

PALESTINIAN TALMUDIC SCHOLAR

The Holy One, blessed be He, has retained in his own hands three keys which he did not entrust to any messenger. These are: the key of rainfall, the key of childbirth, and the key of resurrection.

Quoted in the talmudic tractate Taanit (2a).

Yochanan ben Nuri

FIRST/SECOND-CENTURY TALMUDIC SCHOLAR

He who pronounces God's name according to its consonants (YHWH) has no share in the world-to-come.

Referring to the Tetragrammaton, which in Hebrew is spelled yud, hei, vav, hei, pronounced Yehova (Jehova in English). Quoted in The Fathers according to Rabbi Nathan (36).

Eric H. Yoffie

CONTEMPORARY U.S. REFORM RABBI

I believe in God Who gave Torah to the people of Israel in the process of revelation beginning at Sinai. This belief is the foundation on which all of Judaism is constructed, and without which Judaism—a religious civilization—forfeits meaning, coherence, and the possibility of survival.

From his essay in Commentary, August 1996.

·◆·

Torah is a compilation of both divine command and human response: it is a record of God talking to Jews and Jews talking to God. When I examine the writings of Torah, how then do I know what is divine revelation and what is human interpretation? As a mitzvah-inspired Jew, the only option that I have is to decide for myself what binds me.

Ibid.

Yosi ben Chanina

THIRD/FOURTH-CENTURY TALMUDIC SCHOLAR

Whoever elevates himself by degrading his fellowman has no share in the world-to-come. How much more than when it is done at the expense of the glory of God!

Quoted in Genesis Rabba (1:5).

CHAPTER FIVE

A Personal God

Introduction

Martin Buber (1818–1965), the Viennese-born religious philosopher who together with Franz Rosenzweig published a German translation of the Bible, believed that speaking of God as a concept is both inadequate and improper. Religion, he felt, is not fulfilling its purpose if it merely talks *about* God. God must be personal. The individual must communicate with God directly, even as God communicates with man directly.

There are numerous examples of dialogue between man and God in the Bible itself. Early in the Book of Genesis (3:9) God calls out to Adam, who was hiding in the Garden of Eden with his wife, Eve, and says, "Where art thou?" One chapter later (4:9), God says to Cain, "where is Abel, thy brother?" Still later, God calls out to Abraham, and Abraham responds, "Here I am" (Genesis 22:1). In like manner does God communicate with Moses and the other prophets. In Isaiah (1:18), for example, God invites Israel to engage in a dialogue, even as much earlier Abraham had invited God to a debate, hoping to save the few good souls living in the doomed city of Sodom.

In legends of the Baal Shem Tov (c. 1700–1760) and other chasidic masters, the authors' closeness to God is expressed through prayer, communicating on the most personal of levels, as one would with a dear, close friend. Menachem Mendel of Kotsk (1787–1859), the Polish-born chasidic rebbe, for example, once pleaded with God: "Send us our Messiah, for we have no more strength to suffer." If God does not keep His promise to support Jews as a treasured people, he warned, neither would he, Menachem Mendel, keep his promise to remain loyal to God.

Probably the most famous of supplications to God in modern times is that of the legendary chasidic rebbe Levi Yitzchak of Berditchev (1740–1809), which begins with these very personal words:

> Good morning to You, Lord of the Universe.
> I, Levi Yitzchak, son of Sarah of Berditchev,
> Have come with a complaint against You on
> Behalf of our people Israel.
> What do You have against Your people Israel?

Addressing God directly and personally is not alien even to sophisticated modern thinkers. In an essay in *Commentary* (August 1966), for example, Orthodox rabbi Eliezer Berkovits writes: "I believe that God did, indeed, speak to Moses, as the Bible says. I am, however, unable to imagine how an infinite, incorporeal Being speaks to a man 'face to face.'" His firm belief is tempered by doubt.

Psychologist Erich Fromm offers an answer to Berkovits's dilemma when, in his *Man for Himself* (1947), he associates God with conscience: "[Man's] conscience is the voice which calls him back to himself; it permits him to know what he ought to do in order to become himself. It helps him to remain aware of the aims of his life and to the norms necessary for the attainment of these aims."

Man meets God "face to face" when his conscience has matured sufficiently to recognize that God's laws, as those spelled out in the Ten Commandments and elsewhere in the Bible, must be the guiding light and goals for all endeavors in life.

Many intellectuals, such as historian and Conservative rabbi David Dalin, have less trouble believing that God communicates directly with man. In an essay in *Commentary* (August 1996), he writes:

> I believe in a personal God who listens to our prayers, whether or not He answers them to our satisfaction. . . . I accept as a matter of religious faith the biblical claim that God communicated with Moses directly at Sinai. . . .

In that same issue of *Commentary*, his colleague, philosophy professor Elliot N. Dorff, states:

> "I believe . . . in a personal God Who interacts with us individually and collectively. . . ."

There is evidently a deep-seated craving on the part of many intellectuals, as well as laymen, to believe in a personal God even though that belief might seem irrational.

According to a study released in 1997, upwards of ninety percent of Americans believe in a personal God, although a lesser number believe in a God who parts seas and creates species one by one. Surprisingly, forty percent of American scientists believe in a personal God—not merely "an ineffable power and presence in the world, but a deity to whom they can pray" (*Newsweek*, July 20, 1998).

This chapter gives insight into the many ways that man seeks to reach God personally, as did Abraham, Jacob, Samuel, Jonah, Job, and other great figures in the Jewish past.

Abraham/Abram
FIRST PATRIARCH OF THE JEWISH PEOPLE

Will You destroy the innocent with the guilty? . . . Far be it from you. Will the Judge of the entire universe not deal justly?

Pleading with God not to wipe out the innocent with the guilty in the city of Sodom. Quoted in Genesis (18:23–25).

. ֎ .

My Lord, God, what would you give me for I am going (to die) childless . . . to me you have not given seed.

Addressing God for the first time in Genesis (15:2), complaining that he may die without an heir, despite God's promise that Abram would be amply rewarded.

Arlene Agus

CONTEMPORARY SCHOLAR, TEACHER, ACTIVIST

For me, encountering God has meant addressing God directly in my own words and seeking a direct reply in any form describable as divine revelation—God becoming manifest to humans. However, establishing such a connection is almost impossibly difficult, not necessarily because God is inaccessible—quite the contrary—but because I am.

Quoted in Beginning Anew: A Woman's Companion to the High Holy Days (1997), edited by Gail Twersky Reimer and Judith A. Kates.

Akiba ben Joseph

[c. 50–135]

LEADING TALMUDIC SCHOLAR, ACTIVIST

Everything is given on pledge, and a net is spread for all living people; the store is open, and the storekeeper [God] offers credit; the ledger is open, and the hand writes; whoever wishes to borrow may come and borrow, but the collectors visit regularly to exact payment from man, whether he realizes it or not. . . .

Quoted in the Ethics of the Fathers (3:16).

.◆.

A man should always accustom himself to say, "Whatever God does is for the best."

Quoted in the talmudic tractate Berachot (60b).

Solomon Alami

FIFTEENTH-CENTURY PORTUGUESE RABBI

Avoid listening to love songs which excite the passions. If God has graciously bestowed on you the gift of a sweet voice, use it in praising Him.

Quoted in the Introduction of Nathan and Maryann Ausabel's A Treasury of Jewish Poetry (1954).

Joseph Albo
FIFTEENTH-CENTURY SPANISH RABBI, THEOLOGIAN

Success is an attribute of God available to all. The degree to which a person is ready to receive success is the degree to which God gives it.

Quoted in A Call to the Infinite (1986), by Aryeh Kaplan.

(Rabbi) Alexandri
THIRD-CENTURY TALMUDIC SCHOLAR

If an ordinary person makes use of broken vessels, it is a disgrace for him. But the vessles used by the Holy One, blessed be He, and precisely broken ones, as it is said: "The Lord is near to them that are of a broken heart." [Psalm 34:19]

Quoted in Leviticus Rabba (7:2), where he emphasizes that God supports those who are aggrieved and suffering.

Anonymous
If God lived on earth, people would break his windows.

Yiddish folk saying.

.•.

God gave man two ears and one mouth so he might hear much and say little.

Ibid.

.•.

Oy, if God would only help me until he helps me!

Ibid. Quoted in Henry D. Spalding's Encyclopedia of Jewish Humor (1969).

.•.

The Holy One, blessed be He, fashioned every man in the mold of the first man [Adam] and yet not one of them resembles his fellow. Therefore, every single person is obliged to say, "The world was created for my sake."

From the talmudic tractate Sanhedrin (37a).

257

The Holy One, blessed be He, requires the [sincere] heart.

Quoted in the talmudic tractate Sanhedrin (106b).

A person must bless God for the evil [that befalls him], just as he blesses Him for the good.

Quoted in the talmudic tractate Berachot (54a).

My God, the soul which Thou hast placed in me is pure. Thou hast fashioned it in me. Thou didst breath it into me, and Thou preservest it within me.

Ibid (60b). A prayer prescribed by the Rabbis of the Talmud to be recited upon arising in the morning.

A good wife is a precious gift. She will be put in the bosom of a God-fearing man.

Quoted in the talmudic tractate Yevamot (63b).

Make a beautiful *sukka* in God's honor; a beautiful *shofar*; beautiful fringes [*tzitzit*]; and a beautiful Torah scroll written with fine ink and a fine reed pen by a skilled calligrapher, and wrap it with beautiful silks.

Honoring God through ritualistic acts. Quoted in the talmudic tractate Shabbat (133b) based on the interpretation of Exodus 15:2.

God will provide—ah, if only He would till He does!

Yiddish proverb.

When a Jew breaks one leg, he thanks God he did not break both; when he breaks both, he thanks God he did not break his neck.

A Yiddish folk saying.

If you want to give God a good laugh, tell God your plans.

A Yiddish proverb.

.•.

What about his hat?

A classic punchline of the humorous story of a child who is drowning and the grandmother who prays to God for help. God finally intervenes and brings the child safely to shore, but without his hat.

Bradley Shavit Artson
CONTEMPORARY CONSERVATIVE U.S. RABBI

Having God as my constant companion does not mean there aren't times when I question my beliefs. For example, the horrors of floods, the attacks on large groups of innocent people, the destruction of earthquakes. Yet, with all of that, there is still much love and beauty in the world.

From a lecture delivered at Valley Beth Shalom, in Encino, California, December 3, 1998.

.•.

The salvation of the universe is determined by us through our choices of goodness and mercy in the ways we help mend the world.

Ibid.

Israel Baal Shem Tov
[c. 1700–1760]
FOUNDER OF CHASIDISM

When a father starts to teach his child to walk, he stands in front of him and holds out his hands on either side of the child so that he cannot fall, and the boy goes toward his father. But the moment the child is close, his father withdraws a little and holds his hands farther apart. As the father does this again and again, the child learns to walk.

Responding to a question about God's seeming remoteness, put to him by a disciple. Quoted in William B. Silverman's Rabbinic Wisdom and Jewish Values (1971).

·◆·

When I fuse my spirit to God, I let my mouth say what it will, for then all my words are bound to their roots in heaven.

Quoted in Martin Buber's Tales of the Hasidim: Early Masters (1947).

Menachem Begin
[1913–1992]
ISRAELI PRIME MINISTER (1977–1983)

The Jewish people can exist, with God's help, only by readiness to sacrifice on the part of our finest sons. We have paid a price—woe is me. I need not add another word. And we are unable to console the families who have lost their dear ones; only God can comfort them, and will comfort them.

We pray for the quick and complete recovery and healing of all the wounded. I visited them. I came to comfort them and they comforted me. I left with feelings that have no expression in human language. A wounded, hurting man told me just one thing—be strong and of good courage!

This is the stuff our sons are made of.

From an address to the Knesset on June 28, 1982.

Saul Bellow
[1915–   ]
U.S. NOVELIST

The planet's a school, life's an extended know-thyself course. When you speak to God in your heart, however, you ask if you're simply put among all this to make mistakes, to be a fool. I've made so many mistakes about myself and others. To put it briefly: Socrates said the unexamined life is not worth living, but sometimes the examined life makes you wish you were dead.

From an interview with Desmond O'Grady, quoted in The Jerusalem Post, July 26, 1997.

Eliezer Berkovits

[1908–1992]

U.S. ORTHODOX RABBI, SCHOLAR, AUTHOR

Everything in the Bible is communication between God and man; everything is relationship. God spoke; God commanded; He called; He appeared—it all means an event happening between God and man. In all these situations man experiences the presence of God which seeks him out and addresses him.

From his God, Man, and History (1959).

Chaim Nachman Bialik

[1873–1934]

HEBREW POET

Why do they pray to Me? Tell them to thunder against Me. Let them raise their fists against Me and claim recompense for their shame!

From his classic poem "In the City of Slaughter" (1904), which was inspired by the Kishinev pogrom.

Ben Zion Bokser

[1907–1983]

U.S. CONSERVATIVE RABBI, SCHOLAR, AUTHOR

The function of petitionary prayer is to make us more conscious of our dependence on God, that we may thereby become more receptive to divine influences. God knows our needs before we voice them, but unless we are fully attuned to God, the bounty of His grace does not flow freely into our lives. As we draw closer to God, we come more completely under His providence, and His bounty flows more freely.

From the introduction to his Prayerbook: Weekday, Sabbath, and Festival (1957).

Martin Buber
[1878–1965]
GERMAN THEOLOGIAN, AUTHOR

The description of God as a Person is indispensable for everyone who like myself means by "God" not a principle, and like myself means by "God" not an idea, but who rather means by "God," as I do, Him who—whatever else He may be—enters into a direct relation with us men in creative, revealing, and redeeming acts, and thus makes it possible for us to enter into a direct relationship with Him.

From his Way of Response (1971).

.◆.

The great achievement of Israel is not so much that it told mankind of the one, real God, the origin and goal of all that exists, but rather that it taught men that they can address God . . . that man can say Thou to Him, that we human beings can stand face to face with Him, that there is communion between God and man.

Quoted in Martin Buber: Jewish Existentialist (1960), by Malcolm L. Dramond.

(Rabbi) Chanina
FIRST-CENTURY DEPUTY HIGH PRIEST, SCHOLAR

Everything is in the hands of heaven save the fear of heaven.

Each person has the choice of being God-fearing or an atheist. Quoted in the talmudic tractate Megilla (25a).

(Rabbi) Chiya
THIRD–CENTURY PALESTINIAN SCHOLAR

May it be Thy will, O Lord our God and God of our fathers, that You turn our hearts to complete repentance; that we may not be shamed before our fathers in the world-to-come; that You may inspire our hearts with fear of Thy name; and that You may remove us from that which You hate; and that You may bring us near to that which You love; and that You may be merciful to us for the sake of Your name.

Quoted in Mishna Berachot (4:2).

Arthur A. Cohen
[1928–1986]
U.S. WRITER, THEOLOGIAN

I love God and have mercy upon God as profoundly and as deeply as I trust God has love and mercy upon me and my children and the people of choice and the whole of creation.

Quoted in Anne Roiphe's Generations without Memory (1981).

Hermann Cohen
[1842–1918]
GERMAN PHILOSOPHER, AUTHOR

The Sabbath became the most effective patron saint of the Jewish people. . . . The ghetto Jew discarded all the toil and trouble of his daily life when the Sabbath lamp was lit. All insult and outrage was shaken off. The love of God, which returned to him the Sabbath each seventh day, restored to him also his honor and human dignity even in his lowly hut.

From his Die Religion der Vernunft aus den Quellen des Judentums (1919).

Morris Raphael Cohen
[1880–1947]
U.S. PHILOSOPHER, PROFESSOR, AUTHOR

Men cling to sanctified phrases not only because of the insights they contain but even more because, through ritual and repetition, they have become redolent with the wine of human experience. . . . The ritual may be diluted by English and by modernisms, but the Hebraic God is still a potent symbol of the continuous life of which we individuals are waves.

From his Dreamer's Journey (1949).

David G. Dalin

CONTEMPORARY U.S. CONSERVATIVE RABBI, HISTORIAN

I believe in a personal God Who listens to our prayers, whether or not He answers them to our satisfaction. I believe divine revelation to be a fundamental principle of Judaism, which I unapologetically affirm. . . . I accept as a matter of religious faith the biblical claim that God communicated with Moses directly at Sinai, and in so doing made His divine will and commandments known in the wilderness.

From his essay in Commentary, August 1996.

(King) David

SECOND KING OF ISRAEL, RULED C. 1000–960 B.C.E.

My God [Eli], my God, why hast Thou forsaken me?

From the Book of Psalms (22:2). Christians often change the word azavtani ("forsaken me") to zevachtani ("sacrificed me") and connect it to the Crucifixion.

Benjamin Disraeli

[1804–1881]

BRITISH PRIME MINISTER, NOVELIST, ESSAYIST

Is it more unphilosophical to believe in a personal God, omnipotent and omniscient, than in natural forces unconscious and irresistible? Is it unphilosophical to combine power with intelligence?

From his Lothair (1870).

Elliot N. Dorff

CONTEMPORARY U.S. CONSERVATIVE RABBI,
PROFESSOR OF PHILOSOPHY

I believe in a personal God because I find that construction of reality to be most adequate in describing and explaining my experience. . . . I think that personality is part of ultimate metaphysical reality, and so I need to build personality into my conception of God if it is to be adequate. I believe, then, in a personal God Who interacts with us individually and collectively, as much female as male in characteristics.

From his essay in Commentary, August 1996.

Kirk Douglas
[1916–   ]
U.S. ACTOR

I hope it's not too late.

If God is a patient God, maybe he'll give me enough time to learn the things I need to know to understand what it is that makes us Jews the conscience of the world.

From a 1994 speech at the Los Angeles Synagogue for the Performing Arts.

·-·-·

I have had a tumultuous relationship with God, and he has let me know that he has not been so pleased with me—at least I think that this was the message when I began to experience severe back pain in my old age. C. S. Lewis, a Christian writer, said that "pain is God's megaphone to wake up a deaf world." If that is true, then I was stone deaf.

From his book Climbing the Mountain: My Search for Meaning (1997), describing his difficulties in reaching an accord with God.

Albert Einstein
[1879–1955]
GERMAN-BORN U.S. SCIENTIST

To be sure, the doctrine of a personal God interfering with natural events could never be refuted, in the real sense, by science, for this doctrine can always take refuge in those domains in which scientific knowledge has not yet been able to set foot. But I am persuaded that such behavior on the part of the representatives of religion would not only be unworthy but also fatal.

Quoted in Lothar Kahn's God: What People Have Said about Him (1980).

· ◆ ·

I cannot conceive of a personal god who would directly influence the actions of individuals, or would directly sit in judgment on creatures of his own creation. I cannot do this in spite of the fact that mechanistic causality has, to a certain extent, been placed in doubt by modern science.

> *Quoted in Geoffrey Wigoder's* Dictionary of Jewish Biography (1991).

Ira Eisenstein

[1906–1997]

U.S. RECONSTRUCTIONIST RABBI, AUTHOR,
EDUCATOR, LECTURER

Prayer does not necessarily require a "Thou." In several cultures, prayer is experienced without reference to a personal being or a Thou. . . . When I pray, I confine myself to the kind of text that enables me to achieve what Walter Kaufman called "passionate reflection" . . . I suggest that traditional Jewish values become the central theme of passionate reflection.

> *From his essay "Prayer as Passionate Reflection," in* Reconstructionism Today, winter 1994–95.

(Rabbi) Eleazar

SECOND-CENTURY TALMUDIC SCHOLAR

God will, in the time-to-come, be a crown on the head of every righteous man.

> *From the Midrash Tanchuma on Sidra Ki Tavo.*

· ◆ ·

The Holy One blessed be He says: "The whole world was created for his [each person's] sake only."

> *To which Rabbi Abba ben Kahana added: "He is equal in value to the whole world." Quoted in the talmudic tractate Berachot (6b).*

· ◆ ·

Sovereign of the Universe, among all the things that Thou hast created in a woman not one is without a purpose: eyes to see, ears to hear, a nose to smell, a mouth to speak, hands to do work, legs to walk with, breasts to give suck. These breasts that Thou hast put on my heart, are they not to give suck? Give me a son, so that I may suckle with them.

Quoting the comment of his Master, Yose ben Zimra, on the verse in I Samuel 1:13: "Now Hannah, she spoke in her heart." Shortly thereafter, she gave birth to Samuel.

Eleazar ben Azariah
[70–135]
PRESIDENT OF THE SANHEDRIN, SUCCEEDING GAMALIEL II

One should not say, "I loathe pig meat and I have no desire to wear clothes made of a mixture of wool and linen, but what can I do since God forbade it and commanded me to separate myself from the nations and to accept this sovereignty."

Quoted in Rashi on Leviticus 20:26, "Thou shalt be holy for me. . . ."

Eleazar ben Judah of Worms
[c. 1160–1238]
GERMAN CODIFIER, KABBALIST, POET

If the infinite God had not appeared to the prophets as a King on a throne, they would not know to whom they were praying.

Quoted in his Sodei Raza ("Secrets of Secrets").

Emil L. Fackenheim
[1916–   ]
U.S. REFORM RABBI, THEOLOGIAN, AUTHOR

Judaism believes in the co-workership of God and man, in the covenant between God and Israel, and in God's availability in prayer; and the . . . relationship implied in these beliefs can be thought of only in quasi-personal terms.

From his Quest for Past and Future: Essays in Jewish Theology (1968).

Is God personal or impersonal? To conceive Him as personal is anthropomorphic. Is God, then, impersonal—a "Process"? But this is physiomorphic . . . even *less* adequate than anthropomorphism; for a "Process" is qualitatively *less* than a man. The upshot is that we can think of God only in symbolic terms.

From his Quest for Past and Future: Essays in Jewish Theology (1968).

Marcia Falk

CONTEMPORARY U.S. SCHOLAR, POET, AUTHOR

In the rabbinic view, it is through the soul that we are expected to know and communicate with divinity; immutable and eternal, the human soul belongs to God and returns to God, ultimately giving humanity its likeness to God. In contrast, the body is seen as the work of God but as fundamentally unlike God in its imperfection and in its mutability—as it grows ill, ages, dies, and decays.

From her The Book of Blessings (1996).

Leonard Fein

[1934–]
U.S. WRITER, EDITOR, EDUCATOR

It was always the ethnic impulse that seemed to be a preserver of Jewish identity. A generation back, no Jew had to apologize for being an agnostic or an atheist. Even the Jewish atheists knew what the God in which they did not believe expected of them.

Quoted in New York *magazine*, July 14, 1997.

Louis Finkelstein

[1895–1991]
U.S. CONSERVATIVE RABBI, SCHOLAR, AUTHOR, EDUCATOR

When I pray, I talk to God; when I study, God talks to me.

Quoted in N.B. *Cardin's* Visions of Holiness in Everyday (1997).

Abraham H. Foxman
EXECUTIVE DIRECTOR OF THE ANTI-DEFAMATION LEAGUE

I have no objection to Jews or Christians being elected to public office, but if they are elected they cannot in any way be influenced by their religious beliefs. . . . Legislators should vote against murder because that's what the majority of people want, not because legislators believe God says that murder is wrong.

From a telephone conversation that Pat Robertson reported he had with Foxman after the appearance of David Cantor's Religious Right: The Assault on Tolerance and Pluralism in America, in which Robertson claims that he was attacked without provocation.

Sigmund Freud
[1856–1939]
AUSTRIAN-BORN ORIGINATOR OF PSYCHOANALYSIS

Why the people of Israel adhered to their God all the more devotedly the worse they were treated by Him, that is a question we must leave open.

From his Moses and Monotheism (1939).

David Frishman
[1865–1922]
HEBREW AUTHOR, POET

Brethren, give me a God, for I am full of prayer!

From his poem "Ha-yadata." Quoted in Meyer Waxman's History of Jewish Literature (1930).

Theodor H. Gaster
[1906–1992]
U.S. FOLKLORIST, AUTHOR

Judaism has a central, unique and tremendous idea that is utterly original—the idea that God and man are partners in the world and that, for

269

the realization of His plan and the complete articulation of this glory upon earth, God needs a committed, dedicated group of men and women.

From a speech delivered at the American Council for Judaism conference, April 30, 1954.

Glückel of Hameln
[1646–1724]
GERMAN-BORN AUTHOR, NOTED FOR HER PIETY

The best thing for you, my children, is to serve God from your heart, without falsehood or sham, not giving out to people that you are one thing while, God forbid, in your heart you are another.

Quoted in The Memoirs of Glückel of Hameln, translated by Marvin Lowenthal (1977).

Leib Goldhirsch
[1860–1942]
U.S. JOURNALIST, HEBREW TEACHER

A Jew is a Jew like a Frenchman is a Frenchman. No race of people can survive long without a ritual and some degree of discipline. These people are my people—the people I live with, the people with whom I came to America. My beloved friend Dudya Silverberg goes to shul to talk to God, and I go to shul to talk to Dudya.

Questioning his father about why he attended synagogue regularly. From Harry Golden's autobiography, The Right Time (1969).

David M. Gordis
CONTEMPORARY U.S. CONSERVATIVE RABBI, EDUCATOR

I do not believe that a personal, conscious deity manipulates and controls human affairs. I find myself constantly "in tension" with the nature and reality of what I refer to as God, yet it is satisfying and meaningful for me to speak of God as the ground of all being, as the embodiment of the potential for growth and moral excellence.

From his essay in Commentary, August 1996.

Alexander Granach

[1890–1945]

GERMAN YIDDISH ACTOR, NOVELIST

Mama has blessed the candles, always interspersing prayer with personal conversation; she has always spoken to God like a grown daughter to her father, reminding him of his responsibilities and duties. It is the same every week.

From his There Goes a Man: A Novel about Life (1945).

Rebecca Gratz

[1781–1869]

U.S. SOCIAL WELFARE ACTIVIST

The whole spirit of religion is to make men merciful, humble and just. . . . Unless the strong arm of power is raised to sustain the provisions of the Constitution of the United States, securing to every citizen the privilege of worshipping God according to his own conscience, America will no longer be the happy asylum of the oppressed and the secure dwelling place of religion.

From a letter to her brother Ben in 1844 after Catholic churches were burned in Philadelphia by the Protestant majority, protesting the large influx of newcomers from Ireland.

Joshua O. Haberman

CONTEMPORARY U.S. REFORM RABBI, AUTHOR

I believe that the One, unique, and incomparable God is the core and source of all being. My God is personal, conscious, and self-revealing. The biblical doctrine of man "made in God's image" implies divine attributes such as intelligence, free will, and moral judgment as models for similar human characteristics, however inferior these may be.

From his essay in Commentary, August 1996.

Yehuda Halevi

[1075–1141]

POET, PHILOSOPHER

My God, heal me and I shall be healed;
Let not Thine anger be kindled against me
so that I be consumed.
My medicines are of Thee, whether good
Or evil, whether strong or weak. . . .
Not upon my power of healing I rely;
Only for Thine healing do I watch.

Translated from the Hebrew by Nina Salaman.

Ben Hecht

[1894–1964]

U.S. AUTHOR, PLAYWRIGHT

A man who writes of himself without speaking of God is like one who
identifies himself without giving his address.

From his A Child of the Century (1954).

Will Herberg

[1901–1977]

U.S. THEOLOGIAN, SOCIAL CRITIC

The God of the Hebraic religion is either a living, active, "feeling" God
or he is nothing.

From his Judaism and Modern Man (1951).

Abraham Joshua Heschel

[1907–1972]

U.S. RABBI, THEOLOGIAN, AUTHOR, ACTIVIST

God's dream is to have mankind as a partner in the drama of continuous
creation.

From his Who Is Man? (1965).

. ◆ .

God does not stand outside the range of human suffering and sorrow. He is personally involved in, ever stirred by, the conduct and fate of man.

From his The Prophets (1962).

. ◆ .

To the prophet . . . God does not reveal himself in an abstract absoluteness, but in a personal and intimate relation to the world. . . . Man's deeds may move Him, affect Him, grieve Him or, on the other hand, gladden and please Him. This notion that God can be intimately affected, that He possesses not merely intelligence and will, but also pathos, basically defines the prophetic consciousness of God.

Ibid.

Susannah Heschel

CONTEMPORARY U.S. PROFESSOR OF JEWISH STUDIES, AUTHOR

Today, in celebrating my father's memory, we have to bring to life the joyful and thoughtful aspects of Judaism he taught and exemplified: that we are all made in the image of God, that God's creation is filled with wonder and awe, and that God needs us as partners in caring for our fellow human beings and for all of creation.

From her article in The Jewish Press, February 9, 1998, remembering her father Abraham Joshua Heschel, twenty-five years after his death at age sixty-four.

. ◆ .

His most important and controversial theological claim concerns "divine pathos," the belief that God is not impassive and immutable but, on the contrary, is deeply responsive to human beings. Indeed, God is in need of the work of human beings for the fulfillment of God's ends in the world.

Ibid.

Hillel the Elder

FIRST-CENTURY SCHOLAR,
FOUNDER OF AN ACADEMY OF LEARNING

God says: "If you will come to my house, I will come to yours."
Quoted in the talmudic tractate Sukka (53a).

(Rabbi) Huna

THIRD-CENTURY TALMUDIC SCHOLAR

In addressing God, man's words should be few.
A view based on a verse in Ecclesiastes (5:1): " . . . let thy words be few." Quoted in the talmudic tractate Berachot (61a). Rabba bar bar Chana amplified on this thought and said, "He who praises God more than is necessary deserves to be uprooted from the world."

Fannie Hurst

[1889–1968]
U.S. NOVELIST, PLAYWRIGHT

I wonder what God's thoughts must be concerning those who turn their faces to Him chiefly in times of calamity. The askers. Give me, God. Help me, God. Do for me, God. Protect me, God. Does God separate them from the givers? Has God too much grandeur to look askance at those who come seeking and never bearing gifts? Or is Faith in itself the great meaning, the white cane of groping mankind?
From her Anatomy of Me (1958).

Abraham ibn Ezra

[1089–1164]
SPANISH SCHOLAR, POET

Many are those who wrap themselves in a prayershawl but do not fear God.
By attribution.

.•.

Reason is the angel that mediates between God and man.
Ibid.

Moses ibn Ezra
[c. 1055–1135]
SPANISH HEBREW POET

In spite of those who hate and envy me,
At all times high will rise my eminence.
They aimed their arrows at my heart,
But the hands of God deflected them.
Quoted in Raphael Patai's Jewish Mind (1977).

Solomon ibn Gabirol
[c. 1021–c. 1056]
SPANISH POET, PHILOSOPHER

O Lord, who can comprehend Thy power?
For Thou hast created for the splendor of Thy Glory a pure radiance.
Hewn from the rock of rocks and digged from the bottom of the pit,
Thou hast imparted to it the spirit of wisdom
And called it the Soul.
Quoted in Lothar Kahn's God: What People Have Said about Him
(1980).

.•.

Lord of the world, O hear my psalm,
And as sweet incense take my plea.
My heart hath set its love on Thee
And finds in speech its only balm.
Translated from the Hebrew by Israel Zangwill.

Bachya ibn Pakuda

[c. 1050–1120]

SPANISH PHILOSOPHER, AUTHOR

Thou knowest what is for my good. When I recite my wants, it is not to remind Thee of them, but only that I may understand better how great is my dependence upon Thee. If then, I ask Thee for things that do not make for my well-being, it is because I am ignorant. Thy choice is better than mine and I submit myself to Thy decrees and Thy supreme direction.

An eleventh-century poem expressing complete surrender to God's will.

(Rabbi) Isaac

THIRD-CENTURY TALMUDIC SCHOLAR

To one who is eager to give charity, God provides the means.

Quoted in the talmudic tractate Bava Batra (9b).

·◆·

With what shall I bless you? Shall I wish you Torah learning? You already have learning. Wealth? You already have wealth. Children? You already have children.

Therefore, this is my blessing: May it be God's will that your offspring will be like you.

To Rabbi Nachman. Quoted in the talmudic tractate Taanit (5b-6a).

Judah ben Chiya

THIRD-CENTURY PALESTINIAN SCHOLAR

When a man administers a drug, it may be beneficial to one limb but harmful to another. But with God it is not so. He gave a Torah to Israel, and it is a drug of life for all his body.

Quoted in the talmudic tractate Eruvin (54a).

Judah ben Shalom

FOURTH/FIFTH-CENTURY PALESTINIAN SCHOLAR

If a poor man says something, people pay little attention. But if a rich man speaks, immediately he is heard and listened to. Before God, however, all are equal.

Quoted in Midrash Exodus Rabba (21:4).

Judah ben Simeon

FOURTH-CENTURY PALESTINIAN SCHOLAR

How exalted above His world is the Most High! Yet, let a man enter a synagogue and pray silently, and the Holy One listens, even as a friend in whose ear one whispers a secret.

Quoted in the Jerusalem Talmud, tractate Berachot (9:1).

Alfred Kazin

[1915–   ]

U.S. AUTHOR, BOOK REVIEWER, EDITOR

Religion is a social commodity. Religion is what people do together. Fundamentally it is a collective experience. God is something else. God is always a personal matter.

From an interview with Matthew Goodman in the Forward, December 5, 1997.

·◆·

What always bothers me about Judaism is that the rabbi never says: "What do you believe?" He says, "Come on and get on the train like everyone else!" Yet for me, God is a very personal commitment.

Quoted in The Jerusalem Report, January 19, 1998.

Larry King

[1933–]

TALK-SHOW HOST, COLUMNIST

I didn't see God when I had my heart attack, no flashes of light, no out-of-the-body experiences. I've interviewed many religious leaders and I liked and respected them. But I don't have faith. I wish I did have faith. I wish I could know I'm going to a better place.

> Commenting on his meeting with PLO Chief Yasser Arafat. Quoted in The Jerusalem Report, March 23, 1995.

Harold Kushner

[1935–]

U.S. CONSERVATIVE RABBI, AUTHOR

Only God can give us credit for the angry words we did not speak.

> From his When All You've Ever Wanted Isn't Enough (1986).

Daniel Lapin

CONTEMPORARY CONSERVATIVE ACTIVIST

It's not in the interest of the Jewish community to give the impression to millions of observant Christians that Jews—who introduced God to the world—should paradoxically be the ones most vigorous in excavating him from the public square.

> The head of Toward Tradition, a conservative organization seeking to forge better relations with the religious right, commenting in 1995 on the strong Jewish opposition to a school prayer amendment.

(Rabbi) Levi

THIRD-CENTURY TALMUDIC SCHOLAR

The Haggadah speaks of four sons: One wise, one wicked, one simple, and one who does not know how to ask. Lord of the world, I, Levi Yitzhak, am the one who does not know how to ask. In such a case, does not the Haggadah say that with the child who does not know how to ask, "You must start with him." The father must take the initiative. Lord of the world, are You not my Father? Am I not Your son? I do not even know what questions to ask. You take the initiative and disclose the answers to me. Show me, in connection with whatever happens to me, what is required of me! What are You asking of me? God, I do not ask You why I suffer. I wish to know only that I suffer for Your sake.

Quoted in Martin Buber's Tales of the Hasidim: The Early Masters (1947).

Levi Yitzchak of Berditchev
[1740–1809]
CHASIDIC RABBI

Lord of the universe, see how much Your people love and serve You. Even when oiling cartwheels, they pray and serve You. And yet You dare to complain against Israel.

By attribution.

·•·

Lord of the universe! I saw an ordinary Jew pick up his tefillin from the floor, and kiss them; and You have let Your tefillin, the Jewish people, lie on the ground for more than two thousand years, trampled by their enemies,—why do You not pick them up? Why do You not act as a plain Jew acts? Why?

Quoted in S. L. Hurwitz's Otzar Ha-Torah.

Naomi Levy
[1963–]
U.S. CONSERVATIVE RABBI, AUTHOR

Open my eyes God. Help me to perceive what I have ignored, to uncover what I have forsaken, to find what I have been searching for. Remind me that I don't have to journey far to discover something new, for miracles surround me, blessings and holiness abound. And You are near. Amen.

A personal prayer. From her To Begin Again: The Journey Toward Comfort, Strength and Faith in Difficult Times (1998).

·•·

I long to change the world, but I rarely appreciate things as they are. I know how to give, but I don't always know how to receive. I know how to keep busy, but I don't know how to be still. I talk, but I don't often listen. I look, but I don't often see. I yearn to succeed, but I often forget what is truly important. Teach me, God, to slow down. May my resting revive me. May it lead me to wisdom, to holiness, and to peace. Amen.

Ibid.

Alice Lucas

[1852–1935]

ENGLISH POET

God of my fathers, may it be
Thy will, this night to suffer me
To lay me down in peace and rise
In peace, when morning gilds the skies.

Isaac Luria

[1534–1572]

JERUSALEM-BORN LEADING KABBALIST

Sovereign of all worlds, Ruler over all rulers, Father of mercy and forgiveness, we bow before You in gratitude for having brought us near to Your Torah and to Your holy service, and for having enabled us to understand some of the mysteries of Your holy Torah. What we are, and what merit is there in our life, that You have bestowed on us so great a kindness? We therefore bring to You our entreaty to forgive all our trespasses, that our acts of wrongdoing shall not serve as an obstruction between us and You. And may it be Your will, our God and God of our fathers, to direct our hearts to fear and love You, that You give heed to these our words, and broaden our understanding that we may grasp the hidden meanings of Your Torah. . . .

By attribution. Quoted in Ben Zion Bokser's The Jewish Mystical Tradition (1981).

Moses Chaim Luzzatto
[1707–1746]
ITALIAN KABBALIST, HEBREW POET, AUTHOR

Whatever a man does he should have no other goal in life greater than to be drawn to God as iron is drawn to a magnet.

From his Mesilat Yesharim (1740).

.•.

Man came into the world only to achieve nearness to God.

Ibid.

Jerome R. Malino
[1911–]
U.S. REFORM RABBI

Perhaps the most rewarding aspect [of being a congregational rabbi] is the opportunity for abiding personal relationships. I am able, without hesitation . . . to utter the same prayer of gratitude I spoke after twelve years in my pulpit when I said [that] the rabbi "will feel himself a partner with God in creating souls." As he confirms those he knew as infants, marries those he has confirmed, as he sees his handiwork in happier and better integrated lives, as he grows with his labors and earns the love of those he served, he will say, "The reward was worth the effort."

From his 1980 presidential address before the Central Conference of American Rabbis.

Mar ben Rabina
FOURTH-CENTURY BABYLONIAN SCHOLAR

O God, guard my tongue from evil and my lips from speaking guile.

The prayer he added to his prayers. Quoted in the talmudic tractate Berachot (17a).

Daniel C. Matt

CONTEMPORARY U.S. CONSERVATIVE RABBI,
PROFESSOR OF MYSTICISM, AUTHOR

Without human participation, God remains incomplete, unrealized. It is up to us to actualize the divine potential in the world. God needs us.

From his The Essential Kabbalah: The Heart of Jewish Mysticism (1995).

Menachem Mendel of Kotzk
Also known as the Kotzker Rebbe
[1787–1859]
POLISH-BORN CHASIDIC LEADER

Lord of the universe, . . . send us our Messiah, for we have no more strength to suffer. Show me a sign, O God. Give me the force to rend the chains of exile. Otherwise, . . . otherwise . . . I rebel against Thee. If Thou dost not keep thy covenant, . . . then neither will I keep that agreement, and it is all over, we are through being Thy chosen people, Thy peculiar treasure!

From "Der Rebbe Fun Kotzk."

Moses

BIBLE HERO, LEADER OF THE CHILDREN OF ISRAEL

Please God, make her well.

The short five-word prayer uttered by Moses asking God to heal his sister, Miriam, who had suddenly been stricken with leprosy, as detailed in the Book of Numbers (12:13).

Nachman ben Simcha of Bratzlav
[1772–1810]
CHASIDIC RABBI

May He who thought us worthy to let us see Jerusalem in her destruction, grant us that we may behold her rebuilt and restored, when the glory of the Lord shall return to her. But you, my son, and your brothers and the whole of our family, may you all live to see the salvation of Jerusalem and the comfort of Zion.

One of many aphorisms transmitted through his disciples.

Cynthia Ozick

[1928–   ]

U.S. AUTHOR, PLAYWRIGHT, ESSAYIST

Gotenyu, a way of addressing God when in despair, is a derivative of familial endearment of rebuke as well as despair.

From her "Legacies," an essay which first appeared in the London Times Literary Supplement, *May 3, 1983.*

Isaac Leibush (I. L.) Peretz

[1852–1915]

POLISH-BORN YIDDISH NOVELIST, POET, CRITIC

Life means: having divine imagination, and in a certain measure divine will to carry into effect what is imagined, to change the environment to accord with the imagination, creating new forms—a partner in the work of Creation!

I live—therefore I have a divine spark in me; all who live have it—and I feel that all lives!

He who denies God also has the divine spark. So has the blasphemer.

From his essay "Roads That Lead Away from Jewishness." Reprinted in Joseph Leftwich's The Way We Think *(1969).*

Jakob Petuchowski

[1925–1991]

U.S. PROFESSOR, THEOLOGIAN

We Jews are so much better at speaking to God than we are speaking of God. We speak to God all the time and not just in moments of formal prayer during worship services. We are asked how our children are, and we answer: "Thank God, they are very well."

"Thank God!" "God Forbid!" "Good God!" "Please God!"—those
and similar expressions are constantly on our lips.

From an essay in The Jewish Spectator, *winter 1984.*

Philo
[*c.* 20 B.C.E.–40 C.E.]
ALEXANDRIAN PHILOSOPHER, BIBLE SCHOLAR, AUTHOR

What God is to the world, parents are to their children.

From his Honor Due Parents.

W. Gunther Plaut
[1912–   ]
GERMAN-BORN REFORM RABBI, AUTHOR, BIBLE SCHOLAR

A Jew, by the very condition of his Jewishness, pays the continuing
price of Sinai. If Jewishness remains his fate, Judaism remains the framework of his native spiritual existence and God his partner. And therefore, as long as the people as a continuing organism in history keep
alive the consciousness of Sinai, each Jew can find his roots.

From his Torah: A Modern Commentary *(1981).*

Dennis Prager
CONTEMPORARY U.S. EDITOR, AUTHOR,
RADIO TALK-SHOW HOST

I believe in God, the God of the Bible. This God is good, holy, supranatural,
personal. As good and holy are self-explanatory, I will briefly explain
supranatural and personal.

Supranatural: God created nature and is in no way part of it. . . .
Personal: God knows each of us. If God did not know us, there would
be no practical difference between atheism and belief.

From his essay in Commentary, *August 1996.*

Emanuel Rackman

[1910–]

U.S.-BORN ORTHODOX RABBI, SCHOLAR, EDUCATOR

To be God's partner both in the improvement of Mother Nature and man's own nature endows man with peerless worth. Life is sacred. Suicide is sin. Nirvana is not human. Escape is cowardice. So each new year we celebrate the act of creation—and we pray for life—not in an unknown hereafter but in the here and now.

From his column in The Jewish Week, July 11, 1997.

Yossel Rakover

VICTIM OF THE WARSAW GHETTO UPRISING

My rabbi would frequently tell the story of a Jew who fled from the Spanish Inquisition with his wife and child, striking out in a small boat over the stormy sea until he reached a rocky island. A flash of lightning killed his wife; a storm rose and hurled his son into the sea; then, as lonely as a stone, naked, barefoot, lashed by the storm, terrified by the thunder and lightning, hands turned up to God, the Jew, again setting out on his journey through the wastes of the rocky island, turned to God with the following words:

> "God of Israel, I have fled to this place in order to worship You without molestation, to obey Your commandments, and to sanctify Your name. You, however, have done everything to make me stop believing in You. Now, lest it seem to You that You will succeed by these tribulations in driving me from the right path, I notify You, my God and the God of my fathers, that it will not avail You in the least. You may insult me, You may castigate me, You may take from me all that I cherish and hold dear in the world, You may torture me to death; but I will always love You, and these are my last words to You, my wrathful God: Nothing will avail You in the least."

> Discovered in a small bottle after World War II in the rubble of the Warsaw Ghetto ruins, this is a portion of a testament written on April 28, 1943, hours before the ghetto was finally taken by the Nazis.

Rav
Also known as Abba Aricha
THIRD-CENTURY BABYLONIAN SCHOLAR

God prays: May My mercy suppress My anger!

His response when asked what does God's prayer consist of when He prays. Quoted in the talmudic tractate Berachot (7a).

Paul Reichmann
CONTEMPORARY PHILANTHROPIST

What multiplied my initial success by a factor of a hundred had nothing to do with my own efforts. It was God's will that I was successful on such a scale.

Confiding to his young relative Morris Brenick in the 1980s. Quoted in Reichmann (1997), by Anthony Bianco.

Resh Lakish
Also known as Rabbi Shimon (Simeon)
SECOND/THIRD-CENTURY TALMUDIC SCHOLAR

God gives man an extra soul on Sabbath eve and at the end of the Sabbath takes it back from him.

Quoted in the talmudic tractate Beitza (16a).

Anne Roiphe
[1935–　]
U.S. WRITER, NOVELIST

Today I frequently argue with a God whose existence I question, but I think that the Jewish people has a purpose, a destiny, a reason for being, perhaps only in the wonder of our plot, the continuing effort to make us shape up, behave decently, look at ourselves with a moral eye. I am no longer a mere particle of genetic material spinning out a single life span. I have a past, present and future among my people. Am I ever surprised!

From her article "What Being Jewish Means to Me" in The New York Times, September 12, 1993.

Jonathan Sacks

[1948–]

CHIEF RABBI OF GREAT BRITAIN (1991–)

We [Jews] always were an obstinate people, too obstinate to let go of God; too obstinate to be defeated by history.

From his article "Love, Hate, and Jewish Identity," in the November 1997 issue of First Things.

Maurice Samuel

[1895–1972]

RUSSIAN-BORN ESSAYIST, NOVELIST

It is more revolutionary to believe in God and take Him to task sensibly than not to believe in Him and denounce Him in unmeasured language.

From his World of Sholom Aleichem (1943).

Dore Schary

[1905–1980]

U.S. PLAYWRIGHT, FILM AND THEATER PRODUCER

In the Jewish life I knew there was a trinity to whom we appealed or expressed our fears. A small accident would evoke "Mammenyu" (beloved Mother), a larger mishap would bring forth "Tattenyu" (beloved Father), and a shock would provoke "Gottenyu" (beloved God). A disaster could evoke an appeal to all three.

Mother, Father and God represented the core of Jewish family life. Every home depended on the warmth and care given by Mother, the strength and security given by Father, and the omnipresence and omnipotence of God. Mother was there when you were ailing or hungry or cold, Father was always handy to protect you, and God was available for everything.

From his For Special Occasions (1961).

Solomon Schechter
[1847–1915]
RUMANIAN-BORN SCHOLAR, AUTHOR, EDUCATOR

A certain Jewish saint who had the misfortune to survive the death of his greatest disciple is recorded to have exclaimed: "Oh Lord, Thou shouldst be grateful to me that I have trained for Thee so noble a soul." This is somewhat too bold, but we may be grateful to God for having given us such a great soul as Lincoln, who, under God, gave this nation a new birth of freedom, and to our dear country, which by its institutions and its people rendered possible the greatness for which Abraham Lincoln shall stand forever.

From his Seminary Addresses and Other Papers (1915).

Alice Shalvi
[1930–   ]
ISRAELI ADVOCATE OF WOMEN'S RIGHTS, EDUCATOR

Although I have been a fairly militant egalitarian for most of my life, my place and role within an Orthodox synagogue was something I grew to accept. After all, one can praise God as loudly and wholeheartedly from one side of the *mechitzah* as from the other.

From her article "Eureka!" in Lilith magazine, fall 1994, describing her shift from identification with Orthodoxy to the philosophy of the Conservative movement.

Natan Sharansky
[1948–   ]
RUSSIAN REFUSENIK, MEMBER OF THE KNESSET

Blessed are You, *Adonai*, King of the Universe. Grant me the good fortune to live with my wife, my beloved Avital Sharon, in the Land of Israel. Grant my parents, my wife, and my whole family the strength to endure all hardships until we meet. Grant me the strength, the power, the intelligence, the good fortune, and the patience to leave this jail and to reach the land of Israel in an honest and worthy way.

The short prayer he composed in Hebrew while languishing in the Soviet gulag. He repeated it daily for nine years, especially when he was led to an interrogation. Quoted in his biography, Fear No Evil (1988).

Zalman Shazar

[1890–1974]

THIRD PRESIDENT OF ISRAEL

Give us, Lord God, as much joy
As You have sent us pain till now.
And light our Freedom as pleasantly
As we suffer Golus [exile] now bitterly.

> A poem based on Psalm 90, composed at Lake Success, N.Y.,
> November 19, 1947. translated from Yiddish by Joseph Leftwich.

···

My God, guard my tongue from speaking evil,
And my lips from falsehood.

And if they curse me, let my heart be dumb,
And my soul like the earth, the same to all.

Open my heart to Your Torah,
And let my soul follow Your commandments.

And for all who in their mind plot evil against me,
Frustrate their plans and destroy their designs.
Let salvation come to all who are Your friends.
With Your right hand help me, answer me.

> A translation by Joseph Leftwich of Shazar's rendering into Yiddish ten lines
> from the Shemoneh Esrei (Amida) prayer.

(Rabbi) Shimi

BABYLONIAN TALMUDIC SCHOLAR

Just as The-Holy-One-Blessed-Be-He fills the world, so the soul fills the
body; just as The Holy-One-Blessed-Be-He sees but is not seen, so the
soul sees but is not seen; just as The Holy-One-Blessed-Be-He feeds the
whole world, so the soul feeds the whole body; just as The Holy-One-
Blessed-Be-He is pure, so the soul is pure; just as The Holy-One-Blessed-
Be-He resides in the innermost rooms, so the soul resides in the
innermost rooms. Let whoever has these five attributes come and praise
the One who has these five attributes.

> Addressing Simeon ben Pazzi. Quoted in the talmudic tractate Berachot
> (10a).

Shneur Zalman ben Baruch of Lyadi
[1747–1813]
FOUNDER OF THE CHABAD MOVEMENT

I do not want Your paradise. I do not want Your world-to-come. I want you, O God, and You only.

> Exclaimed in a moment of ecstasy while reciting his prayers.

Simeon ben Yochai
SECOND-CENTURY TALMUDIC SCHOLAR

"You are My witnesses." When you are My witnesses, I am God, when you are not My witnesses I am not God.

> Commenting in Pesikta d'Rav Kahana on a verse in Isaiah (43:10).

Ralph Simon
CONTEMPORARY U.S. CONSERVATIVE RABBI

I do not presume to ask God for 50 years, believe me, not even 25, and not even 10. I have learned a lesson of our faith, and that is that I ask God for one day at a time . . . that I might be and might continue to be a servant of the Lord.

> From a sermon during the year when he was celebrating his twentieth year with Congregation Rodfei Zedek in Chicago.

Isaac Bashevis Singer
POLISH-BORN NOVELIST, NOBEL PRIZE WINNER

The belief that man is the master of his fate is as far from me as east is from west. God is silent, speaks in acts; and we on earth have to decipher his secrets. We long for faith as much as we yearn for sex. Our great hope is free choice, divine gift. . . .

> Quoted in Journey to My Father (1994), by his son, Israel Zamir.

Joseph B. Soloveitchik
[1903–1993]
U.S. ORTHODOX RABBI, SCHOLAR, PROFESSOR

The great encounter between God and man is a wholly personal private affair incomprehensible to the outsider. . . . We certainly have not been authorized by our history, sanctified by the martyrdom of millions, to even hint to another faith community that we are mentally ready to revise historical attitudes, to trade favors pertaining to fundamental matters of faith.

From an article in Tradition: A Journal of Orthodox Jewish Thought, summer 1964.

Alan Steinbach
CONTEMPORARY U.S. REFORM RABBI, POET

God Himself records His need for man.
In braided filigree of bloom and leaf,
In dawns and starshine, cadenced lake and wood,
In glaciered mountains and in coral reef,
He strains to make His hunger understood.
For whom this vast unfoldment of His might,
This drama of creation without end?
For whom this cosmic theme of growth and light,
If not for man whom He yearns to befriend?

From a poem in The New York Times, May 2, 1954.

Hannah Szenes
[1921–1944]
HUNGARIAN-BORN POET, HEROINE

Dear God, if You've kindled a fire in my heart, allow me to burn that which should be burned in my house—the House of Israel. And as You've given me an all-seeing eye, and all-hearing ear, give me, as well, the strength to scourge, to caress, to uplift. And grant that these words be not empty phrases, but a credo for my life. Towards what am I aiming? Towards all that which is best in the world, and of which there is a spark within me.

> From her Hannah Senesh: Her Life and Diary, *written in* Palestine *on September 21, 1941.*

⋅•⋅

Do I believe in God? I don't know. For me He is more a symbol and expression of the moral forces in which I believe. Despite everything, I believe the world was created for good.

> Ibid.

⋅•⋅

I think religion means a great deal in life, and I find the modern concept—that faith in God is only a crutch for the weak—ridiculous. It's exactly that faith which makes one strong, and because of it one does not depend upon other things for support.

> Ibid. *Lines written a few weeks before her sixteenth birthday.*

Stewart Vogel
CONTEMPORARY U.S. CONSERVATIVE RABBI, AUTHOR

I have the distinction of seeing more of life than the average person. I believe that God is active in our lives. I cannot see the hands of God at work, but I can *see* and *feel* His presence in the creation of the unfolding design of the infinitely complicated and wondrous nature and experience of life.

> *Expressing his deep belief in a personal God. From his introduction to Laura Schlessinger's* The Ten Commandments *(1998), of which he is co-author.*

Leonard Weinroth
CONTEMPORARY PSYCHIATIRST

I am a cultural Jew, a secular Jew. I am interested in everything Jewish except God.

> *In answer to the question:* "Are you religious?" *Quoted in Anne Roiphe's* Generation without Memory *(1981).*

Franz Werfel
[1890–1945]
CZECH-BORN POET, PLAYWRIGHT, NOVELIST

The impersonal God is the most wretched reflection of technologized and thought-weary brains, the modern old folks' home of senile pantheism.

From his Between Heaven and Earth (1944).

Elie Wiesel
[1928–   ]
RUMANIAN-BORN U.S. AUTHOR, PROFESSOR

I rarely speak about God. To God, yes. I protest against Him. I shout at Him. But to open a discourse about the qualities of God, about the problems that God imposes, theodicy, no. And yet He is there, in silence, in filigree.

From an interview in Writers at Work (1988), edited by George Plimpton.

. ◦ .

I still have problems with God—or He still has problems with me. Terrible problems. He is God and I am not. On the other hand I believe that I must continue in spite of what happened. I would almost say today that because I have faith in humanity, I must have faith in the Giver of humanity. In other words, it is through the human being and almost for the human being that I cling desperately to God. If I were to give up on humanity, I think I would give up on God. But I am not giving up, and therefore I am not giving up on God, either.

From Civilization, April–May 1998, reporting on his comments at Forum 2000, held in Prague in the fall of 1997.

. ◦ .

Fanaticism is, I think, something that opposes men not only to others, but to God, too. A fanatic wants everybody to be in prison, so that he or she could be free, so to speak. A fanatic would like to put God Himself in prison. I think we must open the gates of that prison to men, to women and to God himself.

Ibid.

Yosi ben Zimra
SECOND-CENTURY TALMUDIC SCHOLAR

Sovereign of the Universe, among all the things that Thou hast created in a woman: Thou hast not created one without a purpose, eyes to see, ears to hear, a nose to smell, a mouth to speak, hands to do work, legs to walk with, breasts to give suck. These breasts that Thou hast put on my heart, are they not to give suck? Give me a son, so that I may suckle with them.

Imagining the prayer Hannah "spoke in her heart," mentioned in I Samuel 1:13.

Meyer Zaremba
CONTEMPORARY AUTHOR

A young boy asks his grandfather, "Zaydeh, why is it that when we talk amongst ourselves we speak Yiddish but when we *daven* [pray] we speak Hebrew? Doesn't God understand Yiddish?"

"Why are you talking such nonsense?" says the grandfather. "God understands all languages and he speaks all languages. It's just that he doesn't like to speak Yiddish."

"But why doesn't God like to speak Yiddish?"

"Because," answers the grandfather, "God doesn't want people to know that he is a Galicianer."

From his Freud un Fargingin, in which he recalls a story he heard told in Yiddish by Joseph Murphy, past president of Queens College in New York City.

CHAPTER SIX

Sin, Suffering, and Repentance

Introduction

THE BOOK OF GENESIS (3:17–19) describes how Adam, encouraged by his wife, Eve, disobeyed God by eating the forbidden fruit of the Tree of Knowledge, thus committing the first sin in human history. For this flagrant violation of God's command, Adam was punished by being evicted from the Garden of Eden and thus denied the promise of eternal life. Sin may thus be characterized, as Rabbi Ben Zion Bokser did in his *Judaism: Profile of a Faith* (1962), as "a betrayal of God . . . that separates man from God."

In the New Testament Paul says, "By one man's disobedience many were made sinners" (Romans 5:12). In Christian thinking, not only Adam but all of his descendants are to be held culpable for that Original Sin. Salvation can only come to them through the blood of Jesus that had been shed at his crucifixion.

This Christian doctrine of Original Sin is unacceptable to Jews, who believe that man enters the world pure and untainted. While some Jewish teachers in talmudic times believed that death was a punishment brought upon mankind on account of Adam's sin, the dominant view was that man sins because he is not a perfect being—not, as Christianity teaches, because he is *inherently* bad (see Shabbat 55a). Judaism teaches that man sins because he makes the wrong choices.

The concept that each person is responsible and accountable for his own sins did not originate with the thinking of the Rabbis of the talmudic era. The Bible itself warns, "Fathers shall not be put to death for the children, neither shall the children be put to death for the fathers; every man shall be put to death for his own sin" (Deuteronomy 24:16).

The sixth-century B.C.E. prophets Jeremiah and Ezekiel, who lived among the Jewish exiles in Babylonia, many of whom believed they were uprooted from their land because of the sins of Jews of their own and earlier generations, consoled their co-religionists and encouraged them with the hope of redemption, impressing upon them that a day will come when it shall no longer be said, "The fathers have eaten sour grapes and the children's teeth sense pain, but everyone shall die for his own sin . . ." (Jeremiah 31:29–30).

Judaism teaches that any stain upon man's soul caused by his having made wrong choices is his to bear. Only the individual, not some outside force, can erase that stain.

"God does not desire sin," wrote Ben Sira in his *Wisdom of Ben Sira* (15:12), to which Maimonides added (*Mishneh Torah*, Hilchot Teshuva 5:2), "Everyone [by choice] can be as righteous as Moses or as wicked as Jeroboam."

Man must personally go about the task of washing away sin by admitting his guilt openly, by expressing contrition towards those against whom he has sinned, and by rectifying the wrong. In *Choosing Judaism* (1981), Lydia Kukoff quotes Rabbi Rachel Cowan as saying, "Though I was taught [in Catholicism] that deeds were important, the stress was on having faith. . . . In Judaism, by contrast, it is the emphasis on action, on righteous behavior, and that I find so attractive."

Judaism emphasizes that a third party cannot bring absolution or salvation to a sinner. After a 1993 visit to Jonathan Pollard, who was incarcerated in a U.S. prison for spying for Israel, Rabbi Ezriel Tauber reported that Pollard said that being imprisoned was a great favor God bestowed upon him because, in his words, "I still have some cleansing to do."

Judaism holds a repentant sinner in high regard. The twelfth-century philosopher Moses Maimonides stated in his *Mishneh Torah* (Hilchot Teshuva 7:4–5) that a sinner who repents is more beloved of God than a person who has never sinned, because the former has tasted and enjoyed the delights of an uninhibited immoral life but has over-come its allure, thus proving his ability to master his evil inclination.

How does one overcome the tendency to sin? The Rabbis of the Talmud believed that this can be accomplished by serving God through the observance of the commandments of the Torah and through prayer. Prayer in the Jewish tradition means more than sim-ply asking God to fulfill one's personal needs. "Whoever has it in his power to pray on behalf of his neighbor and fails to do so is called a sinner," states the Talmud (Berachot 12b). The needs of one's fellow man and the needs of the community are paramount in Jewish prayer. Said the fourth-century Babylonian scholar Abbaye, the correct way to pray is to include the whole congregation of Israel in one's prayers. One should say, "May it be Thy will, O Lord our God, to lead us forth in peace . . ." (Ibid. 29b–30a).

How does one explain the suffering and eventual extermination of Jews and others in Nazi Europe during World War II? For what sins were they being punished? No one is able to offer a satisfactory answer. Perhaps the philosophical suggestion of Professor Eliezer Berkovits, set forth in his *Faith After the Holocaust* (1973), contains the seed of an answer: "There must be a dimension beyond history in which all suffering finds its redemption through God. This is essen-tial to the faith of the Jew."

(Rabbi) Abbahu
Also known as Avahu
THIRD-CENTURY TALMUDIC SCHOLAR

God said: "Sound before Me a ram's horn so that I may remember on your behalf the binding of Isaac, son of Abraham, and consider it [to your credit] as if you had bound yourselves before Me."

> Explaining why the horn of a ram is blown on Rosh Hashana as a mitigator of man's sins. Quoted in the talmudic tractate Rosh Hashana (16a).

· ◆ ·

Better that a man sin secretly than publicly profane God's name.

> Quoted in the talmudic tractate Kiddushin (40a).

(Rabbi) Acha

[c. 280–356]

BABYLONIAN TALMUDIC SCHOLAR

Since the day of the destruction of the Temple there is no laughter for the Holy One, blessed be He.

> Quoted in the talmudic tractate *Avoda Zara* (3b).

Akavya ben Mehalalel

FIRST-CENTURY TALMUDIC SCHOLAR

Better that I be called a fool all the days of my life than that I be made a godless man before God for even one hour.

> When asked by his colleagues to retract four unpopular opinions that he had expressed and thereby become worthy of being made vice-president (Av Bet Din) of the court. Quoted in the Mishna Eduyot (5:6).

Anonymous

On Rosh Hashana all mankind will pass in review before Him [God] like a flock of sheep (kivnei maron).

> The citation is part of a prominent passage in the High Holy Day liturgy. Rabbi Judah said in the name of Samuel, the meaning is "like the troops of the House of David, which are reviewed one by one." Quoted in the talmudic tractate Rosh Hashana (18a).

·◆·

Tragedy comes when we don't do God's will. Look at the way girls dress in the street outside, like prostitutes. Also, we religious Jews have our share of sin: We're guilty of helping cause hatred among Jews. The whole nation needs to repent.

> Comment of an Orthodox Jew owner of a shop on the Ben Yehuda Mall in Jerusalem that was blown up by three Arab suicide bombers in September 1998. Quoted in The Jerusalem Report, October 2, 1997.

·◆·

You [God] wish me to repent of my sins, but I have committed only minor offenses. I may have kept leftover cloth, or I may have eaten in a non-Jewish home where I worked without washing my hands. But You, O Lord, have committed grievous sins: You have taken away babies from their mothers, and mothers from their babies. So let us make a truce. If You will forgive me, I will forgive You.

> A simple tailor speaking to God. When Levi Yitzchak of Berditchev was told the story by the simple tailor, he commented: "Why did you let God off so easy. You could have forced him to forgive all Israel!"

·•·

God chastises with one hand and blesses with the other.

> A popular Yiddish folk saying.

Israel Baal Shem Tov
[c. 1700–1760]
FOUNDER OF CHASIDISM

The Shekinah [God] permeates all stages of life from the highest to the lowest. Even when man commits a sin, the Shekinah is in him, because otherwise he could not have carried out the act nor moved any organ, for it is God who endows man with vitality and power.

> From his Keter Shem Tov.

·•·

When a man has committed a transgression, he should not be sad on that account, for this would only diminish his worship of God, but he should forget about it and resume his rejoicing in God.

> Quoted in the work Toldot Yaakov Yosef, by Jacob Joseph Palonnoge (died 1782), a disciple of the Besht.

Bernard M. Baruch

[1870–1965]

U.S. FINANCIER, PUBLIC OFFICIAL

Even when we discover basic truths about human affairs, it is another thing to overcome human failings—the greed, hatred, sloth, or whatever it is that keeps us from acting on those truths. In a laboratory, men follow truth wherever it may lead. In human relations, men have a supreme talent for ignoring truth, and denying facts they do not like. That is why the ancient messenger who brought bad tidings was put to death.

We would all do well to echo Thomas Huxley's prayer: "God give me strength to face a fact even though it slay me."

From his Baruch: The Public Years (1960).

Ben Sira

SECOND-CENTURY B.C.E. SAGE, AUTHOR

Say not: "God has led me astray," for He does not desire sin. No one is bidden to be Godless, and to no one did He give permission to sin.

From the apocryphal book Wisdom of Ben Sira (15:12).

Eliezer Berkovits

[1908–1992]

U.S. RABBI, SCHOLAR, AUTHOR

God is responsible for having created a world in which man is free to make history. There must be a dimension beyond history in which all suffering finds its redemption through God. This is essential to the faith of a Jew. The Jew does not doubt God's presence, though he is unable to set limits to the duration and intensity of His absence.

From his Faith After the Holocaust.

Ben Zion Bokser

[1907–1983]

U.S. RABBI, SCHOLAR, AUTHOR

Any deed of which one is ashamed becomes a dark shadow that has fallen between lovers, and the one who feels guilty cannot face the one whom he has betrayed. Sin, a betrayal of God, becomes an "iron curtain" that separates man from God.

From his Judaism: Profile of a Faith (1962).

Martin Buber
[1878–1965]
GERMAN THEOLOGIAN, AUTHOR

If a man does not judge himself, all things will judge him, and all things will become messengers of God.

From his Ten Rungs: Hasidic Sayings (1947).

Chanina ben Papa
THIRD-CENTURY TALMUDIC SCHOLAR

The angel in charge of conception is called lailah [meaning "night"]. [At the moment of conception], he takes the drop of semen and places it before God, and says: "Master of the universe, what shall be the fate of this drop? Will it develop into a strong person or a weak one? A wise person or a fool? A rich person or a poor one?" He does not ask whether the person will be wicked or righteous.

Expressing the conviction that each man is responsible for his own actions. Quoted in the talmudic tractate Nidda (16b).

Jacob Cohen
NINETEENTH-CENTURY HEBREW POET

At last I have returned unto my God,
The God I know and you know not at all. . . .

I am a part of the world, and yet with the world I war,
I war and I'll live for evermore!
I am Man!

Quoted in Meyer Waxman's History of Jewish Literature (1941).

Abraham Danzig
[1748–1820]
RABBINIC SCHOLAR

A sin against man is far more reprehensible than a sin against God.

Quoted in The Jewish Encyclopedia, vol. 4 (1905).

David Einhorn
[1809–1879]
GERMAN-BORN U.S. RABBI

Is it anything else but a deed of Amalek, rebellion against God, to enslave human beings created in His image? . . . Can that Book mean to raise the whip and forge chains, which proclaims, with flaming words, in the name of God: "Break the bonds of oppression, let the oppressed go free and tear every yoke!"

A rejoinder to Rabbi Morris J. Raphall's sermon in which he preached that the Bible does not consider slaveholding to be a sin. Einhorn's attack was published in his Sinai, February–March 1861, a monthly German-language journal first issued in 1856.

Albert Einstein
[1879–1955]
GERMAN-BORN U.S. SCIENTIST

I cannot conceive of a God who rewards and punishes his creatures, or has a will of the kind that we experience in ourselves.

From his Ideas and Opinions (1982).

(Rabbi) Eleazar
SECOND-CENTURY TALMUDIC SCHOLAR

Since the destruction of the Temple, the gates of prayer are locked. . . . Yet, though the gates of prayer are sealed the gates of tears are not.

Implying that while it has been more difficult to commune with God since the destruction of the Temple, prayer that is heartfelt is always effective. Quoted in the talmudic tractate Bava Metzia (59a).

Whoever translates a verse literally is a liar, and whoever adds to it commits blasphemy. Thus, one who translates the verse, "and they saw the God of Israel" literally is a liar, for the Holy One, blessed be He, sees, but is never seen. But one who translates, "and they saw the glory of the *Shekhinah* of the God of Israel" blasphemes, for he is constructing here a trinity: the Glory, the *Shekhinah*, and God."

> Commenting on Exodus 24:10. Quoted in the thirteenth-century Yemenite compilation known as Midrash Ha-gadol. *Maimonides made a similar statement.*

Eleazar ben Azariah
[70–135]
PRESIDENT OF THE SANHEDRIN, SUCCEEDING GAMALIEL II

For transgressions of man against God, the Day of Atonement atones; but for transgressions against a fellow-man the Day of Atonement does not atone, unless and until he has conciliated his fellow-man and redressed the wrong he had done him.

> Quoted in the talmudic tractate Mishna Yoma (8:9).

Eleazar ben Zadok
FIRST-CENTURY TALMUDIC SCHOLAR

To what are the righteous compared in this world? To a tree standing wholly in a place of cleanness, but its bough overhangs to a place of uncleanness; when the bough is cut off, it stands entirely in a place of cleanness. Thus the Holy One, blessed be He, brings suffering upon the righteous in this world, in order that they may inherit the future world.

> Quoted in the talmudic tractate Kiddushin (40b).

Yaffa Eliach
CONTEMPORARY U.S. PROFESSOR, AUTHOR

I have no quarrel with God, only with men! . . . I would put on trial each Western university and library, for harboring millions of malicious words written against an ancient people, words like murderous daggers hiding beneath the cloak of science and truth. . . . I want to bring to trial the pulpits of countless churches where hate was burning like eternal lights. . . . I want to bring to trial a civilization for whom man was such a worthless being. But to bring God to trial? On what charges? For giving men the ability to choose between good and evil.

From her Hasidic Tales of the Holocaust.

Eliahu
FRIEND OF THE BIBLICAL JOB

God does not make demands upon a person that are beyond his ability to execute.

During his debate with Job. Quoted in Exodus Rabba, Teruma (34:1).

Marc Gellman
[1947–]
CONTEMPORARY U.S. REFORM RABBI, AUTHOR

We may view all our deeds up to this moment as balanced between good and evil, and hope our answer to God's question to Adam—"Where are you?" (Genesis 3:9)—will tip the balance in our favor among the accountants in charge of the book of life. In this struggle for honesty and courage, for shame and repentance, you should remember that every single biblical hero from Adam to Moses was flawed.

From his First Things (1996).

Neil Gillman
CONTEMPORARY CONSERVATIVE U.S. RABBI, THEOLOGIAN

I insist that God transcends human understanding and language. That is what makes God God. To believe that human beings can comprehend God is idolatry, the cardinal Jewish sin.

From his essay in Commentary, August 1996.

Jacob Glatstein
[1896–1971]
YIDDISH AUTHOR, CRITIC

We've both turned universal.
Come back, dear God, to a land
        no bigger than a speck.
Dwindle down to only ours.
I'll go around with homely sayings
suitable for chewing over in small places.
We'll both be provincial.
God and His poet
Maybe it will go sweeter for us.

> Translated from the Yiddish by Cynthia Ozick.

David M. Gordis
CONTEMPORARY U.S. CONSERVATIVE RABBI, EDUCATOR

God is not responsible for evil, even the depths of depravity represented by the Holocaust. God is not responsible for historical achievements, even those as notable as the reestablishment of the state of Israel.

> From his essay in Commentary, August 1996.

Hayim (Chaim) Greenberg
[1889–1953]
RUSSIAN-BORN JOURNALIST, ZIONIST LEADER

May God not punish me for my words, [but] the fact that in recent months Jews have not produced a substantial number of mentally deranged persons is hardly a symptom of health.

> From "Bankrupt," a February 1943 article about American Jewry. Quoted in Hayim Greenberg: Anthology, edited by Marie Syrkin (1968).

Irving Greenberg
[1933–]
U.S. ORTHODOX RABBI, AUTHOR, EDUCATOR

Faith in the God of History demands that an unprecedented act of destruction be matched by an unprecedented act of redemption, and this has happened.

Quoted in Anne Roiphe's Generation without Memory (1981).

Uri Avi Greenberg
[1894–1981]
ISRAELI POET, ZIONIST LEADER

And if the Redeemer comes and nations beat their swords into ploughshares and throw their guns into the fire, you will not, my son, not you.

From his poem entitled "Holy of Holies," which takes the form of a dialogue between a mother, representing the dead Jews of Europe, and her son, representing the sabras, who is warned to stay alert.

Herschel Grynszpan
[1921–1943]
DEEPLY PASSIONATE ANTI-NAZI

With God's help I couldn't do otherwise. My heart bleeds when I think of our tragedy and that of the 12,000 Jews. I have to protest in a way that the whole world hears my protest, and this I intend to do. I beg your forgiveness.

From a November 7, 1938 Hebrew letter to his uncle in Paris. He then purchased a pistol, went to the German Embassy in Paris, and fatally shot the German First Secretary Ernst von Rath. Quoted in an article by Michael R. Marrus, "The Strange Story of Herschel Grynszpan," in American Scholar, winter 1987–88.

Will Herberg

[1901–1977]

U.S. THEOLOGIAN, SOCIAL CRITIC

Turning [teshuvah] is the fusion of repentance and grace. It points at one and the same time to man's action in abandoning his delusive self-sufficiency so as to turn to God, and to God's action in giving man the power to break the vicious circle of sin and turn to the divine source of his being. . . .

Because it is the delusion of self-sufficiency that must be overcome before the healing work of God becomes available to us, we obviously cannot hope to achieve our salvation through our own works, however meritorious.

From his Judaism and Modern Man (1951).

.◆.

Redemptive history is not merely history of redemption; it is also redeeming history, history with the power to save. The Jew achieves salvation not through purely individual, mystical exercises which somehow bring him into union with God. The Jew becomes a "true Jew" and makes available to himself the resources of divine grace under the covenant by making Israel's past his own, its sacred history the "background" of his own life.

From his essay "Torah: Teaching, Law and Way," in Conservative Judaism and Jewish Law, edited by Seymour Siegel (1977).

Abraham Joshua Heschel

[1907–1972]

U.S. RABBI, THEOLOGIAN, AUTHOR, ACTIVIST

Man is rebellious and full of iniquity, and yet so cherished is he that God, the creator of heaven and earth, is saddened when forsaken by him.

From his The Prophets.

.◆.

From the perspective of the Bible: Who is man? A being in travail with God's dreams and designs, with God's dream of a world redeemed, of reconciliation of heaven and earth, of a mankind which is truly His image, reflecting His wisdom, justice, and compassion.

From his Who Is Man? (1965).

Emil G. Hirsch
[1852–1923]
U.S. REFORM RABBI

Sin is not an offense against God, but against our humanity. It is not a state which came to us and which we cannot throw off; it is an act of our own. Sin is anti-social conduct, due to the want of resistance on our part to the influences of the animal world behind us, selfishness, or to the legacy of a phase of civilization over which and beyond which we should have passed on.

From his article "The Sociological Center of Religion," which appeared in The Reform Advocate, vol. 11 (1896).

Solomon ibn Gabirol
[c. 1021–c. 1056]
SPANISH POET, PHILOSOPHER

I have sinned against Thy law,
I have despised Thy commandments,
I have defiled my heart and my mouth,
I have spoken abomination,
I have done evil,
I have done wickedly,
I have been presumptuous,
I have been violent,
I have dealt in falsehood,
I have given ill counsel.
I have lied,
I have scoffed,
I have murmured,
I have blasphemed,

I have rebelled,
I have trespassed,
I have transgressed,
I have wronged,
I have stiffened my neck,
I have disdained Thy chastisements,
I have done iniquity,
I have perverted my paths,
I have wandered from my ways,
I have turned away from Thy commandments,
I have gone astray.

From his *Keter Malchut* ("The Kingly Crown"), translated from the Arabic by Bernard Lewis (1961). Known as *Al Cheit*, this confession is recited on Yom Kippur.

Isaac ibn Ghiyath
ELEVENTH-CENTURY SPANISH HEBREW POET

Woe unto us that we have sinned! Jews despise or neglect the *Guide* [of Maimonides] nowadays, although the purpose of the treatise is to demonstrate the existence and unity of God. The Christians honor the work, study, and translate it.

One of many instances in his ethical will that he urges his son to study Maimonides' Guide of the Perplexed.

Bachya ibn Pakuda
[c. 1050–1120]
SPANISH PHILOSOPHER, AUTHOR

There is an old saying: If you wish to find out whether your motive is pure, test yourself in two ways: whether you expect recompense from God or anyone else, and whether you would perform the act in the same way if you were alone, unbeknown to others.

From his Chovot Ha-levavot ("Duties of the Heart"), c. 1080.

··•·

He who is humble before God will not only do good to all men, but he will speak kindly to them and about them . . . will never relate anything shameful about them and will forgive them for any shameful things they may say about him.

Ibid.

··•·

If you want to praise, praise God; if you want to blame, blame yourself.

Quoted in Solomon Schechter's Seminary Addresses (1959).

(Rabbi) Isaac
THIRD-CENTURY TALMUDIC SCHOLAR

When a man commits a transgression in secret, it is though he were pushing the feet of the Holy One [off His footstool].

Commenting on the verse in Isaiah (66:1): "The heaven is My throne and the earth is My footstool."

Jeremiah ben Abba
THIRD-CENTURY BABYLONIAN SCHOLAR

Four classes of people are not acceptable to God: jokers, flatters, liars, and slanderers.

Quoted in the talmudic tractate Sota (42a).

(Rabbi) Jonathan
SECOND-CENTURY TALMUDIC SCHOLAR

The Holy One, Blessed be He, does not rejoice at the downfall of the wicked.

Explaining why the words "He is good" are omitted in II Chronicles 20:21 describing the battle of King Jehoshafat of Judah with the Ammonites and Moabites. Quoted in the talmudic tractate Sanhedrin (39b).

Joshua ben Lev
THIRD-CENTURY TALMUDIC SCHOLAR

Anyone who overcomes his [evil] inclination and confesses his sin, Scripture considers that he has thus honored God in both worlds—this one and the next one.

Quoted in the talmudic tractate Sanhedrin (43b).

Harold Kushner
[1935–]
U.S. CONSERVATIVE RABBI, AUTHOR

I believe that the fundamental message of religion is not that we are sinners because we are not perfect, but that the challenge of being human is so complex that God knows better than to expect perfection from us. Religion comes to clean us of our sense of unworthiness and to assure us that when we have tried to be good and have not been as good as we wanted to be we have forfeited God's love.

Quoted in his How Good Do We Have to Be? (1996).

. ◆.

[Real religion is] not familiar hymns. It's coming into a room with an unbearable burden of shame and seeing it lifted.

People want less theology and more religion. They want an encounter with the living God that will change their lives.

From a New York Times interview with Gustav Niebuhr, November 6, 1996.

Yeshayahu Leibowitz
[1903–1994]
ISRAELI PROFESSOR, BIOCHEMIST, BIBLE SCHOLAR, AUTHOR

The phenomenon of individuals returning to *halakhic* [legal religious] practice has nothing to do with the "beginning of redemption"; it is, rather, an expression of spiritual struggles that can arise within individuals in any place, at any time, and under any historical circumstances. Israel's return to its God will only come about from an awakening of the Jews themselves, not by virtue of the Israel Defense Force. There is today no sign of this awakening.

From an essay in David Hartman's Conflicting Visions (1990).

(Rabbi) Levi

THIRD-CENTURY TALMUDIC SCHOLAR

Great is repentance, for it reaches it reaches to the throne of God.

Quoted in the talmudic tractate Yoma (86a).

Levi Yitzchak of Berditchev

[1740–1809]

CHASIDIC RABBI

Show me what this, that is happening at this very moment, means to me, what it asks of me—and what you, God, are telling me through it. It is not why I suffer, that I wish to know, but only whether I suffer for the sake of God.

Quoted in Martin Buber's Tales of the Hasidim: Early Masters (1947).

Moses Maimonides

[1135–1204]

SPANISH RABBI, PHYSICIAN, SCHOLAR, PHILOSOPHER, AUTHOR

I believe with complete faith that the Exalted One rewards those who observe the commandments of the Torah and punishes those who transgress them. The greatest reward is entering the world-to-come and the greatest punishment is extinction.

Based upon his commentary to the Mishna Sanhedrin (10), in which he presents Thirteen Principles (Articles) of Faith every Jew must believe in order to be assured a place in the world-to-come.

·-•-·

We seek relief from our own faults; we suffer from evils which we inflict on ourselves, and we ascribe them to God who is far from connected with them.

From his Guide of the Perplexed (1190).

·-•-·

It cannot be said of God that He directly creates evil. . . . This is impossible. His works are perfectly good. He only produces existence, and all existence is good.

Ibid.

• • •

Awake, ye sleepers from your slumber, and rouse you from your lethargy. Scrutinize your deeds and return in repentance. Remember your Creator, ye who forget eternal truth in the trifles of the hour, who go astray seeking vain illusions which can neither profit nor deliver. Look well into your souls and mend your ways and your actions; let each of you forsake his evil path and his unworthy purpose, and return to God, so that He may have mercy upon you.

From his Mishneh Torah, Hilchot Teshuva (3:4). A prayer traditionally recited before the shofar-blowing ceremony on Rosh Hashana.

• • •

O God I have sinned, I have committed iniquity, I have rebelled against Thee. I have done thus and thus. I regret these deeds and am ashamed of them and will never repeat them.

Ibid. (1:1).

• • •

Pay no attention to those fools among the nations of the world and many stupid Jews who say that God pre-ordains, from birth, whether one will be righteous or wicked. This is not so. Every person can be as righteous as Moses or as wicked as Jeroboam. . . .

Ibid. (5:2).

• • •

Man is given freedom of will. If he wishes to choose the right way and be righteous, he is free to do so. If he wants to choose the wrong path and be wicked, he is free to do so. Do not believe what the stupid people say—that God decides at birth whether one will be righteous or wicked. No, every human being can either be righteous like Moses, or wicked like Jeroboam, for there is no compulsion exerted upon him and nothing draws him to one of the two ways. A person chooses his way with his own determination.

Ibid. (5:2).

. ◆ .

If God decreed that a person should be either righteous or wicked, or if there was some force inherent in his nature which irresistibly drew him to a particular course . . . how could God have commanded us through the prophets, "Do this and do not do that, improve your ways, and do not follow your wicked impulses," when, from the beginning of his existence a person's destiny had already been decreed? . . . What room would there be for the whole of the Torah? By what right or justice could God punish the wicked or reward the righteous? "Shall not the judge of all the earth act justly?" (Genesis 18:25).

Ibid. (5:4)

. ◆ .

Does God know or does He not know that a certain individual will be good or bad? If you say, "He knows," then it necessarily follows that man is compelled to act as God knew beforehand he would act, otherwise God's knowledge would be imperfect. If you say that God does not know in advance, then great absurdities and destructive religious theories will result.

From his Eight Chapters, *a preface to his comments on the Ethics of the Fathers.*

Gil Mann
FOUNDER OF A COMPUTER COMPANY, AUTHOR

Some survivors never were able to accept the notion of God again. Yet others did. Survivors have different answers. One daughter of Holocaust survivors told me that her father regained his faith in God because the Holocaust taught him that he could not believe in people.

From his How to Get More Out of Being Jewish Even If (1996).

Jonathan Pollard
[1954–]
FORMER U.S. GOVERNMENT EMPLOYEE

God put me in prison for a reason, and when the time is right I'll be released. It is a great *chesed* [act of God's mercy] to be in prison because

I still have some cleansing to do. If people really want to help me, they should say Psalms for me.

> On March 4, 1987, Pollard was convicted of spying for Israel. Reported in 1993 by Rabbi Ezriel Tauber after visiting Pollard in prison.

Raba

THIRD/FOURTH-CENTURY BABYLONIAN SCHOLAR

If the Holy One, blessed be He is pleased with a man. He oppresses with afflictions.

> Quoting his teacher Rabbi Hune in the talmudic tractate Berachot (5a). It was believed that afflictions will make a person devote himself more intensely to the study of Torah. The afflictions are considered to be administered out of love.

Rabba bar bar Chana

THIRD/FOURTH-CENTURY TALMUDIC SCHOLAR

Anyone who praises God excessively is uprooted from the world.

> Quoting his teacher Rabbi Yochanan, who felt overpraising God smacked of insincerity. Quoted in the talmudic tractate Megilla (18a).

Resh Lakish

Also known as Rabbi Shimon (Simeon)

SECOND/THIRD-CENTURY TALMUDIC SCHOLAR

There is no Hell (Gehinom) in the next world. God will take the sun out of its sheath; the righteous will be healed by it, and the wicked will be judged and punished thereby.

> Quoted in the talmudic tractate Nedarim (8b).

Leon Roth

[1896–1963]

ENGLISH-BORN PHILOSOPHER, SCHOLAR

It has become fashionable to talk of the relationship between God and man as that of a dialogue. That is as may be; but it should at least be noted that the dialogue involved is not a tea-table conversation. It is rather a call, even a calling to account; and it is curious to observe from the record how some of those called upon found in it terror and suffering, and how some, for varying reasons, tried to evade it.

From his God and Man in the Old Testament (1955).

Saadya Gaon
[882–942]
BABYLONIAN SCHOLAR, LITURGIST

Sin is not sinful because God forbade it, but God forbade it because it is sinful.

From his Emunot Ve-deot (933).

Harold Schulweiss
[1925–]
U.S. CONSERVATIVE RABBI, AUTHOR

Whether you call it [the 1994 Los Angeles earthquake] an act of God depends on your understanding of God. . . . Most assuredly, profoundly and emphatically, this was not punishment from God. I can think of a lot of other areas that are more deserving, like the heart of Las Vegas. Or the headquarters of the Skinheads. . . .

Theology gets into a lot of trouble trying to read God's mind. If the earthquake is to be seen as punishment, then any catastrophe can be seen as punishment, and I just can't accept that.

From an interview with Ari L. Noonan in Heritage Southwest Jewish Press, January 21, 1994.

Harvey Shapiro
[1924–]
U.S.-BORN POET

Where did the Jewish God go?
Up the chimney flues.
Who saw Him go?

Six million souls.
How did He go?
And so still
As dew from the grass.

The poem entitled "Ditty" appeared in Steven J. Rubin's anthology Telling and Remembering *(1997).*

Simeon ben Yochai

SECOND-CENTURY TALMUDIC SCHOLAR

God's name, graven on Israel's shield at Sinai, was obliterated when Israel sinned.

Quoted in Lamentations Rabba *(24).*

Henry Slonimsky

[1884–1970]

U.S. PHILOSOPHER, PROFESSOR

Man has freedom, he can choose God or reject God, he can lead the world to perdition and to redemption. The creation of this being Man with such power of freedom means that God has made room for a co-determining power alongside of Himself. Man is the crossroad of the world.

From his Essays *(1967).*

Arthur I. Waskow

[1933–   ]

U.S. WRITER, THEOLOGIAN

For my grandmother, Rose Honigman Osnowitz Gertz (Rachel bat Hirsch Yaakov v'Chana Hitzel), who punished God for her husband's death by refusing to hold a Passover seder for fifteen years.

From the dedication of his Godwrestling *(1978).*

Simone Weil

[1909–1943]

FRENCH PHILOSOPHER, AUTHOR

If we forgive God for his crime against us, which is to have made us finite creatures, He will forgive our crime against him, which is that we are finite creatures.

From her First and Last Notebooks (1970).

Elie Wiesel

[1928–]

RUMANIAN-BORN U.S. AUTHOR, PROFESSOR

Once, New Year's Day had dominated my life. I knew that my sins grieved the Eternal; I implored His forgiveness. . . . This day I had ceased to plead. I was no longer capable of lamentation. On the contrary, I felt very strong. I was the accuser, God the accused.

In his Night (1958).

(Rabbi) Yannai

SECOND/THIRD-CENTURY PALESTINIAN SCHOLAR

Lord of the world, I have sinned before you! May it be Thy will to grant me a good heart, good desires, a good name, a good eye, a modest soul and a humble spirit. May Thy name not be profaned through us, and preserve us from being the subject of gossip among people.

Recited each morning, thanking God for returning him to life.

·◆·

The Holy One, Blessed be He, carries out a mission of his through anything, even through a snake, even through a gnat, even through a frog.

After hearing a report that a snake had bitten a man who had died immediately, Quoted in Genesis Rabba 10:7

(Rabbi) Yassa

BABYLONIAN SCHOLAR WHO SETTLED IN PALESTINE

God says to Israel, "Open to Me a gate of repentance no bigger than the eye of a needle, and I will widen it to a gate [of forgiveness] wide enough to drive through wagons and carriages."

Quoted in the Song of Songs Rabba (5:2).

Yochanan ben Nappacha

[190–279]

PALESTINIAN TALMUDIC SCHOLAR

Woe to the nation that would be found attempting to interfere when the Holy One, blessed be He, when He is in the process of redeeming His children [Israel]. [It would be as dangerous as one who would throw his garment between a lion and a lioness when they are copulating.

Quoted in the talmudic tractate Sanhedrin (106a).

Yochanan ben Zakkai

FIRST-CENTURY TALMUDIC SCHOLAR

Anyone who observes the Sabbath properly, even if he be an idolater, is forgiven his sins [against God].

Quoted in the talmudic tractate Shabbat (118b).

．◆．

May your fear of God be as strong as your fear of men.

Advice to his son. Quoted in the talmudic tractate Berachot (28b).

Index of Names

N

Nachman ben Chisda, 193
Nachman ben Simcha of Bratzlav,
   136–137, 194, 282–283
Nachmanides, 50, 137, 194, 240
Nachman of Kosov, 137
Nehemiah (Rabbi), 138
Neusner, Jacob, 138, 194, 240
Novak, David, 194–195

O

Olan, Levi, 195
Osha'ya (Rabbi), 195
Ozick, Cynthia, 50, 283

P

Pava, Moses, 138
Peerce, Jan, 139
Penzias, Arno, 51
Peretz, Isaac Leibush (I. L.), 51, 283
Perlmutter, Menachem, 240
Petsonk, Judy, 240–241
Petuchowski, Jakob, 139, 283–284
Philo, 51, 139–140, 284
Pinchas ben Abraham Abba
   Shapiro, 241
Pinchas of Koretz, 241
Plaskow, Judith, 52, 140
Plaut, W. Gunther, 241–242, 284
Podhoretz, Norman, 195
Pollard, Jonathan, 296, 314–315
Popkin, Ruth W., 196
Post, Marlene, 141
Posy, Arnold, 242
Prager, Dennis, 52–53, 141, 196,
   284
Priesand, Sally, 53, 142

R

Raba, 142, 196, 315
Raba bar Rav Huna, 242
Rabba bar bar Chana, 315
Rabbis of the Talmud, 295–296
Rackman, Emanuel, 54, 197, 285
Rakover, Yossel, 285
Rashi, 54, 157, 243
Rav, 142, 197, 211, 243, 286
Reichmann, Paul, 286
Resh Lakish, 54–55, 243, 286,
   315
Riemer, Jack, 143
Rivers, Joan, 143
Roiphe, Anne, viii, 55, 197, 286
Rokach, Yissachar Dov, 244
Rosenblatt, Naomi H., 143
Rosenzweig, Franz, 55, 253
Roth, Leon, 55, 315–316
Rubenstein, Aryeh, 198
Rubenstein, Richard, 56, 198–199
Ruth, 143

S

Saadya Gaon, 144, 316
Sacks, Jonathan, 200, 287
Salanter, Israel, 56
Sampter, Jessie Ethel, 144
Samuel, 255
Samuel ben Nachman, 56
Samuel, Maurice, 287
Schachter-Shalomi, Zalman, 144
Schary, Dore, 287
Schechter, Solomon, 288
Schlessinger, Laura, 145, 200, 244
Schneerson, Menachem Mendel,
   145
Scholem, Gershom, 57, 145, 244

About the Author

ALFRED J. KOLATCH, a graduate of the Teacher's Institute of Yeshiva University and its College of Liberal Arts, was ordained by the Jewish Theological Seminary of America, which subsequently awarded him the Doctor of Divinity Degree, *honoris causa*. From 1941 to 1948 he served as rabbi of congregations in Columbia, South Carolina, and Kew Gardens, New York, and as chaplain in the United States Army. In 1948 he founded Jonathan David Publishers, of which he has since been president and editor-in-chief.

Rabbi Kolatch has authored numerous books, the most popular of which are *Great Jewish Quotations*, *The Jewish Home Advisor*, *This Is the Torah*, and the bestselling *Jewish Book of Why* and its sequel, *The Second Jewish Book of Why*. Several of the author's works deal with nomenclature, about which he is an acknowledged authority. *The New Name Dictionary* and *The Complete Dictionary of English and Hebrew First Names* are among his works on the subject of nomenclature. Other books by the author include *Our Religion: The Torah*, *The Jewish Heritage Quiz Book*, *The Jewish Mourner's Book of Why*, *Who's Who in the Talmud*, and *The Family Seder*.

In addition to his scholarly work, Rabbi Kolatch is interested in the work of the military chaplaincy. He has served as president of the Association of Jewish Chaplains of the Armed Forces and as vice-president of the interdenominational Military Chaplains Association of the United States.